THE 21ST CENTURY SALES BIBLE

ARMINLEAR

Library of Congress Control Number: 2022945143

ISBN (paperback): 978-1-956450-38-5
(eBook): 978-1-956450-39-2

Armin Lear Press Inc
215 W Riverside Drive, #4362
Estes Park, CO 80517

THE 21ST CENTURY SALES BIBLE

MASTERING THE 10 COMMANDMENTS OF MARKETING, NEGOTIATION & PERSUASION

DR. YANIV ZAID

To my amazing kids, Noam and Yoav, whom I enjoy more every day and who give me the greatest inspiration for doing what I do.

My dear parents, Varda and Moty, who have always been supportive and empowering and have wished nothing but the best for me. You are largely responsible for everything that I have achieved in my life.

My family, friends, clients, colleagues, agents and publishers and the people on my team, who have been with me for many years, growing with me and helping me grow and have significantly contributed to my business, professional and personal development.

My wife, Nathalie, the most beautiful woman on earth (inside and outside), whom I love more every day. Thank you for your support and smart advices, and for the journey.

TABLE OF CONTENTS

INTRODUCTION

What are the four most important things in life no one has taught you?

If you pick people randomly off the street and ask them what the four most important things in their life are, all of them (based on international research) will give you the same four answers:

» **Love**
» **Wealth**
» **Happiness**
» **Health**

Not necessarily in this order or phrasing, but the four things most important to all of us are:

» To be loved by others (this notion includes family members, partners, friends, and so on.
» To have enough money to live the life we want
» To be happy, content and fulfilled
» To be healthy, energetic, and strong

There's only one problem: No one has ever taught us in any educational framework or "formal" life track how to obtain happiness, love, health and money! Not in pre-school, elementary school, or in college. Here and there, we've picked up some insights, knowledge and tools from a teacher, parent, or mentor. But in an institutionalized manner, it's rare that people ever teach us how to find the right partner for us, how to make people love us, how to make money, how to live a life of value, how to eat or sleep well and so on and so forth. When in fact, these are the most important things in life for us!

Most people discover this gap between what they were taught in their formal schooling and what they need or what is important in life only at a later stage, after they've completed their formal studies.

I'll give two short examples.

» I'm an economist, I studied for my BA in economics for three years, and no professor ever taught me marketing in any course. I never even heard the word "money" during my degree (in economics!), aside from learning theoretical economic models. **How are people who have completed their academic education and opened a business supposed to know how to make money?**

» I'm also an attorney. While studying for my law
degree, no one ever taught me how to speak
in court, how to write a legal claim, or how
to negotiate.

How is an attorney, who's completed all the theoretical legal studies, supposed to manage in the competitive legal and business world without being given any
practical tools for working with clients and judges?

I can give more examples, but the question now
is, "What should one do?" Meaning, what do people do
when they discover this gap and realize something is
missing in their life—money, health, happiness, love or
all four—and don't know how to obtain them (because
nobody taught them?)

This is where "non-formal" education comes in—
through workshops, conferences, books, consultation,
and/or coaching from experts in the field, from private
settings. In this way, people can make up for the gaps
and obtain the knowledge that was "withheld" from
them in formal institutions.

In this book and in my work with clients, I address
two highly important needs:

» **Improving your relationships with others**:
How to speak before an audience be persuasive
and be skilled in interpersonal communication.
» **Increasing your income**: How to market,
negotiate, sell, and make presentations.

I have three pieces of good news:

1. Any gap you have in life, whether it involves love, romance, money, marketing, health, or happiness does not mean you have to struggle through it alone. There is always someone out there who can teach you. Look for that teacher.

2. Feel worthwhile and productive if you personally supply services or products that provide people with solutions in one of these four areas—love, money, health and happiness—because you are a coach, consultant, therapist, counselor, or mentor. If you are one of these professionals, you address a genuine need shared by many people; you have a lot of potential clients. And as long as the "formal" educational frameworks continue to overlook these topics in their syllabuses, you will always have a lot of work.

3. We are about to narrow the gap between what you absolutely need to know about sales, marketing, persuasion, negotiations, presentations and business in general, and what you were taught (if you studied) at "formal" institutions, in order to maximize your potential and lead you to maximum possible achievements.

The 10 Commandments in this book have can change your life in the following ways:

» Increase your income, whether you are a salaried employee or self-employed

» Increase your chances of success in your career, whether you are now in a senior or junior position

» Increase your chances of success in your business or company, whether you are at the beginning of your business journey, or your business has been around for many years

» Increase your chances of breaking into new markets and new countries

» Increase your chances of creating great partnerships

» Increase your branding, professional authority and status

These 10 principles are **universal**. They work in any country, with any people, and in any field and any market. You can trust me based on my track record and research: I have examined this in four continents over two decades, in over 2,500 workshops and lectures that I have delivered around the world, in consultations to over 1,250 large companies and organizations—from all fields—and in mentorships to thousands of small and medium sized businesses and employees. When you implement these principles—and I'll be generous with you in acknowledging that, even if you only implement a small number of them—people **will buy** more from you, **will talk** more about you (good things of course), **will choose** you more often, **will invest** more in you, **will promote** you more, will be your best "ambassadors" and will **love** you more.

I don't make do just with theory, even though I base my work on many theories and studies; I myself have also been studying the fields of marketing, persuasion, sales, public speaking, rhetoric, negotiation, service and presentation since the beginning of the 2000s.

Beyond having a PhD, and being an economist, a lawyer, mediator, and realtor, I also thrive in the field and I check, in practice, every tool and every method that I write about and recommend. (I have been in sales since I was twelve and I sold flowers at a traffic junction in the town where I grew up.)

Every tip and every tool you will read about in the book has been **tried and tested by me** on my customers and by others countless times (you will get a sense of this by reading stories from around the world throughout the book).

Please read this book as if I am speaking to you from a stage, and we have convened for a practical seminar. Words in bold are those I would emphasis should I be speaking to you from a podium. I hope you can hear me. I sometimes use parentheses and even ellipses. . .it is all part of the strategy I hope to pass on to you in this book.

Implement these tools and you will see success, of course, in everything connected to business, money, revenues, branding and promoting your career but also in other fields of life like parenting, relationships, friendships, relations with family and more.

I believe that the "personal" and the "business-oriented" are connected, and that successful people learn all the time and try to improve all the time in every field. And therefore they achieve a lot more than most people in the world do.

Every expert is also a student. It doesn't matter how senior you are and how much experience you have, and if some of the principles written here sound familiar or known to you, I warmly recommend that you put aside what you know (or think you know), and dive deeply into the stories and examples, to see what you still don't know or don't do and to implement that. And primarily, pay attention to my unique perspective and to how I analyze and see things, including universal and current events that we are all familiar with.

This book distills the 10 Commandments of marketing, persuasion and sales: the best principles and tools available today in my perspective, and, most importantly, the most practical and possible to implement, especially in a digital age as saturated, challenging and competitive as the present age.

At the end of each chapter, I have written a summary of the key rules for that particular principle, for your convenience and to make it easier for you to implement and to remember those principles once in a while.

I want to **shorten your learning curve.**

I truly want you to **succeed in life and business**.

The most important thing for me is that you enjoy the book, find it interesting, laugh, and profit.

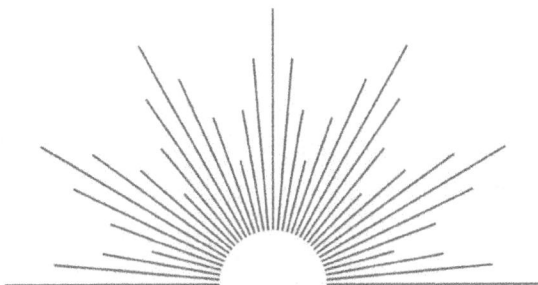

COMMANDMENT NO. 1

Ask and get high prices for your products and services even in a "saturated" market.

WHAT'S THE DIFFERENCE BETWEEN AN "ORDINARY" BOUQUET OF FLOWERS AND A "BRIDAL BOUQUET?"

It's the same bouquet, but in one context, it's used at a wedding as part of the photography session and ceremony.

You will find the answer at the end of this section. But in the meantime, here's a story:

As part of my activity on Amazon.com, which is one place where my books are sold, I periodically check the pricing and promotions of books. During one of my checks, I came across a collection of ninety-nine classic tunes by Mozart selling on Amazon for between $8 and $11. So far so good, right?

Although Mozart's classics are being sold to adults, there is business line called Baby Mozart. (For those of you who don't have kids yet, or whose kids are older, these collections for babies and toddlers ages 0-3. They are supposed to be calming.) A collection of ten Mozart classics in a Baby Mozart box is sold on Amazon for between $39 and $51!

The Baby Mozart collection has the same music as the adult version; Mozart didn't compose anything special for kids. So, for fewer tunes, the children's version costs five times more! Why? Because it's for kids.

Studies show that there are three areas in which people spend a lot of money, disproportionate to the true value of the product. Those three areas are:

» **Health**
» **Weddings**
» **Kids**

Let's start with kids. According to surveys taken around the world, a typical family in the Western world spends a few hundred thousand dollars, on average, on each of their children from the moment they are born until they reach eighteen, regardless of its socio-economic status.

Now you may ask: How can an average family afford to spend so much money on each child?

The answer: It can't. But the parents spend it anyway—because "you don't skimp on kids."

Hence, Mozart for babies is also five times more expensive than Mozart for adults.

And on to the second topic of health. You know how some people work at an ordinary job for relatively low wages, live modestly, and everyone around them keeps telling them they can and should earn more, but they have very low self-esteem? Then, one day, they get sick (or one of their family members) and they need surgery urgently that costs $100,000. All of a sudden, they find a good part of the money by working at more jobs, asking people around them for a loan or donation, and so on. They find a way to earn more and pay crazy sums of money. Why? Because you spend whatever is necessary when it comes to health.

And now to the third topic of weddings. The difference between an "ordinary" bouquet of flowers and a "bridal" one is somewhere between $100 and $200 based on our research. Why? Because the purpose is different.

When a bride and groom purchase a "bridal bouquet" for their wedding, what they are really buying is the bride's feeling of being "a queen for a day."

They are buying the bride's "million-dollar feeling" (together with her dress, hairstyling and makeup, which were all relatively expensive, as it's a wedding). They are buying the "winning picture" that they will show to their kids in ten years' time (or to their grandchildren in thirty years' time) when they go through their wedding albums and say, "Look how beautiful your mother/grandmother was!"

That's why when it comes to a wedding, people pay more.

If you're selling products or services in one of these three areas—children, health or weddings—you're lucky! I don't want to hear any complaints about the "market conditions," "many competitors," and so on. And if you're doing business in other areas, you'll appreciate the importance of "selling the problem before the solution."

The more important (or urgent) the problem or need is to me, the more I, the customer, am willing to pay for a solution.

So, before you sell a customer flowers, for example, you must find out what they need them for.

WHY DO CERTAIN PRO ATHLETES MAKE SO MUCH MONEY?

In June 2009, Ronaldo, already a huge soccer star, won the Champions League. Two weeks later, he moved from Manchester United to Real Madrid for a then absolutely insane record transfer fee of 80 million pounds sterling paid to Manchester United, net wages of 9.5 million euros a year for Ronaldo himself, and a further 10 million euro commission for his agent!

These figures were unheard of at the time and caused shockwaves in the world media and sparked unprecedented criticism of Real Madrid's President Florentino Perez. A few days later, he also signed the

French soccer star Karim Benzema for the small sum of 35 million euros!

Perez said in an interview at the time: The acquisition that seems the most expensive at first, is in the end, the cheapest.

Journalists ridiculed him, but looking back with the perspective of time, Perez was right!

Real Madrid built a complete business model around the time of Ronaldo's arrival at the club, in which they expected to recoup their investment in six years—they made it back in less time—and they significantly increased their advertising contracts with companies such as Coca Cola, Audi and Adidas. They also significantly increased the price of subscriptions and held a series of summer exhibition matches around the world, and managed to bring in 700 million euros in broadcasting rights in the next five years, as well as a further 30 million euros in the three years after that as a primary sponsorship from Internet betting company bwin.com.

Now let's ask ourselves again: Was Ronaldo worth 100 million euros in 2009?

The answer: he was worth that sum to Real Madrid. That's why they paid it.

Let's return to our reality. In my view, customers and consumers are calculated and sophisticated people, far more so than advertising agencies and most businesses believe.

You are in trouble—and it doesn't matter what field you are in—if you think your customers are stupid.

At the end of the day, everyone makes their own calculations. There is a range of benefits that the customers sees if they purchase the product or service, and a range of needs that the product or service answers for them. Some of them are irrational or emotional, but those are needs as well.

Even if you as a salesperson can't always see these benefits and needs, your customers most certainly can! That's why people are willing to pay high prices for products and services. Even if they don't have enough money at the moment.

Not everyone, of course. This only applies to those who are sufficiently flush to make the purchase, and those who see the benefit they will generate from the transaction.

If you want to sell at expensive prices, you have to get inside the mind of your customers, and understand why they are buying from you—and not why you want to sell to them. Sell them their needs, pains and problems, before you offer them your solution.

WHY DO WE NEGOTIATE WITH OURSELVES INSTEAD OF WITH OUR CUSTOMERS?

I had an interesting conversation with a client I was mentoring. She is a lecturer, coach and consultant, and she had received an order from a large firm (thanks to a marketing campaign she carried out as part of the mentorship program). She called me to get advice on how to price the workshop and how to write out a price quote.

I immediately saw an opportunity for her to "step up to another level" and ask for far higher sums than she was used to, and also to work with a much bigger customer than she was used to. I told her the price I thought she should ask from a company of that size.

She had planned to ask for a much lower sum than the sum I had suggested. She "got scared" by what I had said and started to argue with me: They will never agree to that kind of sum! Who pays that much?

I explained to her that people do pay precisely those kinds of sums; I myself received even higher sums from the same company. And in any event, it was worth her while to ask for that amount just to position herself in their eyes.

We debated for a while and she kept trying to explain to me (though I'm on her side) why she wanted to ask for the lower sum. On top of that, she kept saying things like, "Even what I was thinking seems too high to me. To be on the safe side, I'll lower the sum even more."

At one point, I stopped her and said, "Look what you are doing. You are negotiating with yourself in your mind, and with me, your mentor, without having even approached your client, without having any idea what their budget is. Also without hearing their reaction and without knowing what they are used to paying other people."

She was so afraid of the thought that they might say "no" to the price she asked (they wanted her; they had approached her!) that she reduced her price (in her head) again and again, until she reached a sum that in my opinion was very low and not sufficiently profitable, especially for her professional level.

Let me present a few conclusions from this conversation. First, most people price themselves too low, and then they never know (and will never know) how much they could really have gotten. So, ask higher prices for your products and services.

Second, it's all in your mind. The toughest kind of persuasion is self-persuasion.

Believe in yourself, that you are worth the money and are a professional authority, and explain that properly to your customers. Then it will be a lot easier for you to demand high prices.

Third, when you are engaged in financial negotiations, you have to look not at how much money you want, but at the other side: how much they are willing and able to pay, what is the value they will extract from you, budgets, and how important is the knowledge and experience that you have.

IS IT POSSIBLE TO SELL A SINGLE TOMATO FOR $24, AND IF SO, HOW DO YOU GO ABOUT DOING THAT?

In July 2019, HaSalon, a New York restaurant belonging to the international Israeli chef Eyal Shani, received a scathing review in the *New York Post*. The paper's food critic Steve Cuozzo was outraged by the cost of a single sliced tomato, which was $24!

"It was tasty, sure, but this was far from the best tomato I've ever had," the celebrated food critic wrote. He added that HaSalon translates as 'the salon' or, as applied to this venue, 'the living room," but it might as well mean, 'Ha, suckers! The joke's on us.'"[1]

A few immediate questions arose as a result of this incident.

First, is it "chutzpah" to price a sliced tomato at $24?

Second, what is Chef Eyal Shani really selling?

Third, what's the effect of a critique like that on a chef restaurant?

With regard to the first question, let me rephrase it a little differently; How much is a single tomato really worth?

We all know that if we go wander around a farmer's market or go to a supermarket and buy tomatoes, the price will differ from place to place, depending on the type of tomato and the socio-economic status of a particular community. (Not to mention private grocery stores when prices are often out of control—and I haven't even mentioned organic food stores.)

My answer to the question "How much is a single tomato really worth" is: as much as customers are willing to pay for it!

---

1 Steve Cuozzo, "Restaurant charges $24 for a single tomato," New York Post, July 2, 2019.

The HaSalon restaurant in New York is full most of the time. In a free market and in privately-owned restaurants, the rule is supply and demand—if so, then many people are willing to pay $24 for a tomato (and $24 for an avocado bruschetta—which is basically an avocado and $19 for a bag of green beans), so it is worth it to them.

That brings us to the second question: What is a chef really offering diners when he sells a tomato for $24?

The answer, of course, is not a tomato. People are still sane and rational. HaSalon, like other restaurants, offers an experience that is beyond food. Customers come to dance and to be merry, to see the chefs in action. The music is cool and upbeat and the restaurant offers a unique and exclusive experience. In New York, the restaurant offers a special "Middle Eastern" experience.

Twenty-four dollars includes not only the sliced tomato, but also the happy atmosphere, the way the food is served, and the experience that the diner receives—plus the Mediterranean character that cosmopolitan New York seems to love so much.

The third question, and perhaps the most intriguing is: How did the scornful restaurant review impact the number of people dining at the restaurant?

One might think that having a famous critic slam their dishes is a chef's worst nightmare. But, in fact, the review did wonders for the restaurant, and not only did the number of diners not go down, it went up!

Why?

After publication of the review, more people knew about it, and a buzz ensued. Alongside all those who in all likelihood wouldn't want to come and pay so much, there were plenty who would want to see the infamous tomato that costs $24, to see what it tastes like and to talk about it with their friends. (After all, no one pays $24 for a tomato and keeps it to themselves.)

I don't always agree with the statement, "There's no such thing as bad publicity," but in this case I do. What's more, it's not like the review said there were rats in the kitchen, or that the waiters were rude and racist; that could really bring a restaurant down, no matter how successful. The buzz was about its high prices. And high prices are a sign, among other things, of brand. Of high positioning. A different experience. And of a courageous chef who sees himself as an artist and prices his dishes accordingly.

HOW TO BEGIN CONVINCING YOURSELF TO RAISE PRICES

SITUATION #1:

You're a professional or you own a business and you want to raise the prices of your products or services. How do you approach existing clients about the new price (higher than what they've gotten used to) with ease and confidence?

Write the new, higher price on paper. Look at it a few times. Practice saying it out loud, in front of the mirror or to a partner, spouse or colleague, before you begin saying it to paying clients.

SITUATION #2:

You've worked as an employee for many years and you have now founded your own business or company. How do you make the necessary "mental transition" in the smoothest, most practical way?

Make a business card for yourself with the business or company logo, and write "CEO," "Owner" or "Founder" under your name.

What do the two situations and answers I've listed have in common? Both situations involve self-persuasion before you turn to persuading others.

Before I begin to tell clients about a new price, I have to feel confident and comfortable with it myself and be convinced that I'm raising the prices for the right reasons. And before I begin to introduce myself and my position to others, I have to be content with the new position I've "created" for myself. (After all, any entrepreneur, businessperson or company owner creates something out of nothing!)

Unless you feel confident with your messages, no one listening to you will feel confident about you. And, unless you're convinced of your position, it will be very difficult for you to persuade others. That is, your persuasion skills begin in your head, in how you think about yourself, businesswise.

WHY YOU SHOULD NEVER MEET WITH YOUR CUSTOMERS FOR FREE.

One of the strongest objections I receive (to my surprise), is on the subject of "My first meeting with a customer—should I charge a fee or not?"

In every lecture, workshop, or consultation for small businesses, medium-sized business and large firms as well, when I meet with service providers (lawyers, business consultants, mortgage advisors, designers insurance agents, realtors, travel agents, appraisers, architects and more), I spell out my beliefs. When we get to the subject of pricing and establishing a connection with clients, and I note that from the perspective of personal branding, future pricing, and most importantly, the chances of closing a deal, I recommend charging clients from the first meeting, many of my clients jump up and say things like, "In my field of business that would never work." "That might work in other professions." "None of my competitors charges for meetings with clients." "If I were to ask clients for payment for our first meeting, no one would book an appointment with me." The excuses go on an on.

One of the biggest mistakes people and businesses make (including people very close to me on a personal level), is to meet for free with everyone who is willing to meet with them. (By the way, the meeting isn't really for free, it costs you money for parking, gas, a babysitter, time you could have spent doing something else, and so on.)

This issue is very important in my opinion as part of the process of persuasion that customers undergo when they decide whether to buy from you or from someone else. I want to explain to you why you must never meet with a customer for free.

I'm not talking about working meetings, or meetings to discuss cooperation. I'm not talking about a situation in which you are in a store or at a trade show, and customers come to check out your products. What I'm talking about is a situation where a supplier or service provider, who sells (among other things) their time and knowledge, holds an "introductory" meeting with a customer for free, instead of demanding payment for the meeting.

Let me list several reasons for my (very resolute) position (which is backed up by several studies, by statistics, and by two decades of business experience):

» If you are providing value from the first minute, then you should be paid from the first minute. In other words, assuming you are a professional and an expert in your field (which is why the customer approached you in the first place), then from the moment you meet the customer and you listen to their story and identify their problem/need, you will know straight away what solutions they require and what they need to do. And then you will give them tips, explain things to them, tell them who they need to turn to, and so on. In other words, you will be providing them with something of value!

In short, there is no such a thing as an "introductory meeting." It's an invention devised by customers who want to get something for free, as in, "Come to my office so I have a chance to get to know you," "We don't know each other yet," and "I'd like to see some more."

When you meet the customer, (and I'm also talking about managers at large companies) they won't be too interested in your background, and certainly not in getting to know you on a personal level. The customer is interested only in their needs and problems (which is perfectly natural), and during the meeting will try to "squeeze" you for information, tips, tools and help as much as possible (which is also perfectly natural), regardless of whether they have paid or not.

If a customer is receiving something of value, why shouldn't they pay for the meeting? If you don't think you are going to be giving them something of value for your customers, don't meet with them in the first place. Charge a fee from the start.

> » The second reason is that customers who aren't willing to pay for a meeting are customers that aren't good for you.

I call them by the codename or pejorative "the coupon crowd." You will invest in them the same effort you would have in a paying customer. You will get to the appointment on time, you'll learn about them ahead of time, you will read the materials they sent, you will provide them with something of value during your meeting, and you will answer all their questions.

And what will they do? They will be more argumentative because they didn't pay, so they are less appreciative of you (!) even if it's just a subconscious response. They will feel free to cancel the meeting at the last moment, to be late or to fail to turn up without even notifying you because they didn't pay and don't feel obliged. And the chances that they will close a deal with you or purchase your products and services will be significantly lower than if you were dealing with a paying customer doing so.

This, too, is proven by research and statistics. The more your customers pay you, the more they respect you.

The absurdity is that a paying customer won't be angry about the payment and won't complain. In fact, the opposite is true: They will respect you more. This is because, subconsciously, they will justify the price to themselves, especially if the price is high, by the fact that you are expert and professional.

Charging a fee from the start (and I don't care what "common practice" is in your market, or what your competitors do) naturally sorts good customers from "the coupon crowd." It sorts customers who are ripe for the process and want to purchase your service or expertise, from those who aren't yet "ripe enough to buy" and are just "checking" and putting out feelers.

It sorts between those who really want to gain something and are willing to invest to do so, and those who aren't serious enough or don't want it enough. (What really amuses me is people who meet with five different experts or suppliers, give each one the feeling they are about to close, squeeze as much information as they can out of each one, and then try to go it alone.)

Charge from the start.

> » The third reason is, as experts and authorities in your field (no matter what field), your most precious resource is your time. You must value it and price it accordingly, otherwise you will be damaging your image in the customer's eyes.

There is a term in economics called "price positioning."

By defining a specific price for your product or service, you have positioned your product or service, or yourself (subconsciously) in the eyes of your customer at a specific level, or in a specific category.

Getting out of the box that your customer has put you in becomes much harder if you meet without charging. Many businesspeople believe, for example, that "If I don't charge for the first meeting, the customer will see how good my services are and how professional I am, and they will be willing to pay me a lot down the line."

But it works exactly the opposite: The chances of closing a deal with a customer you have met with for free go down, not up! This is because the customer who insists on meeting you for free is not a good customer for you, and because they actually don't think you are good enough and professional enough if you don't ask for money. (All the more so if you come to the customer rather than the customer coming to you.) And because they have (subconsciously) positioned your time as not being worth money—don't be surprised because that's what you did as well!—why should they pay for more time with you? After all, they received your time for free.

Even if some of your customers agree to pay you to continue, why should they pay you a lot? After all, you're probably not "so professional" if you are running around from meeting to meeting and not charging anything, right?

If you want to brand yourself in your market, or to position yourself as an authority in the eyes of your customers who do not yet know you, then **charge them from the start.**

A few years ago, I was approached by a Marketing VP at a very large international company who asked for a meeting with me. She had heard me give a lecture at a major conference and was impressed. She said that the subject of my lecture, Motivating Customers to Action and Penetration of a New Product to Market, was exactly what her company was looking for, as they were about to launch a new product into the market.

I told her I would be happy to meet her, clarified a few details and told her my price for a meeting. She was a little surprised that I had asked for money and said, "No, no, we only want to have an introductory meeting."

I asked her what she meant, and she replied, "We are currently examining the possibility of working with several advisors. Several other senior managers and I will meet with you, and consult with you about our product, and in the end, we will choose whom to work with."

What was the VP Marketing, with whom I had no previous acquaintance, really saying to me? That she and some other managers would meet me (no doubt at their offices, if it was up to her) for free, they'll tell me about the product and the launch and get me to talk. At the same time, they will meet with a few other advisors, and finally, they would decide whether to continue to work with me or not.

I told a few people about the incident and they said to me, "It's okay that they want to get to know you." But what does "get to know me" mean? After all, they aren't going to ask me personal questions, and my private life doesn't interest them. They want me for my knowledge, my experience, my abilities, and so forth.

The same people said to me, "Okay, go and meet them, but don't give them any information. If they ask you professional questions, tell them they will get the answers in a paid follow-up meeting after they pick you."

Really?!? Let's try and imagine the situation. I come for a meeting with a few managers at their company. I'm already in an inferior negotiating position, by virtue of the fact that I have come to them on their terms. By the second or third question (within a couple of minutes), they are already asking me professional questions—after all, that's why we are meeting. And then what? Do I retain the right to maintain silence? While I am sitting there in front of them?

And if I'm there for some kind of audition, how exactly am I supposed to impress them and show them what a professional I am, if I don't answer them and give away my precious knowledge?

My only way to impress them and justify my being there is to give them my best solutions. What will stop them from doing it themselves, then, after the meeting with me? Or from meeting another consultant and speaking with them about my ideas? If they don't pay for the meeting, what's the chance they will appreciate what they received from me and that they will see me as a professional authority?

Of course I wasn't prepared to meet them for free, and I explained to her that I charge for meetings because I conduct myself in the most professional manner possible; prior to a meeting, I study the product and the launch. I research the subject by myself and instruct the customer which materials to send me, and I read all of them. Then, at the meeting, I give them value from the start.

As I've already said, if I am providing value for my customer from the start, then I should get paid from the start.

WHY YOU SHOULD STAY AWAY FROM "GET-TO-KNOW-YOU MEETINGS."

Now ask yourself: what if the customer really does want to get to know you? They have heard about you, they are thinking about it, but they still aren't completely ripe to pay.

No problem! Want to get to know me for free? I have a personal Facebook page, a business Facebook page and a YouTube channel with hundreds of videos and hours upon hours of instructional training, plus LinkedIn, Twitter, a mailing list and countless articles on each of my three websites. Either I or someone on my team will send you links, materials and free videos. In addition, I'll usually have a short telephone conversation with you; we'll get to know each other and I'll get to understand your needs. Perhaps, if we are talking about a big project, I'll invite you to be a guest to one of my conferences.

But if you want to meet me for a personal face-to-face consultation, that costs money. That has been my business model for the past two decades and it is, in my opinion, the right model in any field. Your customers will respect you a lot more, and you will differentiate yourself from your competitors and increase your chances of being selected.

That's what happened in the case I described. It didn't happen immediately, it took a few weeks of conversations and emails, but in the end, the managers of the company met with me for a fee (at the rates I charge) and selected me to work with them. And in the years that followed, I did several successful projects with them that were very profitable for me—and especially for them.

I later learned that they had contacted five senior consultants and I was the only one who had asked to be paid for the meeting.

You are much better off not doing business with a customer that just wants to extract your knowledge, to give you an "audition" (and meet at the same time with several other suppliers for free) and to give themselves the option to use your knowledge without you.

If you are an expert in your field, your most important resource is **your knowledge**. Your second most important resource is **your time**. Don't give away your time and knowledge for free.

That's true for any field, any market and any profession.

WHY YOU SHOULDN'T BE DRAMATIC WHEN TALKING WITH CUSTOMERS ABOUT HIGH PRICES.

Imagine a situation (some of you probably won't have to imagine it) where you come home in the evening exhausted from work and your partner says to you, "We have to talk." You sit on the couch in the living room, tense and stressed. What happened? What have you done? What does your partner want? You are agitated and are sure you are about to split up.

You are already on the defensive and are preparing your "counter-argument" (even though you don't know what for yet), and then your partner says something like, "I've asked you before to take the garbage down every morning when you go out, and you haven't done it now several times. It leaves a bad smell in the kitchen and creates an unpleasant situation. Please make sure to take care of it next time."

What happened here? Unnecessary drama! They made you stressed out and worried for nothing! They made something small and unimportant look like a big and serious problem.

If people do that a lot in the field of relationships (unfortunately), there is another field where most people are far too dramatic—when talk turns to prices.

I hear this all the time from customers—in business consultancy, in meetings, from listening to recorded sales calls, and from working with customers and with call centers.

Because most people don't really know how to sell—nobody taught them properly—they don't like sales. They prefer to focus on conversations about their product or service and not on conversations about price; they feel uncomfortable talking about money. They then create unnecessary drama at the sales stage when they have to talk about price and say to the customer things like, "Now we need to talk about money" (the awful parallel to "we need to talk"). They change their tone of voice or pace of speech when it comes to talking about cost, they lower their gaze or turn down their intensity at this stage, and all sorts of other things.

What happens? First, if you signal that you are uncomfortable talking about money, the customer will definitely feel it! You are making this part of the conversation even more problematic and cumbersome for yourself.

Second, you are increasing the chances that your customer will argue about the price and say, "It's too expensive," will ask for a discount, installments, and so on, all because you are signaling weakness, insecurity and discomfort.

Third, the customer will immediately become tense, agitated and defensive and the nature of the conversation will take a turn for the worse!

What should you do?

Make the conversation about money as "incidental" as possible. Make it a natural part of the conversation, not a dramatic moment. Don't turn down your energy in a conversation about cost. On the contrary, turn up your intensity, speak with the same flow and confidence that you spoke with earlier, when you described your product/service/solution/idea/proposal to your customer.

State your figure out loud, not with a "deafening silence;" keep the conversation flowing with confidence and repeat the benefit that the customer will gain after payment. If you feel comfortable with the price you are asking for, then your customer will feel comfortable as well!

If you relate to payment as something natural, obvious and self-evident (even when prices are high), then your customer will also relate in the same way—and that will prevent unnecessary arguments and expected resistance.

WHY YOU SHOULDN'T GIVE DISCOUNTS TO CUSTOMERS

A famous saying states that "Liars need a really good memory." Why? To remember what they said to whom and when.

Reliable people say the same thing to everybody, so they don't need to remember which version they told and to whom they told it. I have been telling this to people for years, with regard to everything connected to discounts for customers.

Businesses and people who don't work in an organized manner—I'm always surprised by how many of them there are—don't operate with a fixed price list and set terms for customers.

The excuse they give themselves and everyone else is that "it's not important," "I get a sense of the customer in conversation and that's how I set my price," "customers with differing financial means will pay different prices," "I get on just fine without a price list," and so on.

In practice, what this mainly does is create a mess. First of all, you need a really good memory to remember what price you gave to each customer. For the most part, people don't have such good memories, and they end up looking bad in the eyes of the customer. The result for the most part is pricing that is too low or a significant discount (your customers will often take advantage of your poor memory.)

Second, a good and successful sales process, without any connection to results, is one in which you lead the conversation with the customer confidently, and not one in which they lead the conversation.

When the terms are clear to everyone (primarily to you), when there are fixed prices for each product, operation or service, and most of all when you are very familiar with the prices and feel happy with them, you will lead the sales process with confidence—and your chances of closing a deal will increase significantly.

On the other hand, when the client feels they are managing to "sway" you, that you aren't certain of your price, that any price you name is subject to change and that any term you have mentioned is open to negotiation, they will argue with you, be a lot more stubborn and most importantly, they will respect you less.

I argue that you shouldn't give discounts, especially not if you are selling at high prices and positioning yourselves as experts in the eyes of your customers, because customers argue less with experts.

Customers respect experts more merely smart people with interesting opinions, and they spread the word to others. Customers are willing to pay more to experts, and (almost) never request a discount, and even if they do, they don't tend to expect to get one.

If you want to be paid more, to be listened to more, to close more deals and to be argued with less, conduct yourself as a professional and an expert when talking to customers. That way you won't need a brilliant memory.

The next chapter covers branding yourself as an expert.

KEY ELEMENTS OF COMMANDMENT NO. 1

Ask and get high prices for your products and services.

SELL THE PROBLEM BEFORE THE SOLUTION:

✓ The more important (or urgent) the problem or need is to the customers, the more they are willing to pay for your solution.

✓ If you want to sell at high prices, you have to get inside your customer's head, and understand why they are buying from you—and not why you want to sell to them. Most people price themselves too low, and thus they don't know (and will never know) how much they can really receive.

✓ Demand higher prices for your products and services. When you are engaged in financial negotiations, you have to look not at how much money you want, and how much you are willing to compromise, but at the other side, that is, how much are they willing and able to pay, and what value they can generate from you. How much is a product or service really worth? As much as the customer is willing to pay for it! Before you begin to tell clients about a new price, you have to feel confident and comfortable with it yourself and be convinced that you raised the prices for the right reasons.

√ If you are selling your time and knowledge, charge your clients from your first meeting. If you are providing value right from the start, then you should be paid right from the start.

√ The more your clients pay you, the more they will respect you!

√ If you have set a specific price for your product or services, then you have positioned your product/service /yourself subconsciously in the eyes of your customer at a certain level, or in a particular category.

√ If you are an expert in your field, your most important resource is your time and knowledge. Don't give them away for free.

√ Make the conversation about money incidental as much as possible; make it a natural part of the conversation. Don't make a drama out of it and don't drop your energy levels when talking about prices.

√ When you know your prices well and feel happy with them, you will lead the sales process with confidence—and the chances of closing a deal will increase significantly!

COMMANDMENT NO. 2

Brand yourself as expert in your field in creative ways, even in a competitive market.

AS LONG AS YOU'RE NOT A BRAND, YOUR INCOME IS IN TROUBLE!

A few years ago, a client told me an amazing story. He was a computer importer who had tried to market computers to companies. In most cases, he encountered refusals and excuses, and he didn't understand why. His computers were better and cheaper than his competitors, which is supposedly every purchasing manager's dream. At some point, in order to understand and become more efficient, he started asking those who turned him down why they had refused him and one day, a purchasing manager in one of the companies that had turned him down gave a straight answer that shocked him.

He said: Listen, I know your computers are cheaper and better than IBM, but I'll still going to order my next shipment of computers from IBM. Why? Because if I run into a computer problem or malfunction, no one will fire me if I ordered it from IBM. But if I gamble on you and there's a problem, I'll be fired!

An amazing yet not unusual answer. That purchasing manager simply told my client what everyone else who didn't buy from him thought. When that client told me this story, I wasn't surprised. I've seen this before.

When I first started promoting my lectures designed for managers and sales agents, I knew that the training manager was the one to decide if to invite me for a lecture or not. I was certain he really cared about the lecture being beneficial and insightful to the participants, so that over time, they could use what they learned in the lecture to increase the company's profit. Boy, was I naïve.

Because what's the first thing a training manager really cares about? That people will enjoy the lecture at that particular moment and, mainly, that no one will complain to them! That none of the managers would come out of the lecture and scowl: "That was boring." Therefore, they'd rather (generally speaking) not take the risk, and hire well-known, successful speakers—or in other words brand names!

Those "brand names" are highly likely to give a good, enjoyable lecture, and are least likely to be problematic. Even if they are, the meeting planner can always respond to the complaining manager with amazement, "What do you want? He came highly recommended and with his kind of experience. Who would have thought he'd be terrible?"

Just like that purchasing manager who won't be fired if he buys from IBM.

Now, back to that computer importer who is competing with IBM. He has two options.

The first option is to quit, because he doesn't have a chance as a small business to compete with a huge company, and he is better off shutting down his business.

The second option is to stay in the game and shift tactics. Don't try or desire to be IBM, but be the best possible version of himself. He should brand his business correctly vis-a-vis his customers so that they know and feel that he also has successes, a "track record," satisfied customers, has been around for a while, and so on, and that they should be willing to take a "risk" on working with him or ordering goods from him. These are known as **social proofs** and I will expand on their use in Commandment 10.

Therefore, if you want to sell, but are less familiar with the market, or if it's a new client, you must increase the client's certainty in working with you. You will then minimize the fear that something unpleasant may happen if he works with you, or that he may receive a complaint for his choosing to work with you.

WHAT HAPPENS WHEN A TIME MANAGEMENT CONSULTANT IS LATE?

In 2003, I attended a lecture on time management, and the lecturer was late. Imagine the situation: Dozens of people waiting in a classroom for a lecturer who was supposed to begin his lecture at 9 o'clock in the morning.

Everyone was there on time, waiting, and the lecturer ran in at 9:10, panting and out of breath. He arranged his presentation and a few minutes later began his lecture—15 minutes late—saying, "Sorry I'm late, there was an unexpected traffic jam that I didn't take into account when I left home. And now, let me teach you how to manage your time properly."

From that moment on, it made no difference what he said because when he ran late, he had lost his audience, who no longer considered him a professional authority.

After all, what do people expect, among other things, from an expert? That they implement in practice the things they talk about. They walk the talk. If he's teaching people how to manage their time, then he should start on time. If someone is running weight loss workshops, they shouldn't be fat. If someone is lecturing on how to get rich and how to make millions in a particular field, they shouldn't be living at home with their parents.

During my career, I have seen quite a few similar examples.

A few months ago, I was approached by a large and well-known company that asked me to hold a workshop for its salespeople and managers. They wanted a seminar on how to improve sales of their brands, how to ask for and to receive higher prices for their flagship products, and how to correctly respond to price resistance such as "It's expensive for me."

I gave them a quote, and guess what happened? They claimed that I was expensive and that they had planned a much lower budget for the workshop, and asked me to lower my price.

I didn't budge and refused to lower the sum by even one dollar. In our following conversations as well, I would not discuss the price, only the value they would receive from the workshop, as a result of the increase in revenues if only some of the participants in my workshop were to implement just a small part of the content I would deliver and practice with them, and the fact that the workshop was an investment for them—money they would see a return on—and not an expense.

Eventually I persuaded them and they took me at the original price I'd requested. I wasn't arguing out of ego or in order to "educate" them, but because I really believed that the price I had given was justified and that I could make a significant contribution to increasing their revenues.

When it was all over, I found myself thinking about the example of the time management consultant who was late and I thought to myself: how could I have possibly positioned myself as an authority, an expert on selling brands, on overcoming resistance to sales at high prices, if I reduced my own prices and gave a discount in order to sell? That isn't logical and just doesn't work!

If you want your environment to take you seriously, your customers to see you as a professional authority and to buy from you and not your competitors, and to pay prices far above average, for your community of "fans" and "followers" to grow consistently—and yes, for your kids to listen to you and see you as a role model—then you have to live as you educate others to and implement the tips and tools you teach.

HOW DO YOU GET YOUR CUSTOMER TO FEEL THEY ARE YOUR ONLY CUSTOMER (EVEN IF YOU HAVE A LOT OF CUSTOMERS)?

Many years ago, one of my customers, a real estate agent, told me the following story: A few years earlier, when he was a young and hungry realtor, there was a house belonging to a very old man and the rumor spread among real estate agents that the old man wanted to sell the house in order to move to an assisted living facility.

The young real estate agent decided he was going to do everything to sign the old man on an exclusivity agreement. He went to see the old man every day for two weeks, and would spend several hours there every day. Every time they met, he would drink several cups of tea with the man and listen to countless stories— the old man was of course in no hurry to go anywhere and was happy to have company. At the end of every meeting, the realtor tried to speak to the old man and get him to sign the exclusivity agreement. The old man would always answer, "Tomorrow, tomorrow, we'll sign."

Two weeks after their first meeting, as they drank a third cup of tea, the old man informed him that he had decided to hand the sale of the house over to another real estate agent and had already signed an exclusivity agreement with him.

The young realtor was surprised and asked the old man, "Why? I've been sitting with you every day for the past two weeks!" The old man replied that's exactly the problem. You don't seem busy enough I prefer to leave the house in the hands of someone who is busy and has a lot of customers."

From his perspective, the young realtor gave the best service he could and invested a lot of time and effort in the deal, but the more he "invested" and developed a "friendship" with the potential customer, the further the deal slipped away from him and the more his professional authority was diminished.

> » How does a company selling brands conduct itself?
> » How does an expert conduct himself?
> » How does an authority become an authority?

The answer is, first, by the way one conducts himself with his customers. Second, a principle known as the "luxury paradox" plays into the scenario, that is, a brand or authority works with customers using two parallel tenets that complement each other, but also contradict each other.

The first doctrine is: the customer is king. The second is: but only on my terms. There is a sort of contradiction between these two tenets and thus the "paradox."

Because if the customer is king, then in principle, every transaction should be executed the way the customer wants, on their terms, wherever the customer desires to meet, at a price the customer is willing to pay, and so on. That, by the way, is how most businesses conduct themselves with their customers, by adhering to the (incorrect) slogan, "The customer is always right." This means they are willing to adjust their terms, prices and professional standards to suit what their customers want. This is a mistake as it only impedes a deal, diminishes a company's authority, and in the long term leads to financial losses and to a lower quality of customers that are less suitable to the company's business.

Being a brand, though, brings us to the second doctrine: only on my terms. In other words, once a customer has joined your "members' club," they will receive fantastic service, you will fulfill all the promises you made, and you will do everything to achieve good results for the customer.

But—and this is a very important but—in order to join your "members' club," the customer has to meet certain terms such as the price and location you set,

your professional demands, and your terms of payment without compromises and without discounts. It
is precisely these demands and conditions, contrary to
instinct, that will increase the chances of the customer
closing a deal with you, and they will certainly increase
the chances that the customer will respect you and see
you as an authority.

Let's go back to the realtor and the old man.

One of my guiding principles in business is that it
is important for your customer to know that you have a
lot of other customers, but they mustn't feel that you do.
If a customer feels that they are your only customer or
your first customer or that you hardly have any customers, that isn't good. The chances of them closing a deal
with you will decline.

On the other hand, if a customer knows that you
have a lot of customers and are very busy, and they
feel that you don't have time for them, that you aren't
available when they call, you turn up for meetings
unprepared, or you're on the phone with other customers during meetings, that isn't good either. Again, the
chances of them closing a deal with you will decline.

Customers want a personal touch; they want to
feel like celebrities in your world and to be appreciated.

What's the solution? How do you implement the
"luxury paradox" in your relationship with your customer? How do you find the "middle path" in the way
you deal with your customers? How do you increase the

probability that your customer will want to close a deal with you?

The key is balance: Don't be too available and don't be too busy.

When you are meeting or talking with customers, give them your full attention, come to your meeting prepared, show them real "love." Remember what they told you at your last meeting, and make them feel that you have nothing better to do right now, nowhere else to go right now, and no one else you would rather be with—until the time to end the meeting has come. Then make yourself available to sit or talk with another customer, and give them exactly the same feeling!

Set boundaries for your customers. Within those boundaries, give them maximum service and maximum attention. That way, over time, you can create a loyal community of customers that will only grow.

The young real estate agent didn't set boundaries with the old man; he didn't make it clear that his time is valuable, he didn't tell him about his other customers and about the other things he was doing. He agreed again and again to come to the old man's house, even though he didn't have a signed contract.

In practice, despite his sincere efforts, what the young real estate agent did was to discourage a deal, and the customer, and of course, he ended up being offended.

"Invest less," but do so prudently. Brand yourselves properly to your customers and you will see much better results.

THE DAY MY HOUSEKEEPER SENT ME A PRICE QUOTE

A few years ago, I moved within the same neighborhood to a bigger apartment. Any move, as you are certainly aware, involves a lot of expenses and challenges and/or negotiations with suppliers and various service providers.

In my case, I needed to do minor renovations and a thorough cleanup of the house a few days before the movers brought over everything from the previous house.

I'm an organized person, so a few months earlier I had already put together a list of things to do—pretty long from the start, but became longer and longer as the move neared. There were chores and tasks that seemed to me from the start to be difficult and complicated, such as switching bills to my new address, and I was pleasantly surprised by how quickly they went.

On the other hand, there were tasks that seemed relatively simple, that turned out to be complicated, such as finding a housekeeper and people to do general maintenance.

I did a market survey, and called a few service providers that I already knew or that had been recommended to me by friends or on internet sites. I was surprised to hear that all of them refused to give me a price quote over the phone, but would only do so after seeing the house. Some of them "compromised" and agreed that I should photograph the house from every angle and send them pictures and videos to their phones or email before they made a decision about doing the ongoing work. That done, they all gave me a written price quote after viewing the house. The result: All of them asked for prices that were much higher than what I'd remembered, had estimated, and had budgeted. After my initial surprise and "recalculating the route" from a budgetary perspective, I thought about it in depth, and reached a happy conclusion.

Despite the fact that dealing with all the service providers had taken a lot more time, energy and money than I had thought, and had caused me as a client to work much harder with them, I was happy to see that:

» Service providers see themselves as experts and price themselves accordingly; businesses and the self-employed work in a clear and orderly fashion—everything is written down, everything is clear, and there is full coordination of expectations; and

» Service providers. conduct "auditions" for clients, and aren't willing to work with anybody (and certainly not at any price).

Why did that make me happy? Because that's what I've been preaching to my clients for years!

If you want to succeed big time, over time, then you have to conduct yourself properly, from a professional, business, and personal standpoint. You have to brand yourself as an expert and to respect yourself professionally. You have to know how to ask for higher prices for your products and services, you have to work in an orderly and organized fashion. That's the difference between being a "business" and just doing a "job." And you have to determine for yourself which clients you wish to work with, and to fire clients that aren't suitable.

That's a situation that everyone benefits from, including your customers.

If in the short term all of this seemed to me a little, heavy, complicated, annoying and more expensive, in the long term, it was better for me as a customer that all the terms are clear and orderly, that there were no "extras" or additional costs at the last moment, that service providers. came on time and finished on time, and so on.

Branding yourselves as experts in the eyes of your clients is good for you and good for them! It's a classic win-win situation.

WHY AREN'T TOP CHEFS AFRAID OF PUBLISHING THEIR RECIPES?

In 2004, I published my first book, *Persuade and Influence any Audience*. The book was based mostly on lectures that I gave at the time, on presentation, debate-style speechwriting, and public speaking.

Among the many impactful statements I heard from my environment, both near and far when the book came out in stores, one statement was repeated again and again, "Why are you revealing all your tricks and secrets? Why are you publishing all your lectures in the book? You are harming yourself. People won't come to your lectures because they have already read your book!"

I recalled those statements some years later as I was talking with a top chef who was taking part in one of my mentoring programs when she revealed to me one of the most well-known secrets in the world. She said to me, "Do you know why famous chefs publish their recipes in cookbooks, in newspaper articles, on their cooking shows, and on TV? And why they aren't afraid their competitors will copy them, or that people will prepare their special dishes at home and then won't go to their restaurants? Because they never really reveal everything!

Even if the technical and professional explanation is detailed in a long recipe, there is always the "secret ingredient" that won't appear, that 2 to 5 percent of the recipe that the chefs never completely reveal. She gave me an example that frequently appears in cookbooks: Add salt/oil/sugar to taste or in the right quantity or as necessary.

What is the "right quantity"? The chef is the only one who really knows, based on their years of experience. If you make it at home, it probably won't come out as tasty. I agreed with the chef. I've always claimed that you can teach others everything, but no one can copy you exactly, because each and every one of us is unique and special.

The chefs know that, in order to build authority, they have to appear on television shows, be featured in newspaper articles, on social media, at lectures and so on, and to publish their knowledge. But they aren't afraid of being copied, because they are sure about their experience and expertise, and know that if their customers or competitors try, they will never manage to copy or imitate them perfectly. Therefore, the chefs maintain a relative advantage for as long as they publish and are active, innovative, and so on.

What's more, in my experience, even if people theoretically knew everything I know from reading my books, they would still come to my lectures.

Why? Because going to a lecture, workshop or conference—similar to going to the restaurant of a chef whose recipe you have just read in a newspaper—has an importance, meaning and purpose that are far beyond knowledge itself: experience, networking, breaking routine, meeting the lecturer in person, meeting friends, enjoying refreshments, fun and humor, and many other reasons.

Even if people did know everything that you know (and they never do), they will still leave the house to meet you at the office, restaurant, conference hall or wherever.

Put yourself at the front of the stage, and don't be afraid of sharing knowledge (your very best knowledge) on every possible platform—lectures, traditional and digital media, active blogs, YouTube, social media, and more. (Commandment 4 explores this.)

Next, when you publish and share your knowledge, leave your audience with a "taste for more." Whoever wishes to see and learn more of your content will have to contact you, to ask you directly, come to one of your activities or to your place of business.

Next, remember that you are unique and special and that you cannot be replaced.

Every expert, professional, mentor and authority brings with them their own unique perspective and life experience, and therefore people will always seek your company and more if you share your knowledge genuinely.

WHAT WAS IT THAT I SAID WHICH MADE HUNDREDS OF PEOPLE LEAVE MY LECTURE ALL AT ONCE?

A few years ago, I held a webinar at 9 p.m. my time (three hours ahead of GMT and seven hours ahead of US Eastern time, so 2 p.m. in New York) and scheduled to end 90 minutes later. The day on which my webinar was scheduled happened to coincide with a synchronized broadcast of two highly rated programs: soccer semifinals in Europe and the final installment a popular TV reality program in the United States.

The truth is it wasn't so coincidental; it was simply an oversight on my part, because I didn't pay attention to the programming guide and I chose to hold my webinar on that same date. (Otherwise, I, too, would have opted for watching the soccer semifinals.)

But despite the competition, we still gathered for

the webinar—me at my end, and hundreds of people at the other end. I wanted to start my on-line discussion by empowering the audience and complimenting them for taking the time to sit in front of their computer and listen to me, so I began my lecture:

> Hello, everyone. My name is Dr. Yaniv Zaid. First of all, I'd like to thank all of you for participating in this webinar. It's no small matter and it shows a lot about you and about how much you're willing to invest in yourselves. It's no small matter that you chose to listen to me instead of watching the semifinals right now.
>
> (On the right side of my screen was the webinar dashboard, where I could see the number of people online. As soon as I said "semifinals," I saw the number drop by 100 listeners within a few seconds! I admit that at first I didn't notice what was happening and I just went on, saying . . .)
>
> "and that you preferred to listen to me instead of watching (name of the show)."

Suddenly, an amazing thing happened: another 100 listeners left at once! And I was left with a third of my audience after only one minute of broadcasting! At this point, I realized it was my fault and I immediately switched to the content of the lecture.

What really happened here? What was my big mistake? Very simple: I mentioned my competition!

I gave the stage to my competitors. In this case, my competitors were highly-rated shows that, for most of my audience, were a viable alternative to my webinar.

Most of the people who heard me at that moment didn't really make an educated, conscious decision to choose me over those shows. They simply heard about me and the webinar, wrote down the date and didn't bother checking the programming guide to see what was being broadcast at the same time.

But when I told the members of my audience about my competitors, I actually created the competition for myself!!

What can be learned from this episode?

In a sales meeting or when relaying a message to clients, never speak directly about competitors!

Even if you know the competitors or think about them, your client mustn't think about them at that moment, and certainly not thanks to you.

I've heard businesspeople talking to their clients many times, saying "I'm A, and I'm better than B and C!" And then the client innocently asks, "Who is B? Who is C?"

And even if that client had planned to do business with you, now they won't, because they are going to get a quote from B and C, too! When you try to prevent your client from approaching specific competitors, you have in fact introduced your competitors to your client.

What to do?

Talk about yourself, promote your service and the value you offer, explain your relative advantages, and mention, if at all, the market you belong to in a general manner, without mentioning specific competitors.

If I would've said something like, "I appreciate your listening to me right now instead of watching TV," there wouldn't have been any problem and people wouldn't have left because they would only know on a subconscious level that there was competition, that I wasn't the only one in the world they could listen to, and that there was something to watch on TV.

But reminding them of that competition, I cause them to reconsider their moves and doubt their decision. Then, at that point, some of them will leave me.

WHY YOU SHOULD REALLY AIM TO BE THE WOLF OF WALL STREET.

In January 2014, I went to see Leonardo DiCaprio's blockbuster movie, *The Wolf of Wall Street*. It's a true story of Jordan Belfort, a young, ambitious broker on Wall Street in the early 1990s. He was hungry for success and very quickly founded a highly successful company with hundreds of employees that sold stocks to people for hundreds of millions of dollars. The stocks they sold were penny stocks of companies that were worth virtually nothing, and they conned uninformed people, rich and poor, stealing their money and committing a series of criminal offenses and violating the US Securities and Exchange Commission (SEC) laws.

Aside from the movie being excellent, I was mainly taken by the marketing and persuasion methods used by the Wolf of Wall Street (the name given to that broker by the American media).

Now, don't jump at me—I hate dishonesty and strongly object to violating the law— but throughout the movie, one thought about business success echoed in my head: "What if a different person, any person, was to do exactly what the 'Wolf' did, but, unlike him, was to sell a real, legal product that gives value to clients? It would succeed big time!" Because everything the Leonardo DiCaprio character did in the movie was no less than genius—his sales and persuasion methods, the way in which he "hyped" his staffers and instilled motivation in them and how he recruited people and taught them how to sell—was brilliant.

There's a lot you can learn from him! All you have to do is ignore the fact that the "Wolf" sold a corrupt, non-existent product and to imagine him selling a purely legal product that would also be valuable to the clients. Then what he did becomes a perfectly successful, profitable business that can serve as a role model for others.

What's my point in all this? That you can learn from everyone, *everyone*, even people you don't relate to on an emotional level, that you don't believe or whose products you don't believe in, and services you loathe.

As long as something works, as long as people are quick to surround themselves with "believers" and "fans," as long as a product is successful, as long as it manages to create a "buzz" in the market, you can learn from it. You can learn from members of the clergy, from your competitors, even from criminals.

Regardless of what you think about some people, you can learn from them. All you have to do is ignore their product or service and focus on how they do what they do so well.

HOW TO TRULY SUCCEED IN THE GIG ECONOMY.

Welcome to the "gig economy," part of what is known as the "sharing economy," which basically means people selling goods and services directly to other people, through platforms such as Uber (ride services), Etsy (crafts), Airbnb (rooms for rent) and more. Using this format, they bypass the big corporations, the bureaucracy, and the public mechanism; you don't have to use public transport, you don't have to cooperate with the big chains, you don't have to stay at a hotel for a high price, and so on.

On the face of it, the sharing economy is a great idea—everyone can sell anything to anyone. Everyone can be an entrepreneur.

We all have "intangible assets" such as free time,

driving as we do anyway, a room at home that is empty, knowledge we have acquired and aren't doing anything with, and more. The sharing economy helps us to turn intangible assets into tangible ones and to translate them into money, and thus improve our economic and social situation.

I'm in favor. The principle is correct; the byproduct is the "gig economy." A whole generation of gigsters has been created, that is, people who make a living from several parallel jobs (or micro-jobs). For example, someone can be an Uber driver in the morning, in the afternoon they can install Ikea furniture for people, and in the evening, they can host tourists at their home via Airbnb.

On the face of it, fantastic entrepreneurship. Make a living from a few different jobs, spread risks, no one can fire you and you live a free and happy life.

But the gig economy also has a few disadvantages. First of all, despite the fact that people are self-employed and supposedly are in control of their lives, they still need to manage their connections with other people through mega-platforms.

Criticism of the "gig economy" around the world claims that it is, in fact, these platforms that are "in control," and that the gigsters basically become sort of robots that serve the platforms, and are de facto employees, only without the benefits and conditions of company employees. Even though the ride driver is "independent," in practice, Uber sets the price the driver takes. And despite the artist selling their work on Etsy, it is the platform that controls their ranking as a seller, determines the rules and work procedures, and it is the platform that can close the seller account at any moment if the seller does something that it doesn't like.

But what interests me is a more significant disadvantage: the fact that it is very hard to specialize in the "gig economy."

If you are doing several things at the same time and if you are making a living off of a different gig all the time, then you have neither the time, the opportunity or the strength to specialize in what you are doing, and you have no time to develop a long-term relationship with the platform, which in practice provides you with your living. You can also lose everything in a moment (if a platform is "angry" with you and, for example, moves you down the search rankings for people in your field from page two to page fifty—automatically making you nearly irrelevant for consumers looking for goods and products on that platform.

In fact, the gig economy is a complete contradiction to the expert industry. Why? Because if you are experts, you have developed a uniqueness, your own knowledge and differentiation, and you cannot be replaced. But if you are a gigster, you are replaceable: Someone can replace you at any time.

If you are an expert, you are in a *value market*. You can easily charge high prices and your market value is high. If you are a gigster, you are in a *price market* where it doesn't matter who is providing the service; the customer's main consideration is price.

If you are an expert, you can focus, plan ahead, evaluate how much you will earn in the future, and charge high prices.

If you are a gigster, it is highly difficult and even impossible to plan ahead for time and revenues, and you will find yourself chasing the next job all the time.

I choose expertise, and I recommend to my clients to be experts; it doesn't matter in what discipline, it doesn't matter which field, and it doesn't matter what products and services you are selling. The important thing is to specialize in one field and to be really good at it, and not to spread yourself over many fields and professions.

WHY DO CELEBRITIES POSE FOR SELFIES WITH THEIR FANS?

Every time I go to a basketball game, I like to watch the following scene play out. About half an hour before the start of the game, the players come out onto the court to warm up. The fans who have arrived early and sat down in the seats near the court ask to have a selfie taken with some of the players.

In most cases the players are happy to do so. Most of the time it is the "stars" who are most willing (even though they are probably busier and more stressed ahead of the game) to have their photo taken with the fans—even if there are just ten minutes to go to until the game starts.

The selfie phenomenon of taking a photo of ourselves with other people or with something nice in the background has become so common and so prevalent that we barely stop to ask ourselves, "What interest does a celebrity have in taking a unpaid selfie with anyone who asks?" And what interest does a mentor or counsellor or business owner or entrepreneur have in taking a selfie with customers or with participants at a lecture?

Beyond the usual reasons for agreeing to a selfie— it isn't polite to turn down someone who asks, it's a nice ego rub, it only takes a few seconds, and it doesn't cost anyone money—there are the "marketing" reasons:

» Over the past decade, taking a photo with clients who ask you to, before or after a show, lecture, game or meeting, has become seen as part of the service you provide, and in particular, it generates for you much stronger viral marketing.

» Because those customers or fans who have their photo taken with a celebrity (more than likely) post the photo on Facebook/Instagram/Tik Tok or other social networks used by young people that I don't even know about because I'm over 40, then all at once, all their friends are exposed to the photo of the celebrity at their best and then their friends share it.

» The star gets dozens or hundreds or thousands or even tens of thousands of "ambassadors" (depending on the size of the photographer's audience) who talk about the star, tell stories about them, compliment them and think of them, and all of that without having asked them and without having paid them any sales commission.

Not a bad deal, right?

After all, celebrities, entrepreneurs, and business-people spend a fortune on marketing, sales, public relations, website promotion, social media, and so forth. But here, you have a free marketing funnel—the selfie—which creates a lot of traffic online, a lot of buzz and indirectly, a lot of paying customers.

Someone who thinks good things about you is also more likely to buy from you. Someone who asks for something "extra" (like a selfie) and straightaway receives a positive response with a smile will talk about you more and will provide you with free publicity.

By the way, viral marketing (discussed in Commandment 8) can also work negatively. I still remember an incident that happened a few years ago at a book fair I was taking part in, when I invited a colleague to a "behind the scenes" event put on by the publisher, where I signed my books.

Standing next to me was a very famous author. (I won't reveal his name as I don't want to shame him.)

My colleague was really excited to see him and told me that she was a really big fan of his and had all his books at home. She went up to him, smiled and asked to have her photo taken with him. He turned her down with a scowl.

To this day—many years after—my colleague who was very offended at the time hasn't forgotten the incident and has spoken about it many times. This is negative publicity for the author, and when his new book came out a couple of years later, she didn't buy it.

You may ask, "What's the connection between the way he reacted at that event and the quality of his writing?" After all, my colleague liked his books, right?

Liked. Past tense. Now she won't buy his books and won't read them anymore, because he once behaved toward her unpleasantly. Good or bad, that's the way it works.

Let's go back to the basketball game and, with your permission, I want to make the question difficult for you. It's clear what interests a business owner who sells products, a lecturer who sells lectures, an author who sells books or a performer selling tickets to a show has in being nice to their customers and giving them good service: It increases the number of people following them and, over time, it increases their sales and revenues. But why should a salaried basketball player whose salary is paid by the team be nice to fans and take selfies with them? And what's more, before the game?

The answer is personal branding. In our day and age, salaried employees need to brand themselves and to build a "community" because then they are worth more money at their current place of work and in future places of employment. (In Commandment 5, I'll talk more about building a "community" of followers and customers—one that is "educated" to buy from you.)

Talent alone isn't enough. Neither is hard work. You also have to market yourself.

If we take the field of sports as an example, teams pay their players, and certainly their stars, not just according to their ability on the field, but also according to what they do off the field, that is, how many subscriptions and tickets will the fans buy because of them, how many jerseys and hats and merchandising will the club sell with their name and number, how popular are they with the fans, their behavior off the field and off the court, and more.

All the big stars, in every field of sports, have understood the importance of building a community of fans and investing in the development of personal branding and their social networks, even though someone else pays their salaries because their salaries are also derived from the number of fans following them on social networks.

HOW TO PREVENT YOUR CLIENTS FROM BYPASSING YOU AND DOING YOUR WORK THEMSELVES

Imagine the following scenario: A realtor meets with a potential client, to show them a property they are representing, although not exclusively. They meet for the first time outside the building and the realtor says to the client, "Susan Lewis lives in an apartment on the third floor of this building and she wants to sell."

Here are two scenarios that could happen (and quite often do):

» Scenario #1: The client says, "Susan? Great. I know her, she went to school with me thirty years ago. I'll get in touch with her myself and speak to her. Thank you."

» Scenario #2: The client says, "I don't know, I don't like the look of it," without having even seen the apartment and they go their separate ways. The following morning, the client knocks on Susan's door(even though they don't know each other) and negotiates with her directly.

Let's say that after a month of meetings, phone calls and negotiations, they close a deal and the client buys the apartment from Susan. Now let's say that the realtor hears about this by chance, calls the client and says, "What about my commission?" The client will say, with some measure of justification from their perspective, "What commission are you talking about? You didn't do anything! I did everything myself directly with the seller."

What do the two scenarios have in common?

In both situations, the client bypassed the realtor to save on the commission. In both of them, the client did, or at least tried to do, the work themselves without the help of the professional. In both scenarios, the client was dismissive of the most important detail in the deal—the realtor's knowledge.

In order to know that Susan was selling the apartment and in order to be familiar with the apartment itself, and to be able to negotiate a fair price professionally, the realtor invested countless hours, days and nights in getting to know the neighborhood, searching through various databases, and checking deals that had already been closed in the neighborhood, and so on.

And the most important information they have in hand is their knowledge! The knowledge about the little details of the deal. But as soon as they give their knowledge for free without an agreement, then that knowledge becomes public knowledge and the client could become dismissive and think that they know how to do it themselves and can do the deal alone.

Continuing with the example from the real estate sector, what do realtors who conduct themselves professionally do to make sure their clients don't bypass them? The realtors make sure to sign the purchaser on an agreement regarding the house and/or representation before the meeting with the or seller.

The realtor can meet with the client at the corner of the street, sign the forms and then proceed with the client to the building to prevent them from seeing the "for sale" sign on the building and calling the seller themselves. The realtor can also sign Susan (the vendor/seller) on an exclusivity agreement, and then even if the client does approach her directly, the realtor will still be in control of the deal. And there are more and more steps, all of which are aimed at protecting the realtor's most expensive product, that is, unique and specific knowledge that they've accumulated with great effort.

From many years of experience, there is something a little tricky in selling knowledge.

You would never imagine going into a grocery store or a shop belonging to a friend or colleague, taking a few items or products and leaving without paying, right? You would certainly never imagine doing that over and over without paying for those products, right? But when it comes to tips, business knowledge, connections, advice and ideas, people sometimes feel comfortable milking the service provider, the vendor or the expert, squeezing as much free information as they can, and then feeling great about it.

As we already said, in the present era, the "commodity" that most people trade in is their knowledge. And every expert, entrepreneur and business owner—chef, attorney, insurance broker, commander, senior manager, consultant, lecturer, realtor, plumber and more—is measured by their unique knowledge, or the value of their commodity.

And that's why we mustn't, under any circumstances, give it away freely.

Of course you can release a little of your knowledge for free—in the form of clips, newsletters, posts, podcasts, media interviews, e-guides, recipes, tips, short phone calls with customers, and so on. But only if that is part of your business model, and only if the goal of free knowledge is at the end of the day to awaken a desire for more and to cause some of your customers to pay for the rest of your knowledge.

As experts, your "commodity" is your time and knowledge. Don't give them away for free to anyone that asks.

WHAT'S THE FIRST THING EMPLOYERS DO TODAY WHEN DECIDING IF THEY SHOULD HIRE YOU?

In the early part of 2013, I participated in a conference in California. One night I met up with a good friend who lived in Silicon Valley and was looking for a job at the time. At the start of the conversation, this friend, who for years had been closely following anything that was published about me and everything I put out, asked me to explain to him in greater detail how the expert industry that I'm a part of actually works.

I explained to him that these were people who

brand and market themselves in a specific field of expertise, a field they are very good at and in which they have a relative advantage over the majority of the population. To succeed in a field, I added, "It's better if your expertise is unconventional and falls under the category of what we call life skills."

Life skills are fields that are very important to us as human beings, such as enjoying success, creating financial abundance in our lives, finding love, developing excellent interpersonal relationships, living a healthy and peaceful life, upgrading our romantic relationships, developing our bodies, and so on. And what these all have in common is that they are not taught in any formal educational institution—not in kindergarten, not in school, and not in a university.

This is where the expert industry comes into the picture, because it teaches these things in a type of extra-academic track.

My friend listened carefully to my explanation, and from his point of view he was hearing these things for the first time.

Later on, I asked him how his job search was going. (His CV and experience were very impressive, certainly for someone under the age of 40.) I expected to hear stories and details about job interviews, phone calls, emails going out and more, but instead I was shocked to hear him say, "I've already published some articles, my blog is ready now and my website is under construction."

"Excuse me?" I asked in amazement. "Why does a

salaried employee, as senior as he may be, need to set up a blog and a website?"

And my friend explained to me that, since the market was highly competitive these days and since there were many people eager to pounce on every position, you had to do more than just send out your résumé and hope for the best. He told me that you needed to define a field of expertise for yourself, to create a type of professional calling card that characterized you and your activity in the field to date, to stand out in this field of expertise.

He went on and said that you have to set up a blog and a website sharing information in this field of expertise, to write articles and posts that scan the market situation in that same field of expertise and get them published in highly-acclaimed newspapers and journals and on websites in your particular industry, to respond to articles written by other people and give your professional opinion. Only then can you begin to stand out as an "opinion leader" in your particular industry so that instead of a résumé or in addition to it, you can send your potential employer links to your website, your blog and your publications.

In Silicon Valley, the first thing employers do upon receiving your job application is to check your online presence and to get an understanding of the nature of your expertise from the material you've published. Only if the information they see satisfies them and arouses their interest and curiosity, will they invite you in for a job interview.

"You have just described exactly what we do in the expert industry!" I said to him. "Everything you have told me means you're actually doing and implementing yourself!"

And I thought to myself how amazing it was that the "expert industry" had also reached the market of salaried employees and job seekers, and that those who don't create for themselves a field of expertise, a differentiation, branding, and a virtual identity—those who just continue to send out CVs via email—are still living in the twentieth century and do not have much of a chance finding work in today's competitive market.

KEY ELEMENTS OF COMMANDMENT NO. 2

Brand Yourselves as Experts in Your Field

√ If you want to sell to new clients, you must increase their certainty in working with you.

√ People expect an expert to implement the content they are they talking about and for them to walk the talk.

√ Brands operate according to the luxury paradox: two parallel doctrines that complement each other but also contradict each other. The first tenet is the customer is king. The second tenet is only on your terms!

√ It is important that the customer knows that you

have a lot of other customers, but he should never feel it. The key is balance; don't be too available and don't be too busy.

✓ Put boundaries in place for your clients. Give them maximum service within those boundaries.

✓ An expert should define for themselves which clients they wish to work with, and "fire" clients that aren't suitable.

✓ No one can copy or imitate you perfectly, because each one of you is unique and special, and therefore you will always have a relative advantage as long as you are active, innovative, publish, and so on.

✓ Put yourself at the front of the stage, and don't be afraid of sharing knowledge (your very best knowledge) on every possible platform, but always leave a taste for more.

✓ In a sales meeting or when relaying a message to clients, never speak directly about competitors. Talk about yourself, promote your activity or service and the value you offer, explain your relative advantages.

✓ You can learn from everyone. Focus on how they do what they do so well.

✓ If you are an expert and you have developed your own uniqueness, knowledge and differentiation, no one can replace you.

✓ If you are an expert, you are in a value market;

you can easily charge high prices, and your market value will be high.

✓ Someone who thinks good things about you is much more likely to buy from you.

✓ Someone who asked you for something extra, and you immediately responded positively with a smile, will talk about you more and will provide you with free publicity.

✓ Salaried employees also need to brand themselves and build a community of customers (or fans) because then they are worth more money—at their present place of work and in future places of employment.

✓ The commodity that experts trade in is their knowledge.

✓ You need to create for yourselves a field of expertise, a differentiation, and a virtual identity.

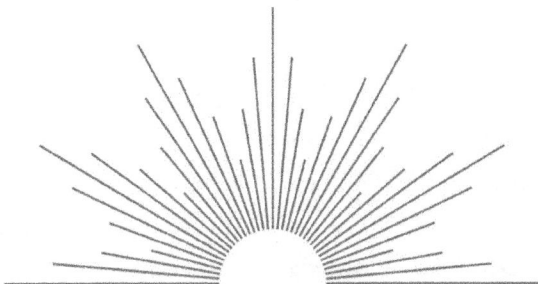

COMMANDMENT NO. 3

Turn compliments into income, motivating people to buy from you, even if they weren't planning to.

WHAT MOTIVATES PEOPLE THE MOST TO GET VACCINATED?

In the 1960s, researcher Howard Leventhal examined to what degree fear motivates people to take action. He took a group of students and handed them pamphlets about the importance of vaccines and the dangers of not getting vaccinated.

When he checked in a month later, he discovered that only 3 percent of the students had gotten vaccinated. He found out that the students who read the material he distributed realized the importance of vaccination and the dangers of avoiding vaccines. Some of them even expressed an explicit desire to get vaccinated, but didn't follow through with it.

The research breakthrough came when Leventhal handed the students directions on how to get to the clinic and specified its operating hours. The percentage of students who got vaccinated grew from 3 percent to 33 percent—a 1,100 percent increase!

What does that mean for you? It means that, although fear, knowledge and desire are powerful engines, people's actions are often determined by the little things. Thus, if people have to do something and you show them how easy and simple it is, they will go ahead and take action.

In recent years, many people I have met at various events and whom I wanted to stay in contact with have told me, "I don't have a business card on me. Just Google me and you'll find all the details."

And I say (to you, not to them): Save your breath. Most people won't Google you.

It's too "complicated." By the time I reach my computer, I won't even remember your full name, and if I do try to search for you on Google, I'll give up very quickly unless I can find your contact information on your website in less than a minute even though I wanted to keep in touch with you.

Why not simply bring a business card along with you to the event?

Another example: A research study conducted on Internet registration showed that if you write "For further details about the conference" on the sign up button, for example, there will be a relatively low conversion rate.

However, if you write "For details about the conference, click here," the conversion rate increases significantly, and, if you write "For details about the conference, click here now!" the conversion rate increases dramatically. What has happened here? We simply explained to people exactly what we expect of them and what exactly they should do.

Not because they're stupid or lazy and not even because we're not important to them.

It is what it is: "I just got an Outlook message so I left your page..." or "My wife just called me so I left the computer..." or "I just remembered I have an exam in two days I must study for..."

Life happens. And it's stronger than you.

The students in Leventhal's experiment really wanted to get vaccinated. They really did. And they understood what could happen if they didn't. They had an exam... their girlfriend just left them... You get the point.

WHY IT IS SO IMPORTANT TO BRING REFRESHMENTS TO AN EVENT (OR, WHEN CAN YOU GET OUT OF JAIL)?

A few years ago, I conducted an extensive client survey in which I asked the participants, among other things, why they sign up for workshops and lectures.

After all, some of the products I sell are workshops and lectures, so it's important for me to understand why clients buy the products and services I offer them.

The answers I received were diverse and even surprising in part, but I particularly remember that one of the reasons (the fifth most important one) was refreshments. Respondents noted that they go to a conference, event or workshop because of the refreshments being served there!

This answer surprised me, but then I read a study that showed that when an event is held and food is mentioned as part of the event, the conversion rate (the actual percentage of signups to the conference out of all those exposed to the information about the conference) increases by 20 percent. So, 20 percent more people will show up for a conference if they are promised food!

Note: It's not really about the food. No one who comes to a business or professional event is starving, and even if they were, the event probably costs them more than a meal would have. So, what is it? Why would more people arrive at an event if they were promised food?

There are three reasons:

1. The *investment principle*. If people invest in me as a client—and people love to be invested in and catered to—and prepare food for me, then I'll invest in return by signing up.

2. Showing up becomes less challenging and more practical. Say my workshop is held between 5 p.m. and 9 p.m. If there are no refreshments, potential clients will figure they have to stop off at home first to eat something

COMMANDMENT NO. 3 | 79

before they can show up. They get home and
bam! TV, spouse, kids, unwinding—the client
will never leave their house again that day,
and so they don't show up for the workshop.
However, if the client knows a light dinner
is waiting for them, they'll plan to get to the
workshop straight from work and then we
don't "lose" them to external temptations.

3. People are more alert and focused when
they've eaten something and are no longer
hungry. A study conducted by three
researchers from Stanford University examined
decision-making on parole committees. These
are professional committees that review
appeals for early release from prison and hold
long days of deliberation from morning until
afternoon. Each day of deliberations is divided
into three segments, with two breaks for
meals in between. Analyzing the committee's
decisions showed an interesting fact: When
the committee members had eaten and were
alert, they were more inclined to release the
prisoner or detainee whose case they were
reviewing. When they were hungry, they
tended to be indecisive and choose the default,
the status quo. They kept things as is, which in
their case was keeping the prisoner in jail.

In other words, to get people out of their "comfort

zone" and make them think and act differently, you must fill their stomach.

What does that mean for you?

» If you're reading this while you're in prison, and your parole committee is coming up, ask to be the first case reviewed in the morning or the first case after a meal break.

» Spoil your clients; give them food and drink. It will pay off!

WHY IT IS IMPORTANT TO SELL EVEN "FREEBIES" TO PEOPLE.

In October 2013, at the International Frankfurt Book Fair I participated in, I noticed an interesting phenomenon: All the publishers, authors and book agents bring their best books to the fair in order to sell and buy rights, and sign distribution and publishing agreements. They display them at their pavilions during the five days of the fair. In the first three days, the fair focuses on the business clients and is closed to the public. (Note well: It was in those first three days of the 2021 Fair that I met the publisher for the North American edition of this book.) In the last two days, the fair is opened to the public and hundreds of thousands visit it during one weekend.

What is the interesting phenomenon?

In the last two days, and mostly on the last day of the fair, most publishers and agents leave their pavilions and return to their home countries. They don't want to carry the merchandise back, so they leave the books on display as is, with a note that allows anyone to take any book they like.

Yes, you heard right. The leftover books are free for all to take. You can show up with a suitcase and fill it with bestsellers. And still, contrary to what you may think, few people do that.

I watched in amazement as the pavilions full of excellent books were left deserted, and no one came to pick up the books. Then I remembered an important principle I've been teaching my clients for years: Even freebies must be "sold."

Say I invite a friend or colleague as a guest to my lecture. If I simply say, "I give a really cool lecture; you should come," one of two scenarios will occur. Either the guest is 90 percent likely to not show up because he simply didn't understand from me how it could benefit him, or in the worse of the two scenarios, he is 10 percent likely to show up because he wants to please me and "do me a favor." That is, the guest will come to the lecture, cost me money, and in his mind, he's coming to help "fill the auditorium" in order to "support me" so that I will feel good.

And why is that not good for me? Because that guest will arrive to "do what he has to do," and it will show: He will arrive last, leave first and derive nothing from the content. Perhaps he might even interrupt the others at the lecture. Finally, he may even think, after doing me this "favor," that now I owe him something.

I'm all for inviting strategic clients and colleagues for free to your events and lectures, but on one condition: They appreciate the gift you've given.

And how will they appreciate it? Well, that's up to you. You need to explain to them how they will benefit from your invitation, and why it's in their own best interests to come. Yes, even though it's a freebie for them, if it's important for you that they show up and take an active part in the event, you need to invest time and energy in convincing them to come.

This is just like the free book lying on a table at a book fair which is less likely be picked up because there is no salesperson or publishing house representative present to describe the book and motivate a person to take it. The potential reader doesn't understand what good the book will bring him without someone explaining the benefit he might gain from it.

WHERE ARE LIONS AND GIRAFFES PLACED IN A ZOO, AND WHY?

Here's a marketing insight that you probably haven't thought about too much. You visit the zoo: What do you see at the start, nearest to the entrance, and what do you see furthest from the entrance? When I ask this question at my lectures and conferences, a lot of people reply instinctively, " lions," or " elephants," or " giraffes." But the truth is that giraffes, elephants, and lions are placed farthest from the entrance to the zoo! Why? Because they are the real reason you came to the zoo!

A sophisticated rule of marketing says that for any shopping experience people engage in, you must build the experience in a circular route—it starts and ends in the same spot—and put what they most expect and what is most important to them at the furthest point from the entrance. Place whatever is less important to them is by the entrance.

At first glance, that would seem illogical. But it contains a lot of marketing logic. Let's take for example a local supermarket. What do people need and buy most from the supermarket? Bread and milk. What do they need and buy least? Sweets and all the specials that the supermarket offers.

So if supermarkets were to place bread and milk right by the entrance, near the cash registers, most customers would enter, pick up bread and milk, pay and leave. They wouldn't walk around the supermarket and they wouldn't see the abundance that the supermarket has to offer. But the bread and milk are placed at the back of the supermarket, at the furthest point from entrance, and by doing so the store profits three times:

1. The customers are "forced" to pass through the entire supermarket on their way to the basic products because that way they have to pass by all or most of the aisles and see what the supermarket has to offer (and to buy things they hadn't planned on buying).

2. This route engenders in the minds of the customers a sense of expectation, curiosity and a certain excitement, as it takes them time to reach the product they wanted. The shoppers don't reach their item immediately and, because of their unconscious sense of expectation, they buy more things than they had planned to buy.

3. When the customers finally get to the cash register, what do they see at or near the cash register? All tantalizing items they don't really need such as candy and batteries.

Let's go back to the zoo.

When you begin your visit to the zoo, what do you see? The little animals: the parrots, turtles, snakes and special exhibit of night creatures like bats. Then you'll see larger and most animated animals like monkeys and eagles. After that, there will be "cool" animals like flamingos and alligators, and then at the furthest point from the entrance you'll experience the peak moment of your visit to the zoo—the lions, the elephants and the giraffes.

Why are they so far away? Because they are what you came to see.

To show your kids snakes, parrots and even monkeys, you don't need to go to the zoo. You can go to the closest pet shop to your home. But at the beginning of your visit to the zoo, you and your kids are "turned on" by the small animals, your expectations get built up and your excitation threshold is increased, so when you and the kids finally reach the lion exhibit, your excitement is at a peak and your customer experience is maximized.

And you will buy more.

Do you want your customers to buy more from you and be exposed to a greater shopping experience in their relationship with you?

Create an "expectation effect" when you offer them your goods and services. Increase their excitation threshold and make them admire you and be pleasantly surprised by you. This is essential today given the abundance that the current era offers us as customers.

WHY DO OUR CHILDREN BEHAVE BADLY?

Every parent is familiar with the following situation: You are driving with your kid on a trip or to a museum or a show, going to a family event or maybe a class birthday party, and before or during the drive you say, "I'm reminding you to behave well" or "It's important that you behave well." At some point, either during the event, or even afterward, when your kid does something you don't like, you reprimand them and say, "But I told you to behave well! You aren't behaving well!"

That's a situation that is very frustrating for a parent. But there is one thing we forget: the young child doesn't know and doesn't understand what it means to behave well.

Think about it: Behave well is a theoretical and

unclear statement for a young child. Even for adults, the concept may not be clear.

What will help? Clear directions. Precise instructions. A few examples:

» "You're travelling with your brother. I'm asking you not to argue with him and not to hit him, and if he teases you, don't react. Just come and tell me."

» "We are going to dinner with the family. Even if you have finished eating, you don't leave the table before everyone has finished and I have given you permission."

» "When we get to Grandma's and Grandpa's, run over and give them a hug and a kiss, and if they give you a present, say thank you."

What happens now? The child knows exactly what is expected of them! And has clear instructions that they understand and knows how to implement. And these are quantifiable instructions; in other words, you can easily test the child and see whether he has "behaved well" or not.

Your chances of enjoying yourselves with the children increase significantly. The chances that your children will behave well increase significantly. The child's education, including the issue of setting boundaries, has improved significantly.

When you expect children to behave well and they don't know exactly what that means, it's difficult for them to implement and even more difficult to debrief and improve their behavior for the next time. But when you have clear instructions, you can school your child on next steps with specifics such as "I asked you to remain at the table until everyone has finished. The family isn't together that often, so it's important you are patient and wait until we're done."

If you want the people around you (whatever age) to do something, explain to them exactly what needs to be done. Spell out precisely, step-by-step, what is expected of them and what actions they need to take. This applies to any human behavior, and of course is also true when it comes to sales.

In too many cases I see landing pages on the Internet, hear sales calls to customers, or am present at sales meetings that end in sentences such as, "We'll be happy to assist you," "Please contact us," "We'll see you again soon," and so on.

No! That's not good enough. The call to action must be clear and precise. The final statements that you make at the end of a conversation or meeting, and the final statements that you write at the end of a post or sales page are the most important, and must include clear, precise and practical instructions.

Precise instructions are critical to drive people in your environment to action.

When a sales consultant says to a business owner he is advising, "You can do more" and doesn't say exactly what "to do more" means, the business won't grow.

When a doctor tells a patient, "You must lose weight. Start eating properly," but doesn't explain what exactly "eating properly" is, the patient won't lose weight. When an attorney tells a client, "Pay attention not to make any mistakes and incriminate yourself when talking with the other side" and doesn't explain what would be a "mistake" and what exactly the client can and can't say, they not only aren't helping the client, they're creating confusion.

I experienced another example of this at my kids' end-of-school and nursery parties. After the end-of-year ceremonies, shows and thankyous to the staff, end-of-year certificates are handed out to all the kids. There are a lot of kids at these events, which usually go on for longer than planned and at least some of the parents are in a hurry to get home, and some of them are there with little siblings who lost their patience when they walked through the front door. So from my experience at the events, the situation is that almost every parent whose kid gets a certificate, gets up, says goodbye to the other parents, speaks with their kid and some of them start to go home.

What happens is that while the first kids to get their certificates (the order is incidental, usually by where they are seated or alphabetically) receive the full attention of all the parents and other kids, the last kids receive their certificate amid noise and disorder with some of the other parents and kids already having left, and the only people still listening and clapping are their parents.

This is of course very disrespectful and even insulting, from the point of view of the remaining children and their parents.

Most people have a tendency to look out first of all for their own narrow interests unless they are managed differently. What happens at events that are managed properly is that the school or kindergarten teacher tells all the parents before the start of the certificate award ceremony that they are requested to stay seated until all of the children have received a certificate. The teachers describe situations that have occurred in previous years, such as the one I described, they explain how frustrating it is for the last remaining children and parents and how it harms their experience, and then they add two important sentences: "Applaud each child as if they were your child" and "Imagine that your child was receiving the last certificate."

It works consistently. Every time that I have been at events where the participants received an organized briefing such as the one before the award ceremony, there was applause and a great atmosphere for all the kids. No one got up before the end and all the kids felt important and that they were being respected.

Why did people behave differently?

First, preparation. The teachers didn't wait for parents whose children had already received their certificates to get up and start leaving before telling them, "Please stay." That is a lot less efficient. They described to the parents before the ceremony exactly what was going to happen and what was expected of them, so people complied.

Second, they were made to think—not about themselves and their narrow perspective, but about the overall picture, about the other kids and parents and about the situation.

Third, they were made to feel—to feel about other kids what they feel for their own children, and to be worried that their kid will be the one left standing last with no one to applaud.

Fourth, the teachers spoke assertively. It may have been a request and not an order, and made in a pleasant fashion, but the message was clear: not one parent was to get up before all the children had been awarded their certificates and everybody was to applaud all the children.

No compromises, no concessions and no exemptions. Once you set clear boundaries, people will stick to them.

You can motivate, persuade and drive anyone to action—if you just make them think, if you instruct them clearly and precisely what they need to do and if you do all of that confidently and with faith in what you are saying.

HOW THE WAITER AT THE RESTAURANT KNEW EXACTLY WHAT YOU WANTED TO DRINK

A few years ago I sat at a restaurant in Madrid, Spain. At the table next to me, a cheerful bunch of friends sat down. The waiter approached them and, as he began setting the table, he asked them: "First off, what wine would you like to drink—red or white?" Some ordered red, others ordered white and the waiter went to bring the menus.

What was amazing to me at this point was that the guests didn't even ask for wine; they didn't even think of wine before the waiter asked them the question. He phrased the question in a sophisticated, marketing style: He didn't ask them if they wanted wine, but immediately jumped to the next question as to which wine they wanted.

This is called *anchoring* in the world of persuasion techniques. The waiter planted an idea in their head about wanting wine and made them take it for granted and think about which wine they wanted rather than if they wanted to drink wine at all.

A similar question can be, for example, "How are you paying—by cash or credit?" That is, you create in the client the feeling that she's already decided to buy and you make her decide only about the method of payment. For those who think this is simply a case of tricky manipulation, let me assure you: Nobody buys if they don't want to. Nobody orders wine if they don't drink wine or don't want to, even if the question is phrased in a smart way.

The anchoring increases the conversion rate (the amount of people who will actually do as you ask) but doesn't cause everyone to do what you want. The waiter saw the cheerful people at his table were in a good mood and steered them to a product he knew would suit this specific group at that moment.

WHY DOESN'T THE FLIGHT ATTENDANT MAKE EYE CONTACT WITH YOU?

Anyone who travels in an airplane on vacation or on a business trip internationally recognizes the following series of events:

» Stage 1 – The pilot and the flight attendants go over safety instructions and a briefing about the flight.
» Stage 2 – Takeoff, waiting for the airplane to reach flying altitude and balance in the air.
» Stage 3 – The airplane crew serves drinks and perhaps a meal.
» Stage 4 – No one pays you any attention for a long time.
» Stage 5 – You're served a drink and perhaps a meal again and are offered duty free items.
» Stage 6 – Preparation for landing—safety belts, filling out forms for customs, and so on.

Everything I said surely seems logical to you, aside from Stage 4. You are probably asking yourself why I am saying, "No one pays you any attention for a long time?" After all, you argue, "We're paying customers!"

That's just it, Stage 4 goes exactly like this, and you've all experienced it on a flight of any duration, whether domestic or international. This the stage where the airline and its staff want you to rest, watch movies or listen to music, and mostly bother the crew as little as possible, so that they can rest as well and get organized for the next stages of the flight.

What do they actually do during Stage 4?

They ask you to close the window shades so that the sunlight doesn't bother you or others when falling asleep. They may turn off all the lights in the main cabin if it's nighttime. And what mostly happens in Stage 4 is the crew doesn't walk around the cabin and you don't see the flight attendants.

On international flights, the crew can be out of sight for hours. If you have an emergency, you press the assistance button and a flight attendant will come to you. And then, she will quickly walk past the passengers, looking down, avoiding any eye contact.

Why?

Because there's a simple principle in marketing that says "a look is an invitation."

When you look at someone straight in the eyes, you're telling them you want their company and would like to communicate with them. It's pleasant, welcoming and makes us feel good as clients.

When the flight attendant on the plane looks us in the eyes, we'll immediately remember we want something more—ask a question, have a drink, an extra snack. During Stage 4, the crew doesn't want you to remember something extra if it's not critical for you; therefore, they avoid contact with you, and, even if the flight attendant must walk through the aisle as part of their job or to help a passenger, they'll avoid making eye contact with other passengers, so as not to make them suddenly "remember" they need more things.

Until Stage 5 comes along. Then, the lights come on all at once, the pilot will address you, and the flight attendants will once again walk around smiling and welcoming. And you will wake up, smile back, eat something, and fulfill your role as expected at this stage.

What's my point? You determine your clients' agenda! You can "manage" them while you provide them with your product or service, just as they do to you everywhere—on a flight, at a restaurant, at the movies, at a hotel, on a trip, and elsewhere.

When you want to communicate with your clients, address them, make eye contact and invite them to communicate with you. And when it's not the right time, all you have to do is be less available.

Most clients won't "harass" you as long as you've catered well to their needs in the previous stage. Think about it on your next vacation, and note how you implement these principles at work or in your business.

Why don't restaurants offer you their entire menu?

You've come to a good restaurant, perhaps one with a well-known chef. All the dishes on the menu look delicious. Let's say that the waiter managed to sell you everything on the menu. You've eaten everything.

What happens? You're not feeling well. Your stomach aches. Even though every dish in itself was really good, you leave with a bad taste, that is, not the customer experience the restaurant would like to have remain with you.

WHAT HAPPENS IN A GOOD RESTAURANT?

You are offered a main course, an appetizer, something to drink and a dessert. You end your meal with a good feeling and, most importantly, with a taste for more. You want to come back to the restaurant and taste more of their dishes.

The same applies to lectures and consultations.

One of the most common mistakes I see lecturers making is to give the audience a lot of information and content throughout the entire lecture. Lecturers do this for a positive reason and with good intentions: They want to teach the audience as much as possible and to give them as much value as possible.

But from my experience, and research I have conducted and research conducted by others, an audience that comes to a lecture is looking first and foremost for an experience and for fun, and only then learning, which they want to be purposeful and high quality. A lecturer who squeezes in a lot of material, especially new material that the audience isn't familiar with, is doing himself and his audience a disservice.

It's a disservice to the audience because the audience can't take in all that knowledge and doesn't absorb most of it. (Note: Studies show that people only take in around a third of the knowledge transmitted in a lecture, and even less if the material is new to them. The audience members then get bored, lose their concentration, their attention suffers, and they don't sufficiently value the knowledge they are receiving.

It's also a disservice to the lecturer because, beyond the fact that the lecturer causes the audience to be fed up with them (TMI!), it will also be difficult to sell them additional products and services afterward because the lecturer has already told them "everything." Or at least that's what the audience will feel, and then they won't want to come back because their shopping experience won't have been good.

The same thing goes for consultations. In recent years I have noticed that the less I speak at meetings the more the customer is satisfied.

On the face of it, that isn't logical. The customer meets me to hear what I have to say and also pays me quite a lot for my time. But there is a logic to it because the customer isn't just buying my knowledge; he is also buying my attention, the opportunity to say objectively and discreetly what is on his mind, to engage in the ping pong of conversation with me, and more.

If I speak nonstop for two hours during a consultation, the client will come out less satisfied, even though I have given him a lot of content and knowledge.

So what, then, is the right way to go about consultations and lectures?

Remember that these are conversations with an audience and with customers, not a "speech to the nation." Separate the wheat from the chaff and remember that not everything is important. Relate just a little of what you know so that they will want to come back and hear you or meet with you again and buy your products and follow-up services.

The chef at the restaurant wants very much for you to taste all their dishes. He has worked extremely hard on each and every one of them. But if you eat them all at once, you will be sick, but if you eat them one at a time, you will come back again and again.

"NO ONE WILL BUY YOUR BOOKS."

A few years ago, I was invited to lecture at a very big firm that employs tens of thousands of people. The lecture took place as part of a series of lectures that the company offered to its employees and managers as a bonus; the name of the lecturer is published along with the topic of the lecture and participation is optional. Anyone is interested in the topic or lecturer and could spare a couple of hours away from work or willing to stay late may register for the lecture and come to hear it.

As is my habit, I turned up at the lecture hall about an hour before the lecture was scheduled to begin. No one was there, not even the training manager who had invited me to speak and whom I had arranged to meet there. I called her and she said she would finish her meeting and come down to meet me.

As someone with a lot of experience, I started to get things ready by myself in the lecture hall. I hooked up the computer, set up my presentation, checked the sound and laid out my books on the table by the speaker's podium.

After that, when I saw that no one had turned up yet—later I learned that the employees always turn up for lectures at the last moment—since I had everything ready, I went to do a few chores like go to the bathroom.

When I came back a few minutes later, the hall was mostly full. The training manager had been looking for me and when she found me, she told me straight away, "Look, it's too late now to take the books down, but just so you know, we don't allow books to be sold after lectures."

I explained to her that I don't actively sell my books during the lecture; I just note at the end of the lecture that I have all of my bestsellers here. Then, if anyone is interested in purchasing a book and having me sign it, they are invited to do so and the same goes for anyone who just wants to ask me some questions.

She replied, "I'll allow you to leave your books there because I only found out at the last moment, but on the condition that your lecture isn't too sales-oriented." And then she added just before I went on stage, "In any case, no one will buy your books. They are salaried employees, and I have never seen anyone here buy books after a lecture."

The hall was filled to its capacity of 200 people. I lectured for an hour-and-a-half and really felt that the audience was connecting(even laughing and enjoying themselves and at the end of the lecture I invited them to come over and ask me questions and buy books.

There was hot interest that even I was surprised by, especially given the comments the training manager had made. Around 40 people—one fifth of the audience—came to speak with me after the lecture, some of them waited patiently for a long time. I sold 22 of my books and ended up staying another hour after the lecture.

The commotion was so great that I saw the training manager trying to make her way over to talk to me, but she didn't succeed. She waited a few minutes and then left.

When I finally left the company's building, I called her. "Listen," she said, "I was really surprised. It's the first time I've seen so many people crowd around a lecturer." I then told her that I had sold 22 books and she replied, "Now I'm even more surprised!"

I couldn't resist, and asked her, "Tell me, how many

of the hundreds of lecturers you invite to your company every year have written a book?"

"Only a few," she replied. We are talking about first-class lecturers who are strictly screened before they come to talk at that company.

"I have another question for you," I said. "How many of the few that have written books, displayed their books to the audience?"

"None of them," she replied, "because I always warn them not to."

"So what you are really telling me," I said, "is that no one has ever displayed books to the audience at your lectures. How could you have determined that no one will buy books from me?"

My conclusions from this event:

» Don't be shy and don't be afraid to make a call to action at the end of a lecture or presentation. If the lecture was good, the audience will still like you if you devote a few minutes to sell to them. If the lecture was no good, they won't like you in any case and they won't buy anything.

» People are often stuck in their views and "restricting beliefs." The training manager had impeded any possibility of lecturers selling something to participants, as if their pleasure would be impeded if someone offered them something. The training manager had told herself a story that "salaried employees don't buy books." If they aren't offered anything, then they certainly won't buy anything.

The key to motivating people and customers to action is initiative and proactive interaction.

More on the rules of engagement with people and clients in the next chapter.

KEY ELEMENTS OF COMMANDMENT NO. 3

Motivate people to act.

- ✓ If people have to do something, show them how easy and simple it is.
- ✓ Twenty percent more people will show up for a conference if they are promised food.
- ✓ The investment principle: If you invest in your clients, they'll invest in return by signing up or buying from you.
- ✓ People are more alert and focused when they've eaten something.
- ✓ Even freebies must be "sold."
- ✓ What customers most expect to buy, place at the furthest point from the entrance. What is least important to them, place by the entrance.
- ✓ People obey road signs, so explain to them exactly what they need to do.
- ✓ Anchoring meaning planting an idea in your clients' head and making them think what and how they want your products and/or services, rather than *if* they want it.

✓ When you want to communicate with your clients, address them directly and make eye contact.

✓ Leave your customers with a taste for more after your activity or their purchase from you.

✓ Don't be shy and don't be afraid to call to action at the end of your lecture or presentation.

COMMANDMENT NO. 4

*Put yourself center stage, in front of an
audience, and in front of your customers.*

THE EXCUSES YOU TELL YOURSELF WHEN YOU'RE IN FRONT OF AN AUDIENCE:

Situation #1:
You arrive at a professional conference in your
field, or at a business event. You were sent by
your firm, or you came on your own initiative.
One of the main goals you have set yourself
for this conference (and certainly if you paid
for it yourself) is to network. Meaning, to get
to know as many new people as possible and
to identify potential customers and partners.

You spend most of the time standing at the
side of the room or near the coffee station,
sitting all day in the same seat in the lecture

hall and speaking mainly to the people you came to the conference with, or people you already know.

Situation #2:

You're in a sales meeting with a customer. There's chemistry and the customer is connected to your message, but maybe they are the one who set up the meeting. You present your product or service and talk about it with a lot of enthusiasm, expecting to close the deal in that meeting.

At some point the customer says something like "It's too expensive for me," "I'm not interested," "I'll get back to you," "Okay, we'll be in touch," and the meeting immediately runs out of steam. You leave the meeting with a sour taste in your mouth, obviously without having closed the deal, and you ask yourself, "What went wrong?"

Situation #3:

You're speaking in front of an audience, sharing valuable content in your field of expertise. Some of the members of the audience are really on board, and at the end of your talk, you want to offer them some sort of additional activity with you—consultation, a workshop, the purchase of your products and services, or the exchange of contact information.

At the last minute, you worry that some members of the audience won't like it if you try to sell something to them and so you don't motivate the audience to act. You leave the lecture, which was good from your point of view, with no significant results and no work for later on.

What do all three situations have in common?

In all three, you did not fully realize the potential of the situation, on both the personal and business levels, and you got zero results.

In all three cases you immediately justified your behavior and actions to yourself and "sold" yourself excuses as to why you didn't act differently—instead of selling to your audience.

You did not motivate anyone to act!

If you want to promote things, you must put yourself forward and you must actually offer those things. No one else will do this for you, and certainly no one can do this better than you, if we are talking about your own personal "agenda" or about a product or service you're selling.

In this chapter, I explain the "rules of engagement" with clients, and how to take your initiative and call to action to the next level.

WHAT'S THE DIFFERENCE BETWEEN THE HOST AND THE WAITER IN A RESTAURANT?

Here's a dilemma that is taught in business management schools around the world:

Let's say you're managing a company and you need to hire another salesperson, a junior manager as your subordinate, or a skilled employee for an important role. You have two options:

You can hire an employee who is a "noble steed," meaning someone who is refined, who is very good at what they do, but who is not willing or able to do other things, and is also not prepared to try anything beyond their abilities. Or you can hire a "wild horse," meaning someone's who is a little more difficult to manage, but who has a lot of energy, passion and motivation and is prepared to do whatever is needed, even if it is not in their area of responsibility and authority.

Whom would you choose?

Studies conducted in large companies around the world have found that most managers choose "noble steeds;" they are more disciplined and less threatening, easier to manage and are less hungry to climb up the corporate ladder. They will not take too much initiative and will not overstep their manager's authority. In short, this is the "classic" employee for managers who do not want any problems, especially if they work in the public sector or in a large corporation.

I have a very different approach.

As a manager, if I need to choose employees for my

company, I would always choose the wild horses. I want employees and team members who will challenge me, criticize me when it's appropriate, and, mainly, I want them to have a lot of passion and energy, so that I won't have to spend time motivating and convincing them every day about why they need to work hard for me.

And this is doubly true if we're talking about salespeople.

To succeed in sales, you need something I call *positive chutzpa*, the ability to pick up the phone and sell to someone, the will to follow up with that person over and over again, and the motivation to go up to people you don't know at an event.

These are all things that noble steeds would never do because it's not their job or they feel uncomfortable doing such a thing, they don't know how or they can't deal with getting "no" for an answer. But wild horses will do all these things because they have the drive to do whatever it takes to succeed!

When you go to a fancy restaurant, a host greets you at the entrance and inside you're served by wait staff.

Do you know what the difference is between the two?

The host is a noble steed and the waiter is a wild horse. Hosts don't sell you anything. Their job is to smile and to usher people into the restaurant. They don't need to sell you anything because you have already come to the restaurant's door. In some cases, they can even be sales "repellents" and can cause people who have already come to the door to turn around and go to another restaurant.

And what about wait staff?

Waiters are skilled salespeople because their tips depend on their skill. They will encourage you to order the more expensive entries on the menu, they will ask you over and over again if you'd like anything else, and, with every dish you order, they will suggest a side dish or a beverage to go along with it. In short, they do everything to make you spend more money at the restaurant, and of course to ensure that you also enjoy the food and the service.

The next time you hire an employee, a manager or a salesperson, even if you do it through outsourcing, I recommend that you choose the wild horse.

WHAT DO YOUR SHOES HAVE TO DO WITH YOUR INCOME?

(Or: What do you do if your competitor's office is right in front of your customer's office?)

People tend to think that marketing and sales are very complicated, that when it comes to these skills, "you either have it or you don't," that there's some "sophisticated mechanism" that affects the customer, that you need highly sophisticated "creative thinking," and so on. But the truth is that in most cases it's a lot simpler than what people think. Here are the things you really need:

> » **Initiative**
> » **Diligence**
> » **A personal relationship**

A customer of mine, an interior designer specializing in branding offices, once told me that she had once arranged to meet a very big potential customer, namely a chain store with a lot of office space, and that when she arrived for the meeting, she found out that exactly across from the customer's head office was the office of another interior designer. It even had a big sign on it!

She was upset and thought that her meeting was now pointless, that this customer was probably already working with her competitor. She asked herself why this customer should want to work with her and not with the interior designer whose office was located directly opposite.

But at the meeting she was amazed to learn that this customer didn't even know the competing interior designer, and was not even aware that there was an interior designer in the area!

Now, I'm willing to bet that the interior designer located opposite that customer's business invested a lot in marketing: website, Facebook page, Google campaign, pamphlets, and so on. However, ultimately, some of the work you would like to get is located "right under your nose."

You just need to know where to look, to take the initiative, to say the right things at the meeting, and to be willing to wear out several pairs of shoes as you market yourself.

WHY ISN'T IT SMART TO HIDE BEHIND THE KEYBOARD WHEN WE WANT TO CONNECT WITH SOMEONE?

A few years ago I saw a charming movie, *The Intern*, starring Robert De Niro. The plot is about a 70-year-old widower whose wife had died a while ago, as had a lot of his friends. He was looking for meaning in his life and wasn't willing to just retire and grow old slowly.

As part of a program that takes in retirees as interns, he joins a young and dynamic high-tech firm with a 35-year-old CEO and employees aged between 20-35. The movie portrays intergenerational gaps in a light-hearted and enchanting way, and the complexity of Generation Y (people born in the 1980 and 1990s, and also referred to as the "Internet Generation" who have grown up into the reality of the internet and a digital world).

In one of the scenes which I remember vividly, one of the young interns tells De Niro that there is a girl at the company he dated in the past and would really like to date again, but he upset her and she won't talk to him.

De Niro asks if he talked to her: "Did you apologize?" and the young man answers "Sure! I texted her a billion times, I emailed her, I even sent her a sad emoticon."

De Niro makes the obvious suggestion that he just go over and talk to her.

The young man falls silent, thinks about it and wonders, "Do you think it would help?"

From my perspective, the scene illustrates the challenges of the present generations, not just Generation Y, but people of all ages. We have transitioned from an environment of constant interpersonal communication, to hiding behind the keyboard—sending emails to potential important clients instead of calling or setting up a meeting, sending text messages and WhatsApp messages to friends and family instead of calling or going to visit, and I haven't even talked about the world of dating and relationships.

Even in the digital age, and perhaps precisely because of the digital age, there is a growing importance of our ability to speak before an audience. Of all the marketing and sales methods I know, the highest "conversion rate" according to studies is still lectures and presentations before an audience.

The best way to convince the highest percentage of people to buy from you is still if they meet you and hear from you, face-to-face, with the real possibility to converse with you and ask you questions.

Following that, in second place is one-on-one, in-person meetings.

In third place are telephone calls.

In fourth place is WhatsApp or something similar.

In fifth place, text messages via mobile phone.

You may ask why WhatsApp and similar apps convert at a higher rate than text messages? These messages are perceived as more intimate. You broadcast to the customer that you are close and have a friendly relationship, not just a working relationship. The close relationship is hinted at subconsciously by using the app. Right now, I am bringing it up to a conscious level.

Take a look now at your mobile phone for a moment. Your WhatsApp or similar app notifications contain messages from friends, family neighbors, parents of kids at your children's schools and nursery, and more. Your text message (SMS) notifications, on the other hand, may contain more formal messages related to transactions.

So, if I'm sending a message to a client, which group do I want to be in? Naturally, in the group that is seen by the client as the more intimate and personal. Even if my message was more professional or "formal" and not necessarily friendly.

Email came in at sixth place.

And only then, in seventh place, are messages via social media, such as personal messages via Facebook, or use of Twitter.

Some of you may be reading this and saying that's ridiculous. "What is he talking about? I'm in touch with people all day only via email and social media, and it works just fine." Well, it doesn't work just fine for everyone. Even those it does work just fine for, this just shows the greater potential that exists if they were to operate a little differently.

If you want to be different—which by the way, according to research, is what Generation Y and Generation Z most want—and to generate exceptional, personal, professional and business results, you need to conduct yourself differently.

That means seeking to engage with clients, creating direct contact with them, developing a relationship with them, telling them about yourself in a correct and accurate manner, and not hiding all day long behind the computer screen or phone, aka the comfort zone. People today have gotten used to sending messages rather than calling. People send emails, even to those physically located very close to them, instead of meeting with one another. People spend a lot of time recording voice messages to each other, listening to the message they received from the other party and then recording a new voice message, instead of simply talking to each other.

In the past, I used to get dozens of incoming phone calls on work and business affairs, not including friends and family. Today, now that I have a higher profile from a business perspective, I receive only a few calls a day, but my WhatsApp and Facebook are overflowing with dozens or even hundreds of messages a day.

The world is changing, means of communications are changing. But people are still people, and the human brain still works in the same way as it did decades years ago.

Do you want to stand out from your competitors? Meet your clients once in a while face-to-face and not from behind the keyboard.

Do you want to conduct negotiations over money or to give a price quote for your product or service? Pick up the phone and talk with your clients and don't just write your price in a message and wait for your client's response. During a conversation, you can defend your price if it's high.

Do you want to differentiate yourself in a difficult market? Initiate physical meetings with your existing and potential customers—conferences, lectures, presentations, visits to your company, factory, offices, and more.

Do you want to establish your professional authority? Publish a printed book in your field of specialty. Podcasts, e-books and webinars are all also recommended, but a printed book is still the king of information products, even today.

Precisely because most of your competitors avoid taking these steps, your customers will be more appreciative of a telephone call, book, meeting or "frontal" lecture.

It will strengthen your authority.

It will make you different.

It will make you more memorable.

And it will close you a lot more deals.

Stop hiding behind the keyboard. There is a real world out there, and it is fun and important.

BY TAKING WHAT ACTION WILL YOU BE MORE LIKELY TO GAIN CUSTOMERS?

One of the most important things in the world of sales is the conversion rate: How many people bought your products and services out of all those whom you approached? If you sent an email to 1,000 people who opened and read it and 20 people made a purchase, the conversion rate is 2 percent. If I appeared before an audience of 100 people and 20 people made a purchase after the lecture, the conversion rate is 20 percent.

All firms, everywhere in the world, be they large or small, market their products and services by diverse means, methods and platforms: websites, launches, conference sponsorships, lectures and presentations, sponsored campaigns on the Internet, advertising, social media activities, direct mailing and more.

As every company at the end of the day has limited resources—time, money and energy—the important question is where is the highest conversion rate to be found? In other words, in which platform is it worth investing the most, as that platform will generate the maximum number of customers?

In the previous section I wrote about the order in which marketing and sales methods convert based on my own research in the past decade and on research conducted around the world; a lecture or presentation in front of a large audience will be more efficient from a perspective of conversion rate than face-to-face meetings. A face-to-face meeting will be more efficient (than a telephone conversation. A telephone call has a higher conversion rate than sending a text message and a text message has a higher conversion rate than email. If I want to increase my conversion rate to the maximum, I therefore need to bring my customers every time to the highest "converting" platform.

If a client approaches you on Facebook, make telephone contact with them. If a client has until today been in contact with you via email or telephone, invite them to a meeting, and so on.

The clients you have today, who are "intangible assets," can easily and quickly become (with zero marketing and advertising expenses) very tangible assets from a revenue perspective.

A client who participated in one of my personal mentoring programs, deals with promoting businesses on Facebook. One of his clients is a toy store chain that also sells costumes. My client wrote a few posts on the chain's Facebook page a few weeks before Halloween inviting parents to come to the stores and buy costumes.

When we met, there had been few responses and very little interest. He showed me posts that he had written, which, in general, said something along the lines of "We invite you come and have a look at the wide range of costumes we have in the store," "Costumes for adults, costumes for kids, and a range of accessories," "Competitive prices."

I changed the posts completely.

I explained to him that the posts were selling the solution, while he needed to focus on selling the problem or the need (I spoke about this principle in Commandment 1 of the book and will expand on it in Commandment 6.)

Because what are parents troubled by two or three weeks before Halloween?

First of all, most of them aren't troubled because they don't even remember that in another couple of weeks it's going to be Halloween. Most of them will only remember the week of the holiday when the kindergarten or class teacher updates them as to when the kindergarten or school is on vacation and when the Halloween party is taking place.

But by then it could be too late because then they will find themselves at the store at the last moment together with the majority of parents, won't necessarily find the costume they were looking for, and will have to compromise or make do with what's left.

We wrote new posts that began by "selling the problem" and looked something this: "To all parents who think Halloween is still far off and think there is still time to buy costumes, to all parents whose child has asked for a specific costume and you don't want to disappoint them, and to all the parents who want the right to choose and not to buy the costumes that others have left on the shelves—if you don't hurry up, there won't be costumes left! Now is the time to head to the store and choose the most appropriate costume for your child, one that is the right size!" And then we added a few more words about the costumes, and a call to action with the address of the store and contact details at the end of each post.

Of course this post touched a lot more parents and the exposure and responses were a lot greater. By the way, on a post like that there isn't even a need to write "Competitive prices," "Discounts" or "Attractive prices."

As soon as I solve the client's real problem, the price will be a secondary consideration.

But our story continues. You've written up some good posts, you've gotten a lot of reactions on Facebook, and now the question is: Wwhat do you do with those reactions?

What did that toy store chain do with those reactions up until now? Almost nothing. A few likes in response to comments, answering a specific question here and there such as "what's the address of the store?" but they didn't create any real connection or call to action. This is where a fantastic marketing tool comes in, which few people know about and even less make use of; something called *buying signals*.

That's a situation in which someone is "signaling" to you that they are interested in what you are doing, writing or selling, without actually asking specific customer questions, or showing a desire to buy.

The right way of dealing with them is to seek to engage, that is, to respond actively to buying signals and to transfer the customer to a higher converting platform—to flatter the customer, to ask them in a Facebook message for their phone number so that you can tell them more about your service or product, and when they send you their number (and response rates are very high, if you act correctly), call them.

My client used this tool and, within a few hours, had received several phone numbers of customers interested in the shop's costumes and wishing to hear more.

He transferred these hot leads to the store manager with a clear instruction to call the customers.

A week goes by and he asks the store manager what the customers purchased, and she answers, "Nothing."

"Did you call them?" he asks her.

She replies: "No, I sent them a brochure on Facebook with a list of our costumes. They never got back in touch with me."

That's a mistake that cost a lot of money. The customers were waiting for a phone call. These are customers who wanted to buy a costume and were willing, more or less, to purchase anything being sold.

The chain had already invested a lot of effort in creating these leads, and had made personal contact with the customers. And then it took a step backward in the process, moving to a less-converting platform, instead of calling the leads. They hid behind the keyboard and again sent them a notification on Facebook, this time without any personal touch, just a general brochure of the kind you send to everyone.

It's hardly surprising that these "hot leads" didn't make contact, and certainly didn't make a purchase.

I call this "leaving money on the floor."

The store manager will probably end up saying things like, "Facebook marketing doesn't work," "We spent all that money on Facebook for nothing" and "The market is really difficult, you just can't make money from costumes."

That's a shame, because things could be different.

You can seek to engage with customers and provide them with services and a relationship that no one else in the market provides—such as phone calls—and they will buy from you, not your rivals.

YOU'VE BEEN TAGGED ON FACEBOOK ALONG WITH ANOTHER 50 SUPPLIERS: HOW CAN YOU GET THE JOB?

If you are active on Facebook professionally and commercially, then you are surely familiar with posts such as the following, "Looking for an entertaining lecturer for a company event. Tag if you know anyone," "Looking for digital gurus who can get my business ranked top," "Anyone know an air-conditioning technician who can be trusted. Let me have their contacts," "I want to buy a large screen TV for my living room, any recommendations?" and so on and so on.

Any post like that (assuming the person who posted has friends) will, within a short time, receive dozens and sometimes hundreds of tags of suppliers or relevant professionals. Sometimes there are suppliers who will appear again and again in several recommendations, but you will still get a large list of potential suppliers that will leave whoever put up the request needing to choose the person most suitable for them or for the job.

On the one hand, this is the wisdom of the crowd at its best and testimony to the collaborative power of Facebook. If you are a professional that has been tagged in the post, it's nice to know there are clients and colleagues who are complimenting you, are appreciative of the work you have done for them and share that with others.

But—and this is a big but—what are the chances that you will actually get the job?

On the assumption that dozens of professionals were tagged by friends of the person who put up the post, many of whom they don't even know, and most of the tags contained no resumé or CV of the person being recommended, how is someone supposed to choose?

Price.

On the assumption they will even approach a few of the suppliers on the list, when a customer doesn't differentiate between you and your competitors, and from their point of view you are all the same (after all, you've been tagged in the same post) the only difference between you is a line above or a line below is price. Whoever offers the cheapest price will get the job.

A *price-based market* is bad for everyone, especially if you are a brand, expert or authority in your field or you want to be, or if you are selling expensive products. Because then if someone tags you several times, which is better than nothing and shows the good work you have done in the past, the chances of someone approaching you are very low amid a sea of competitors. And if someone does approach you, you are going to be in an inferior position when it comes to price because there will always be cheaper offers than yours.

What can you do? You can initiate an approach yourself, and more importantly, speak on the phone with the person who put up the post.

Yes, a phone call!

Don't hide behind the keyboard.

Don't just post a like for anyone that tags you and hope for the best.

Don't just be flattered: take it forward.

And certainly don't write a few lines about yourself and the price in a Facebook post.

You want to differentiate yourself from the dozens of other competitors and colleagues who have been tagged in the same post.

Your aim is to increase your conversion rate and the chances of the customer closing with you, so you really want to talk with them on the phone. In a telephone call the conversion rate increases significantly.

How do you actually do it in practice? After all, you don't have the phone number of the person who published the post. (If you do, then call as soon as you see the ad.)

Here's what you do: Send a personal message to the person who published the post (not to the person that tagged you). You write a message that goes something like this:

Hi, Kevin. Nice to meet you. I saw you are looking for an SEO for your company.

I have a lot of experience in the field and I would
be happy to collaborate with you.

Can I get your cell number, please?
Best, Yaniv

That's it. No additional details. No resumé, no
mention of cost. The goal of an announcement like that
is one goal alone: the person who published the post
gives you their cell number and that you will be able to
call. To increase the chances of that happening, share
your mobile phone number. That's known as the *reciprocity principle*; if you want someone to do something
for you, do something for them first. If I want you to
smile at me, I have to smile at you first. If I want you to
reveal something about yourself, I will reveal something
about myself.

If I want to get a telephone number, I will give
mine out. Statistics at my company and at many companies where we have implemented this rule, point
to 50-80 percent of people giving you their mobile
number in their return message. A few will also call you
themselves, because after all, you left them your mobile
number and that works even better.

When the person that published the post leaves
you his mobile number, call them.

By the very fact that you're holding a telephone
conversation, two wonderful things will happen:

1. You have created differentiation between yourself and others. You are probably the only one to have requested a phone number and certainly the only one to have moved to a higher converting platform and have not gotten "stuck" just on interaction via Facebook.

2. In a telephone call, it is a lot easier to explain how good you are, how experienced and professional you are, and to listen to the other party and understand their needs, and to give a high price and defend it.

It is possible that, sometimes, since you are the only one talking with the job poster, even if your price is significantly higher than others, the job poster won't even know that! He hasn't gotten into a conversation about price with anyone else from the tagged list.

In this way, way you get yourself in above the crowd and maintain the high prices you deserve.

Even in the digital age—especially in the digital age—there is enormous importance to talking on the phone, giving a more personal relationship, to creating differentiation and to moving up to a higher converting platform.

WHAT DO OUR CHILDREN KNOW ABOUT CUSTOMER RELATIONS THAT WE HAVE YET TO LEARN?

In June 2014, my two adorable kids, Noam (then five-and-a-half years old) and Yoav (then three) were playing at home with a friend. They were playing "waiter and customer" in a restaurant. Noam was the customer, Yoav was the waiter, and their friend was the owner of the restaurant, which was located in their room. At some point Noam as customer was standing at the door of the room, and Yoav as waiter was sitting and looking at him. Then the friend playing the owner told Yoav in a rather critical tone: "Go over to him and ask him if he'd like to come in! Don't wait for him to come in on his own. You need to ask him!"

I just happened to witness this situation and thought it was funny. However, I was also positively surprised by the fact that their friend had these great and basic skills and displayed them so brilliantly:

» **Taking the initiative.**
» **Motivating others to action.**
» **Leading and conducting a conversation.**

Don't wait for your customers to come in on their own; some of them will probably take a peek and walk away. Just invite them in!

How simple it is for kids, how complicated for adults. At some point in life, when we get older, it seems to us really complicated to act in such a simple way. "Sophisticated" thoughts go through your head: "I don't want to annoy the customer," "I don't want to sound desperate."

Nonsense. The key to persuading people is to take the initiative.

You must be the driving force behind processes, you must motivate people, you must initiate conversations instead of waiting for others or waiting for your audience to respond.

The bad news is that you always need to have your finger on the pulse. You need to market and to keep reinventing yourself all the time. The good news is there are clear formulas and tools that can help you do it right. And if you do it right for long enough and consistently enough, your success with customers and people is guaranteed.

HOW DOES A MEETING THAT YOU INITIATED WITH CUSTOMERS INCREASE YOUR REVENUES?

One of my firm's clients is a company that manufactures industrial products and components for factories and heavy industry—a company that has a cash flow of hundreds of millions of dollars a year and works with the industrial sector.

The company's clients are purchase managers and manufacturing managers from big factories, such as food companies. They are the decision makers who decide whether to purchase from it or from its competitors.

As part of the consultancy services we provided to them, which included tours with field sales agents, visits to customers, constructing sales scenarios for employees, listening in on the call center, workshops for sales peoples, strategic consultancy to the CEO and more, we were asked to find additional, creative ways to increase the company's revenues without increasing its marketing expenses.

One of the first ideas we raised was a get-together with customers at the company's offices.

The company has a very interesting manufacturing floor, the section of the factory where you can see how the parts are prepared; a gift shop; and a training room that has been remodeled and stands shiny-but-empty most of the day. We suggested they take their fifty best customers and invite them for a day-long visit and training: Give them a tour of the factory and the manufacturing floor, explain to them how you work, get them together in your beautiful new training room with some food and refreshments, introduce them to each other. The CEO can say a few words and the VP will give a professional review of the field.

From my perspective this is a very obvious and routine idea that I have already implemented successfully with many customers, but to them it sounded absolutely revolutionary; they were even against it at first.

We asked them "How many of your customers have visited your factory or have been at your offices?" Their answer was "none," which was really astounding for me.

Initiating customer meetings increases revenues.

Why?

First, it is an opportunity to connect with customers for an original reason: "I want to invite you to an event" and not for the regular and annoying reason of "What's happening with that price quote I sent you?"

Second, if you call, say, fifty customers and in practice only fifteen to twenty turn up, those who didn't turn up will give you credit for inviting them and thinking about them.

Third, the fifteen to twenty customers who do turn up will definitely find things out about your company that they didn't know such as your expertise, your professionalism, the number of customers you have. (Remember, you are putting customers from different fields in the same room.)

Fourth, it is an excellent opportunity to ask customers to refer other customers to you, to close additional deals with them, and to prompt them sign an agreement that may have been delayed for some time.

In other words, a meeting like that can only do good things for you and increase your revenues in the short and long term. And the best thing is, it's a move that doesn't cost the company much! The factory is there, the training room is there, the employees and management are at work anyway. The only thing it does cost is a little management time to call the right people and invite them, and a few hundred dollars for food and drinks.

If it's so simple, why do hardly any businesses and companies do it? Because they haven't thought of it. Because it's difficult for them to implement it. Because they are too busy with "survival" and aren't able to think outside of the box. Because they are blindly chasing after their next customers (including buying new "leads" for a lot of money) instead of investing in existing customers. And, because they don't value their intangible assets, and don't know how to make them tangible (in terms of revenues).

WHY YOUR FIRST PRESENTATION IS ACTUALLY THE EASIEST.

Many of my clients have started giving their own presentations and holding their own conferences and events.

It's not surprising, considering the fact that this is why some of them come to me for consultations in the first place, and considering the fact that one of the things I push my clients to do is to put themselves in the forefront—center stage, in front of an audience and in front of their customers.

Where's the challenge?

In the first presentation.

I recognize a consistent pattern among my customers, when they set up their first conference or to give a lecture aimed at their customers: The fear that people won't come.

Before that first conference, you are afraid that no one will be interested in what you have to offer, that you'll work hard preparing the presentation and the conference and that, in the end, very few people will show up, and so forth and so on.

This fear causes you a lot of worry, sometimes "paralyzing" you; in extreme cases, it can even stop you from getting started. Fear that people won't come can cause you to postpone giving that first presentation over and over again, so ultimately, you might never do it!

I always tell those customers: The fear that people won't come is always there. Every artist, every speaker, every marketer, every politician who holds an electoral event and every company that holds a business conference—they all experience it.

But your first presentation is actually the easiest one. When you market your first presentation to your customers and the people you know, many of them will come because of the personal relationship they have with you. Many people will come out of curiosity and many people will come because, as you will discover, they hold you in high regard from a professional standpoint and they have been waiting for some time to hear what you have to say in your field of expertise.

The second, third and fourth presentation are the ones that are a lot more difficult to promote. For those, you will have to get members of your "third circle," "fourth circle," and so on to attend, including people who don't know you at all. And that is a much more challenging task.

My message is quite simple here: Just get started!

Set a date for your first conference, mark the date of your first presentation on your calendar and start getting your message out to the world. In a competitive, digital and global age such as ours, you can't afford another year without getting your voice and your professional agenda heard.

"I DON'T FEEL COMFORTABLE SELLING TO AN AUDIENCE."

A few years ago, I was in London for a professional convention and I participated in a workshop held by one of the most veteran and well-known mentors in the world. The workshop was quite intimate, with just around eighty businesspeople who had come from around Europe, and took place over two whole days. The mentor was very charismatic and entertaining and gave us a lot of important business insights.

As I am used to products or follow-up services being sold at the end of every workshop, (certainly long and successful workshops) and since I knew that that particular (American) mentor comes to London once or twice a year for two weeks and that the next day he would be starting a new workshop with a different audience, I expected that he would sell follow-up workshops at the end of this particular workshop and I was even curious to see how he would go about it.

The final hour of the workshop arrived and the quality of the lecture peaked. The energy was high, and the session offered a lot of material, including energizing exercises for the audience. I was sure all this was a build-up to a sales pitch. To my surprise, the presenter ended the lecture all of a sudden, precisely at the moment when the audience was at a high level of energy and standing on its feet, and just said, "Thank you very much! Good luck!"

That was it. The audience left quickly and I was surprised. Why didn't he sell anything? Why didn't he leverage the audience's energies in order to at least tell them about additional activities? After all, a lecture is the top selling platform!

I couldn't help myself; after the lecture I went up to him and asked why he hadn't sold us his next workshops in London.

The answers I received during our conversation surprised me:

"I don't feel comfortable selling to an audience. I did it in the past, and I received some not-so-good feedback from some of the audience."

"People don't like it when you sell to them from the stage."

"People already know me and they will come in any case."

"Anyone who wants to do the next workshop will find the way to register."

Despite the pleasant, and long, conversation, I wasn't convinced. My only explanation (which I gave to myself) for the fact that he didn't sell on stage was the fact that he probably wasn't "hungry" like he used to be. He had already been doing this for at least 40 years and perhaps he was winding down and had enough activities going on around the world and enough money that he didn't really care how many people turned up to his London workshop or bought his books.

Okay, I thought to myself, it's up to him. Everyone should do what's good for them.

But then something interesting happened.

Before I left London—I still had another two days to spend there—I received an email from his team, congratulating me on taking part in the workshop and offering me the opportunity to participate in another workshop that was about to open in London.

It was a proper sales email, with a sales link and everything.

Over the following days, I received an email like that every day, and a telephone call from one of his team who wanted to hear about my experiences at the workshop, and of course to offer me something extra. To this day, once every few months I get a phone call from his team member, and once every couple of weeks I get an email from him—mostly just sales emails, with no real added value.

This kind of follow up has confused me, and even made me feel disappointed in him.

In my opinion, it is a wrong business model. If I were already satiated and he didn't want to push me as a customer to register for further activities, I can sort of understand that. But to consciously give up on some customers, because of unwillingness to do any kind of sales pitch seems foolish.

The email follow up indicated he did, in fact, want

me as a customer. He just wasn't willing to do anything personally to close the deal. That is a lot more annoying and troublesome to me than if he had devoted several minutes at the end of the workshop to tell the audience about follow-up products.

What's more, doing it that way is a lot less efficient for the presenter. During a presentation, the audience is energized, the atmosphere is optimistic and creative, the attendees out of their "comfort zone," they have high "esteem" for the lecturer, they are laughing and enjoying themselves—optimal conditions for making a sale.

And the audience is already in London! Some people would have extended their stay for a follow-up workshop if the lecturer had only explained to them why it would be worth their while to do so.

When I receive an email a few days after an event, when I have already returned home to my country, I am already back in routine, my mind is elsewhere, and it is a lot more difficult to motivate me to action. I'm all in favor of telephone calls to customers, and emails, letters, and so on, but as a complementary marketing tool.

At the end of the day, the best way to market with the highest conversion rate is when people meet you and experience you closely, receive a personal touch from you, and receive a verbal explanation from you and can ask you questions.

The more you put yourself in center stage—in front of an audience and in front of customers—the more your revenues will grow, and the more your brand and professional authority will strengthen.

WHY DID THE CHIEF OF STAFF OF THE ISRAEL DEFENSE FORCES PROHIBIT MAKING PRESENTATIONS IN INVESTIGATIONS AND BRIEFINGS?

In 2005, the Chief of Staff of the Israel Defense Forces sent an order down the entire military chain of command that all use of PowerPoint presentations be stopped during briefings and investigations, aside from in a few senior forums and certain situations.

Why did he give this sweeping instruction?

Because a custom had developed in the Israeli military—he found it unacceptable, and so do I—whereby soldiers and commanders would prepare highly elaborate PowerPoint presentations, loaded with "pyrotechnics" (colors, flashes, images, bouncing lines) to the point where the essence was overshadowed by the non-essential fluff.

What's the purpose of a briefing? Any briefing? That the people who are listening to you get the message you are conveying to them and implement it properly and effectively.

And what is the purpose of an investigation? Any investigation? That people will learn and internalize the lessons and conclusions, that they will preserve for the future what's needed and what worked well, and that they will improve upon what didn't work well in the past.

That is the main point, the essence.

But when you focus on the quality of the presentation, both when preparing for the briefing or investigation and while it is taking place, then the "background" becomes the main act, and overshadows the message.

The speaker, not the presentation, needs to be at the center. When people are busy reading your presentation, being bombarded with the "flashes" and the bouncing images, this comes at the expense of their understanding of and integrating your messages. But more than that, it also comes at the expense of the professional image of the person making the presentation, because that person is perceived by the audience as less professional, less connected to the message and less interesting.

That's why the presentation needs to include your key messages and why you need to be the center of your presentation.

WHAT'S THE BEST THING YOU CAN DO AFTER GIVING A BAD PRESENTATION?

There's a famous saying among public speakers: You're only as good as your last lecture.

Which means that the audience always remembers your last appearance that they saw, and that they will judge you by that, for better or worse.

For worse: You held a workshop that included four sessions, and at three of them, you were at your best and the participants really enjoyed them. Then the fourth didn't go so well. It will be the fourth and last work-shop that the participants will "take" back home with them. They will remember only the bad session. Yes, it's true, people have short memories. Audiences are very demanding, and at times, they can even be treacherous.

For better: Let us say that you just gave a lecture that was not so great in one place, and that, immediately after that, you gave a lecture somewhere else. Here is your opportunity to start over and to have a "corrective experience" with a new audience.

By the way, in case you were wondering: Once every few presentations, every speaker gives one that is not that great. There might be external circumstances, such as an audience that is not interested in the topic or has had a bad experience moments before. There can also be personal reasons that are connected with you: tiredness, lack of energy, a phone call you got right before your lecture that upset you, and so forth.

The difference between an excellent speaker and a mediocre speaker is expressed in two ways:

1. How often it happens to you. Among excellent speakers, about 5 percent, or one in twenty, of the presentations will not be so great. Among good speakers, about one in five will not be so great. And among mediocre speakers, the percentage is up to about half. We're all human, and we all have our bad days. But you need to significantly minimize the number of bad days.

2. What you do after giving a presentation that didn't go so well. In my experience, the best thing to do is to give another as soon as possible. Sometimes it's already marked on your calendar; there are days when I give lectures three times a day in front of different audiences. Other times you need to create the situation. The main thing, from a professional point of view, is to have a corrective experience as soon as possible so that you can get back on track and so that you don't wallow in depressing thoughts about the lecture that didn't go so well.

WHY MY YOUNGER SON IS MUCH MORE PERSUASIVE THAN MY OLDER ONE.

As I have already told you, I have two adorable sons, Noam, my eldest, and Yoav, my younger son. They are both funny, energetic and a bit mischievous (of course, I'm completely objective). But I have noticed an interesting phenomenon: The little one (Yoav) is much more persuasive than his older brother (Noam)!

Yoav is better at "manipulating" those around him, he gets his way with greater ease, he knows how to "read the situation" and he gets along with every-body much more easily. If I'm "Dr. Persuasion" and Noam is "Post-Doc Persuasion," Yoav is definitely "Professor Persuasion."

And I have asked myself: Why? Why is it easier for my younger son to be persuasive and why does he know how to make better use of interpersonal communication?

My answer, after giving the matter a lot of thought, is: Because he has to. The second child is born into a different reality from the first. The first immediately gets attention from those around him without having to make an effort, while the second child was born into a reality where there's already someone else who's getting much of the attention, and where, if he doesn't work hard and go out of his way, he won't get noticed as much. So he adapts and learns how to get by in what, from his point of view, is a challenging environment.

My older son is still in his comfort zone and needs to "wake up"; he still does not realize that the conditions have changed and that he too needs to adapt. In other words, my younger son's key to success is "hunger."

It doesn't come easy to him. He needs to make an effort to get what he wants. That's how it is in life, too: In order to succeed, on both business and personal levels, you need to really want it, you need to make an effort, you need to be hungry and you need to understand that no one is going to give you what you do not work for and take for yourself.

You don't have to operate from a place of distress, a bad financial situation or a challenging and unsupportive environment. You can also generate this hunger from the inside—an inner passion that makes you want to "eat up the world" and always move on to the next level.

And this is true at any age. In fact, adults go through a process that's similar to the one my kids are going through. Because at the age of forty, fifty, and above, if you've quit your job, were fired, or were forced to retire, you find out—maybe for the first time—that "it's cold out there." You've joined "the world championships of sending out résumés," only you are on the wrong side of the competition, that is, the résumé-sending side and not vice-versa.

What do you do?

You can get sad, get mad, and drag your family and kids down with you, along with your savings. But if you're hungry for success, you can take charge of your destiny and, even if you have some disadvantages, you can turn them into advantages!

Let us take the issue of age, for example. As someone who prepares clients for job interviews and tenders in the public sector, I'm surprised to see people lose hope because of their age, and it makes no difference how old they are.

A young man who just got his degree says to me, "Why should they hire me? I have no experience in the field and I just finished my degree. They always prefer people with experience."

And another man, who's over the age of forty-five says to me, "Why would they hire me? I'm already 'old' and my asking salary is probably too high for them. The market prefers those young guys who are fresh out of college."

It's all a question of your state of mind: You always need to think positively and to continually persuade yourself that you can succeed. If you think of your age as a disadvantage, then turn it into an advantage.

Although the young graduate does indeed lack experience, he is (to make a gross generalization) very up to date, he has just studied the latest information in the field, he is hungry to succeed and gain experience, and he has not yet been "ruined" by a previous workplace. That's what he needs to market.

The older man does indeed "cost" more, but he has a wealth of experience. He has had the time to make mistakes and correct them. His kids are already grown up and he doesn't need to go to any ceremonies at their kindergartens and schools and to therefore absent himself from the office every so often. He will appreciate the opportunity he receives and won't be quick to leave his job for a few extra dollars somewhere else.

If you're hungry for success and you show up with the right and patient attitude, there's no reason for you not to succeed.

KEY ELEMENTS OF COMMANDMENT NO. 4

Put yourself at the front.

✓ If you want to promote things, you must put yourself forward and offer those things.

✓ Maintain *positive chutzpa*—have the drive to do whatever it takes to succeed!

✓ Even in the digital age, businesses and people

appreciate the personal touch, initiative and speaking face-to-face.

✓ It's important to seek to engage customers, to create a direct connection, to develop a relationship with them, to tell them about yourself accurately and correctly, and not to hide all day behind the computer screen or phone.

✓ Move your client onto a higher converting platform.

✓ Even on buying signals, seek to engage and be proactive.

✓ The conversion rate on telephone calls are significantly higher than by just corresponding in writing with customers.

✓ Use the reciprocity principle to get vital information.

✓ Initiating a meeting with customers at your company will increase revenues.

✓ Your first presentation is actually the easiest one.

✓ A presentation is the best-selling platform.

✓ The speaker, not the style of presentation, needs to be at the center.

✓ You're only as good as your last presentation; after a bad one, have a corrective experience as soon as possible to get back on track.

✓ In order to succeed, you need to be hungry.

✓ Think positively and to continually persuade yourself that you can succeed.

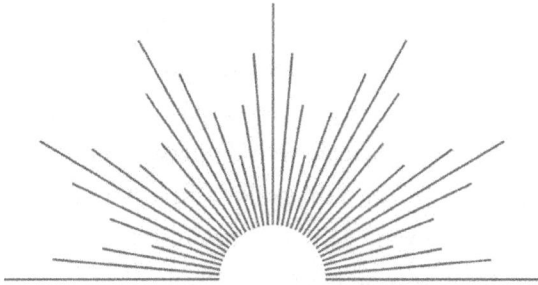

COMMANDMENT NO. 5

Create a community of relevant clients and teach them to buy from you, not your competitors.

HOW TO EDUCATE YOUR MARKET TO BUY FROM YOU AND NOT FROM YOUR COMPETITORS.

Let's take a simple product as an example. Let's say you're selling plasma TV screens. You have an electrical appliance store and there are a few other electrical appliance stores on the exact same street, also selling plasma TVs.

I'm a customer and I walk into your store. One of your salespeople approaches me and tells me about the TV I happen to be looking at.

"Look at the high definition you get on this screen. Check out how great the image looks. This screen has 8 dribbles, 12 pixels and 12 decibels!" (I'm making this stuff up.)

I, the customer, am not an expert in the field of TV screens; I don't really understand what dribbles or pixels are mean, and the truth is that I don't really see that the definition on the screen the salesperson is showing me is so great. When customers don't understand what your professional advantage is and they must decide whether to buy from you or from your competitors, what will they consider? The price, of course.

I, the customer, say to myself, "I don't really understand why this TV is better than the one I saw in the store next door, but I do understand prices. Here, they're offering me this screen for $300, and next door it's going for $200, so I'm going to buy the one next door."

When customers don't understand your value, you're in a "price market" where the only thing that matters is who's selling for a dollar less. In a price market, at the end of the day, everyone loses. Obviously you and your competitors lose, but I'm claiming that the consumer loses out as well, because ultimately some of the "players" in the market will collapse and the quality of the product or service provided to the customer will decline.

Let's take a look at another situation.

One day, you, still the owner of that plasma TV screen store, write a free guide titled "The 10 Secrets for Choosing a Plasma TV Screen for Your Living Room." You print a few dozen copies, or maybe hundreds of copies, and you physically hand them out to every customer that walks in the door. In addition, you post the guide on the store's business Facebook page, you email the guide to all your customers, and so on.

These are relatively simple actions, they would take up only a few workdays at the most, and you already have the knowledge in your head; you only need to put it in writing.

And here's the interesting part: What happens now?

1. You have differentiated yourself from the other stores. You are now perceived as an expert, because you wrote a professional guide and you've done something none of your competitors has done. In my own and others' experience, your level of authority rises amazingly fast as soon as you put out professional information products.

2. You have greatly increased your viral (word-of-mouth) market because your customers are passing the guide around among themselves and/or to others. It's really easy for them to do that online.

3. You are motivating people to come to your store. Because on every page of your guide, and, of course, on its cover and last page, you have made sure to include your store's address, email and phone number so that people know exactly where to go after they've read the guide.

4. This is the really important point: You are educating your market.

Because if your relative advantage is, for example, the high definition of your plasma screens, what is the first secret you'll share in "The 10 Secrets for Choosing a TV Screen for your Living Room" guide? Obviously: Choose a plasma screen based on its level of definition.

You'll need to add a few tips and a number of sections on how to tell when a screen has high definition and when it doesn't, which part of the screen people need to look at to see whether the image is clear or not, and so on. But now, customers who walk into your store after having read the guide are better-educated customers. They know what part to look at on the screen, they will have a better understanding of your salesperson's professional explanations, and they will appreciate the fact that your televisions have really high definition.

Clients who understand the value they are getting, are quite likely to buy from you and not from your competitors. And more than that, they will also be willing to pay you more even if your competitors offer their products at a lower price. In other words, the guide positions you in a *value market* rather than a *price market*. Moreover, those customers will also serve as loyal "ambassadors" for your store because they will remember you better, thanks to the guide and because they appreciate the fact that you have gone to the trouble of teaching them how things really work.

I'm sure you'll agree with me that if I were to show up now in a conference of electrical appliance store owners (and I actually do so every once in a while, because I also work with leading electronics chains) and if I were to explain to them what I have just explained to you now, I would probably hear a lot of responses along the lines of:

"Things work differently in our store. A customer walks in, gets an explanation and chooses whether to buy or not."

"Our customers are different. In our market, everything is based on price."

"What you're saying may be true for other markets, but not for ours."

But all this is simply not true!

Market education is currently one of the leading trends in marketing and it is a prominent feature in every industry, market and field today.

Where are you?

Do you want to be in a value market and enjoy professional recognition and high prices? Or in a price market and find yourself just lowering prices as your competitors do?

HOW DO YOU "EDUCATE" PEOPLE TO RUN?

In an age when "content is king," each product or service that you wish to sell, you can and should sell via professional, high-quality content regarding that product. Especially in the event that the product is you, or you are the principal service provider, and you wish to position and brand yourselves as an expert in a specific field.

Content should be provided over a period of time in order to create a community of loyal customers, who not only purchase the product, coming back again and again, but also recommend it, tell their friends and acquaintances about it and write about it themselves.

Professional, quality content is the most efficient way to create viral marketing; the information is transmitted by word of mouth and people share your content and talk about it. By doing so, they indirectly also talk about you without your asking them to and without getting a commission from you. (Viral marketing is covered in depth in Commandment 8.)

I have advised every company I have consulted for in recent years, no matter what field the company is in, to publish professional content (via lectures/presentations, regular posts on social networks, starting a blog, updating the company website, publishing professional articles, writing newsletters to customers, preparing presentations for important customers, and more), and I almost always run up against resistance such as, "It doesn't suit us," "It doesn't work in our field," "Our customers are different," and so on.

I always respond by giving examples from a range of fields, with diverse operations and different types of customers, who have successfully educated the market.

A great example is marathons.

Every year, large cities around the world—New York, Sydney, Berlin, Tel Aviv, to name just a few—together with sponsors and production companies, hold marathons and races of various distances, with tens of thousands of people registering for each event. The runners (or customers) register, pay, receive a kit with a number, a shirt, and various other items and turn up to run on the day of the race.

It's an incredible experience; I've participated in dozens of races like that. It's a big party, with great service—an absolute joy.

The question is: How do you get so many people to sign up anew every year, pay their dues and show up? And how do you get someone who has paid and will show up to recommend the race to their friends and get other runners (customers) to come along?

This is where viral marketing comes in. You can give a boost to word-of-mouth promotion and speed up the process, rather than waiting for people to go to the trouble of telling their friends. To the credit of the marathon organizers, they reinvent themselves every year from a marketing perspective with cool gimmicks that create great viral marketing.

There is one particular important marketing tool that they have been employing for years—lectures focused on fields connected to sports, health, diet, fitness, and so on. An audience that takes part in races is, by nature, an audience that is interested in these topics. These sessions take place at the same spot where the runners will pick up their race kits, in the same city where the race will take place. Every one runner of the tens of thousands of runners participating in the race will have to go there at least once on set days to pick up his race kit, otherwise they won't be able to enter the marathon kick-off area on the day of the race.

So the organizers put together a series of lectures at the race kit collection spot (entrance is free for the general public) on topics such as "how to eat right," "how to prepare for long-distance races," "how to keep your body in shape at any age," and so on.

What's the advantage of lectures like these when it comes to market education of the participants?

First of all, the organizers create a great customer experience and give the participants (their customers) the feeling that they care about them.

Next, people talk about these lectures, they bring friends to listen (including people who aren't registered for the race, leading some of them to register) and they share notifications about when the lectures are scheduled, causing more people to come to the lectures and register for the race.

Third, and most importantly, beyond the marketing aspect, a customer who has heard these lectures, learned from them and implemented what he has heard, is a better customer for the organizers; he or she will take better care of his or her body and prepare in the right way for the race. The risk that this person will get injured during the race, whether it's pulling a muscle or dehydrating and fainting, is much lower. The chances that he or she will enjoy the race, achieve the result he or she desired and feel good at the end of the race is much higher.

Therefore, a series of professional lectures over a period of time annually generates for the marathon organizers market education, viral marketing, an "active community of customers," marketing buzz, and all the rest of the professional terms that translate into increased revenue, more participation, and more exposure and branding.

WHAT DO YOU DO WITH A CUSTOMER WHO ISN'T "RIPE" TO BUY FROM YOU?

Let's say I'm driving, and suddenly my cell phone rings. I reply (hands free, of course) and it's someone who is interested in my giving a lecture, workshop or business consultation to their company.

I speak with the prospect for a few minutes, get some basic information from them, offer some details, and then, at the end of the conversation, they say something like, "Okay, I see. Let me talk to my partner," or "I'll talk to management and get back to you," or "We are also checking other possibilities," or "I'll get back to you with some possible dates."

The conversation ends without closing a deal, and now, control is seemingly in the hands of the potential customer, and I am supposed to wait for them to get back to me in order to continue the process.

Why is the power "seemingly" in the hands of the customer? Why is it not completely in their hands?

Because during the conversation, or as it neared the end, I did another little something: I asked the client for their email and a few other contact details. Now I also hold power.

What do I do next?

In addition to registering the conversation and uploading the client's details to my Customer Relations Management system, I add the client to my mailing list.

I next send them *email zero*—the first email in a series of messages—with a best-selling guide that I wrote, and the client will start to receive emails that add value and contain a call to action from me, about once a week.

What happens then? What is the real importance of a mailing list?

I remain in the client's mind. I am different from the others. I am branding myself as an expert.

If the contact person at the company called three or four other suppliers in addition to me, and now she is going over the various proposals, I will be the only one to have got back to her "elegantly."

Assuming that the client hasn't got back to me, I can follow up like everyone else—in slightly annoying ways. I can call a few days later and say, "Hi, it's Yaniv, we spoke a few days ago, have you considered my proposal?" And then, a few days later, I can call and say, "My schedule for the next month is getting really busy.

Are we going ahead?" And then, a few weeks later, I can call and wish the customer "happy holidays," if there is a holiday coming up.

Doing that is tiring, annoying, exhausting, bothering for the customer and, most of all, not effective.

Now we come to the real power of a well-maintained mailing list. A mailing list sorts between interested customers, who will pay at the end of the day (the goal of every business), and customers who are not "ripe" to accept your quote for their purchase.

If customers are ripe, then they will close a deal with me on our first telephone call or a few days later. But if the customers are not ripe to make a purchase from me, because it isn't particularly urgent for them or because they don't yet know me or aren't aware of the scope of their need or problem, then they will start receiving materials and messages from me on a long-term basis.

They may not be ripe today, and they may still not be in another month or even two, but in another six months when they urgently need a business consultation, a mentorship, a lecture, a workshop or books as a gift for employees, whom will they call?

Will they just do a Google search or start looking anew for suppliers? Or will they simply send a return email to the expert who has been continuously writing to them over a long period of time, and who is easily accessible and available?

They will most likely call me. That is the real power of a mailing list.

There is huge importance to educating the market and to persistence—not writing a few emails and then disappearing for months, but remaining in constant contact with your community and your customers.

I receive reminders of this all the time. For example, a few weeks before writing this, I held a workshop for managers at a well-known pharmaceuticals company. (I prepared them for appearances in the media and before a committee made up of members of parliaments and officials from the Health Ministry.) When I asked during the course of the workshop how they had found me, it turned out that the VP of the pharmaceuticals company had been reading my newsletter for the past five years consecutively!

For five years I hadn't known that she even existed and had never received an email from her company. But one day, out of the blue, when the company had a real need for a service that I provide and they were ripe, she gave the instruction to contact me and the deal was closed pretty quickly.

There are many other customers out there who I am unaware of, but "they are stewing on a low heat" at this very moment.

WHAT'S THE NUMBER ONE REASON CUSTOMERS LEAVE YOU?

What makes customers leave us, assuming they are happy with the service or product they get from us?

What makes companies that are downsizing fire certain employees and hold on to other employees, assuming that there are no professional complaints against any of them?

And what makes people with nothing in their bank account decide to cancel their gym membership or stop one of their children's afterschool activities, but not to even dream of giving up their cell phone or cable TV?

The answer depends on how necessary the product or service is perceived to be. Products and services are divided, to make a gross generalization, into two categories—must have and nice to have. I perceive a product or service that I must have as absolutely necessary, whereas a product or service that's nice to have is not an absolute necessity for me.

This is not an exact categorization, of course. We all have certain products and services we perceive as necessary and that we also like to have. On the other hand, there are certain products and services we would be happy to have, but we don't have enough time, money, leisure or energy for them, and we would have to give up something essential in order to have them; so these are things, that we go without. These products and services vary from one person to the next.

In addition, what we define as a "must" is not always really "necessary." How do I know this? Because studies show that most of our daily expenses are for products and services that didn't exist twenty-five years ago!

Think about this: Until the mid-1990s, the Internet was a tool for academics and people in the intelligence and military communities. Cell phones were no more popular than that, and plasma TVs and many of the food, transportation, and clothing brands we have today hadn't been invented yet. And believe it or not, we got by pretty well without them!

People today think of their cell phone or Facebook as a must and could not even imagine canceling their cell phone or Internet account, even if they are chronically in need of funds. Not because they can't live without these things, but because they have gotten so used to the product, have become addicted to it and understand the advantages it gives them and because someone has marketed it, and keeps marketing it, to them in a highly effective way.

So if customers tell you they do not have the money to start buying or to keep buying from you, and if a company tells you it does not have the budget to work with you or keep employing you, question the logic. They probably have the money and they're spending it all the time. But they're spending it on things that seem more important to them and on employees who seem more necessary to them.

And you? You're only in the nice-to-have category.

To move yourself to the must-have category, turn your product or service (or yourself) into something that is absolutely necessary for your customer.

Do a better job of explaining what you do or what you're selling.

Talk to the customer in terms of benefits.

Explain the "cost" of making the mistake of not working with you, and make your customers understand that without you they will be worse off on a personal, professional or business level, depending on what product or service you're offering.

WHO IS YOUR "IDEAL" CUSTOMER, AND HOW DO YOU "FIRE" YOUR NOT-SO-IDEAL CUSTOMERS?

One of the biggest mistakes made by entrepreneurs, small businesses and salespeople is that they don't choose their customers, but work with whoever comes along, sell to anybody that contacts them and serve only people who turn to them on their own.

Instead of focusing, being active, deciding who they want to work with, and defining target audiences to whom they will direct their marketing and sales efforts, and marketing proactively mainly to them, people and businesses conduct themselves passively. They don't define for themselves who they want to work with, and in practice, they work with everyone. Everyone who approaches them. Everyone who is willing to buy from them.

The result is the business finds itself working with less-than-ideal customers. They are customers who drain their energy and resources, that they lose money on— even before they have started working with them—and are essentially irrelevant to their success.

I have been preaching a contrary approach for the past two decades: instead of customers choosing you, you should choose your customers. Instead of working because there is no other choice with customers who are "bad" from your perspective, work only with customers who are "good" from your perspective.

Instead of working only with clients who approach you, direct and focus your marketing resources, which are limited in time, money and energy, and work with people that you *truly* want to work with.

Instead of wasting time on customers who aren't ripe or suitable, clarify your target audience and create time for potential customers with perfect timing, when the chances of closing a deal are the highest.

Instead of compromising on bad customers who you are already working with and feel bad about leaving, fire them. Stop selling them services and products, even if they want to continue buying from you).

The worst thing that can happen to your business when you are working with a bad customer (who will cause you to lose time, money and energy) is that the customer will also bring their friends, who most likely will also be bad customers.

What is the difference between a good and bad customer?

The criteria to know whether a customer will be good for your business over time, or whether they will cause your business to collapse changes from business to business, from person to person, and from field to field. But here are two important tests regarding customers, in order to know if they are right for you over time: the *fun test* and the *money test*.

Let's start with the fun test.

I believe that in order to succeed at what you are doing—in any field, in any job, be it as a salaried employee or self-employed, as service providers or selling products—it's very important that you feel great when you get up in the morning and like the people you work with.

The world isn't perfect, but I believe that we have to take control of our lives, and especially our careers and businesses, and we have to choose over time who we want to work with. And as all of us (big companies included) have limited time, money and energy, it's not worth wasting our resources on customers who drain our energy, who deplete all our positivity and optimism and will cause us to want to switch fields.

The fun test, aka the telephone test, that helps you sort between customers that are good for you and your business and customers who are bad requires you check one very simple thing: what you feel when the customer calls and you see their name on your mobile phone screen. If when the customer calls and you see their name on the screen, you feel pleased or happy, or have a pleasant feeling, or you think to yourself, "How nice that they called," or even say, "I was just about to call you to ask whether you had a good time at the event," or "We haven't spoken for a while," then that's a good customer.

On the other hand, when the customer calls and you see their name on the screen, if you immediately feel angry, low on energy or patience, nervous, tired or frustrated, and you think to yourself, "What do they want now?" or some other expression of annoyance, then that's a bad customer.

In our personal, professional and business lives, many people insist on making it complicated this determination complication; it isn't.

The money test involves The Pareto Law, aka the "80-20 Rule, which is one of the most well-known laws in economics. Among other things, it addresses two implications that are relevant to our discussion.

» One is that 20 percent of our customers are responsible for 80 percent of our business's revenues.
» The second is that 20 percent of our customers take up 80 percent of our energy and time.

What's interesting is that they are almost always not the same customers. The customers that are good for the business are the 20 percent that are responsible for 80 percent of revenues; they are usually those that argue less about the price, are more appreciative of service, pay on time, bring along other customers, recommend you, and so on.

Customers who are bad for business are the 20 percent that drain most of your time and energy; they are also the ones who "will squeeze you for every drop" until they close a deal, they will argue with your professional advice, they are cynical, there are problems getting them to pay, and so on.

Almost everyone has customers of both kinds. Now the interesting question is, (and I would ask that you answer yourselves honestly) on a daily basis, whom do you devote most of your time and attention to? Your good customers or your bad ones?

Unfortunately, the answer is often that we spend a lot more time, effort and energy on our bad customers, even though they are destructive to our business (and also to our health and joyfulness) and we invest almost nothing in our "good" customers.

If a customer pays on time, we usually don't thank them or even appreciate them. But if a customer is late in making payments, we chase them, and probably get others in the office to assist with the chase.

If a customer always receives the product or service with a smile, for the most part we don't give them a good word in return.

But if a customer starts shouting or arguing or

complaining, then immediately, all the focus of our employees turns toward that customer and they will receive more attention, help and/or personal treatment, despite achieving it in a negative way.

Contrary to our instincts, we should invest in our good customers, giving them some bonuses, complimenting them, giving them some extras—specifically because they didn't

And what do you do with your "bad" customers? Stop working with them.

At first glance, this seems illogical, and in contradiction to everything you have been taught about the customer always being right, and so on. The truth is, however, that a bad customer leads to a huge loss of energy, resources, and time and money for you and your business. It costs you your health and the loss of other customers, and at the end of the day, you will lose a lot more money on that customer. Therefore, let that customer go as quickly as possible.

There is a right way, a way to end it nicely, without insulting them and without burning bridges. What the two methods have in common is that, in both situations, it is the customer that quits; they leave because of your initiative, but not because you kicked them out the door.

» The first method is *worsening of conditions.*

Let's assume that you have allowed a customer to get used to being able to call you whenever they wanted—big mistake—and you were always available for them. Customers will naturally take advantage of this, they get used to it very quickly and don't appreciate the service, and most of the time they will also complain and use up a lot of your time.

Simply update that customer about your new terms. For example, "From now on, I will be available from 8 a.m. to 5 p.m. on weekdays." It's important to follow through on this commitment; when a customer calls outside of accepted hours, don't answer them, and get back to them during the working hours you spelled out.

One of two things will happen: Either the customer will fall in line and will call you only during normal hours (your problem is solved), or the customer will complain. They will say that it's very important for you to be available as before, and that the new conditions aren't acceptable to them. With the latter one, if you are strong enough in the short term, and don't break and return to the previous conditions, the customer will quit by themselves.

Another example of worsening of conditions is, say you are working with a company, private or government, that pays you two months after you have completed each job. That is obviously destructive for your business and its cash flow, and companies take advantage of that when working with some firms and the self-employed, saying things like, "That's the way it is," or "Those are our terms."

How do you fire a company like that? You update their representatives (purchasers, the marketing department, your professional contacts—whoever you deal with on the money side) that from now on, your terms have changed and you wish to receive a paid deposit in cash immediately following completion of the job, for example, or demand payment no more than one month later, for example. Again, they will likely quit all by themselves.

> » The second method to fire customers is to raise prices.

If there is a customer you don't want to work with, then just raise the price for that customer. I'm talking about an increment that really catches their attention— and depending on your produce or service, maybe that's 300 percent!

There's not much of a chance the customer will agree to work at your "outrageous" new price, and if they do, then the high price will compensate for the fact they are a bad customer.

Most likely, they will refuse to pay your new high prices and then they will quit by themselves.

To summarize, in order to succeed in business and in life, you have to focus your energy and effort in marketing, in service, and in educating the market on good customers and people who contribute to you and create profit for you, and not on bad customers and people who waste your time and energy and cause you financial losses.

A TRICK TO IDENTIFY GOOD CUSTOMERS AND BAD CUSTOMERS.

Now is the time to look reality in the eye, and to examine, from a financial point of view, who exactly are the customers responsible for the majority of your revenues. Not who you think they may be, not what your gut feeling is. Not a rough estimate, but an evaluation based on spreadsheets and the accounting reports of your business.

Define a specific period of time, let's say a year, last year, or two years back from today. Make a list of all your active customers, and for each customer write down how much money they actually brought into your business in that period. You will be surprised to discover that customers that you thought about or talked about a lot, in fact hardly brought in any revenues for you over the past few years.

Now that you have your list of winners of the money test, do the fun test.

Write down for each customer, from a perspective of the time and energy they consume, whether they are a good or a bad customer for you. It's safe to assume (and you may be surprised, or perhaps not) that you will discover the following:

> » You have bothersome and annoying customers who drain a lot of your time and energy and you think mostly about them, when in fact

they buy relatively little of your products and services.

» You have some customers who were never paying customers, or that perhaps were paying customers for a short time, but that hasn't prevented them from continuing to drive you crazy to this very day and to approach you all the time.

» You have a few superb customers who bring a lot of money into your business, take up almost none of your time and with whom you really like to work—and you don't invest enough time in them.

After defining who your good customers are, (the 20 percent that create 80 percent of your revenues) the time has come to invest more in them. Nurture them. Call them. Send them professional materials. And ask them for referrals, because there is a high chance, they will bring along more good customers just like they are.

Why is there a high chance of good customers coming to you via an existing good customer who recommends you and refers you? This is where a nice marketing principle called like attracts like comes in.

Let's say you take the cell phone of the CEO and senior executives of a particular company, and you take a look at their contacts list. What are you likely to find? Lots of other CEOs. Take a taxi driver's cell phone. What are you most likely to find in his contacts list? Other taxi drivers.

People tend to be in contact with people like them—who earn a similar salary, are in the same field of business, have a similar family status, and so on. Take a generous customer and a mean customer, for example. It would be reasonable to assume that, on a personal, day-to-day level, they the disgruntled complainer and the nice guy wouldn't be friends. Why? Quite simply, they won't have a good time together.

The good customer probably knows a lot of other good customers, just like them, so it's the good customer you should ask for referrals.

For the stability and prosperity of your business, the health of your revenues, and your peace of mind, build on the good relationships and eliminate the bad ones.

WHY DON'T LAS VEGAS HOTELIERS PUT A BIBLE IN YOUR ROOM?

A few years ago, while I was attending a conference in the United States, I paid a visit to Las Vegas, aka Sin City. Great branding! An incredible place that provides one with a lot of insights on life.

If I had to sum up Las Vegas in one word, that word would be "bubble." In Las Vegas, they do everything so that from the moment you land at the local airport, you will forget the home and family you left behind, your values, how much you get paid, and you will spend money.

A lot of money. Mostly of course on gambling, but

not just; food, shows, stores, souvenirs, and so on. Las Vegas has everything, all the time, and plenty of it. You are motivated to action all the time.

As someone who consults with companies and has been lecturing for years on the topics of persuasion, broadcasting messages and motivation to action, I have never seen all the rules of marketing, sales, and persuasion operating in one place with such impact.

Las Vegas gave me a lot of insights and things to think about. At this point, though, I would like to talk about one small thing with enormous significance that I noticed while I was there: Unlike hotels throughout the United States, in Las Vegas, the hotels don't put a bible in your room.

A brilliant marketing slogan that characterizes no-bibles Las Vegas says, "What happens in Vegas, stays in Vegas." In other words, no matter what you did in Vegas, Las Vegas will keep your secret as long as you do. I don't know who coined that slogan, but it is absolute genius. Because that slogan brands Las Vegas as a town where anything goes.

If visitors to Las Vegas were to suddenly see a bible in their hotel room, they would think about home, their environment, their church, mosque or synagogue, about the laws in their state, about their customs at home, about what's permissible and what isn't.

It's one small thing, that together with a lot of other small things, quickly "educate" tourists in Vegas that here you can behave differently, and all these little details as one create the big picture (or the big "bubble") that is called Las Vegas.

WHY DON'T CANNIBALS MAKE GOOD BUSINESS PEOPLE?

In the 1980s, Starbucks decided to take over Manhattan. Yes, at the tail end of the 20th century, a large coffee chain named Starbucks decided that it wanted to be the biggest coffee chain in the United States and that it would eliminate competition in one of the most prestigious and expensive areas in America—New York City.

Their strategy, simply put, was to establish a Starbucks on every street corner in Manhattan. At that time, the rival chains had not developed enough to be that aggressive in establishing dominance.

This phenomenon, which is quite exceptional in the world of business, has been labelled in economic literature as *cannibalism*: At the same time, they were trying to shut out competition, the strategy created competition between its own branches.

Why? Because every new branch established eats up the profits of the previous branch. Once you have a branch on every street corner, when a customer walks down half a block from one branch and then feels like having a Starbucks coffee, they won't have to double back; they'll just continue walking and there will be another branch on the block.

Starbucks invested huge sums in establishing more

and more branches, losing money in the short term in order to generate (potential) profit in the long term, and to educate customers that the only place to drink coffee in New York is Starbucks.

The method of cannibalism remains controversial to this day. Among economists, there are diverse opinions and schools of thought regarding whether cannibalism works from a business perspective.

I object to cannibalism for three reasons. In my view, it ties in with competitive thinking, in other words, thinking all the time about your competitors, before you think of yourselves. I also object out of a belief in creative thinking, and because of a principle that says, "Let customers miss you a little!"

Longing is also part of educating the market. I once had a meeting with a brilliant entrepreneur who had written a number of books and wanted to publish them one after the other. His material had all been prepared as a rough draft and he wanted to publish all three books as a trilogy on similar subjects, to be published within a short time of each other. I explained to him that from my experience, it is better to give each book its own time in bookstores and in front of the audience. I recommended to him that he leave a minimum of a year to a year-and-a-half (and even two years) between publishing and launching a marketing campaign for each book.

Otherwise, he would be cannibalizing. The first book would be published, reach bookstores, and the entrepreneur would launch a full-on marketing campaign. After a month or two, even before he has maximized marketing activities for the first book, the second would be published.

Sales for the second book would be lower and take a bite out of sales for the first book. People won't even have had time to buy, read and react to the first book, when another product would land on them. That confuses the customer and a "confused" customer buys less.

As an example, I told the entrepreneur about the *Lord of the Rings* movie trilogy.

Lord of the Rings was shot in New Zealand and out of budgetary considerations, all three movies were filmed together during the same period of several months. So the producers had nine hours of edited film ready at the same time. They could have just released all three movies at the same time, or released the sequels a few months after the first movie. But they didn't do that. They didn't want to cannibalize, so they waited. They waited three years between each movie, even though they already had all the materials ready.

What happened? The fans went crazy, and audiences were left with "a taste for more" after each movie. That allowed the producers time to do a proper launch for each movie in the trilogy—each time, a premiere, marketing campaigns, articles in the media and interviews with the actors, and more. They maximized sales for each movie in the trilogy, they educated the fans to wait patiently for each film and they made the audience into passionate ambassadors, talking about the movie and waiting for the next one.

WHY DIDN'T I VISIT MY SON AT SUMMER CAMP?

My eldest son, Noam, was at summer camp with Cub Scouts. Three days out of the house (for the first time in his life). But don't worry, the counselors sent us photos all the time, from the time they met at the scout house, all through the trip to the camp, arrival at camp, activities, meals, evening activities, and everything else.

They sent hundreds of photos every day to the parents' WhatsApp group because, after all, each parent had to see that their kid is still alive. That's the spirit of our times, that's what everyone does, and it is legitimate and understandable.

I also look at all these updates on WhatsApp as a marketing move.

First of all, camp costs quite a lot of money. Through the photos and updates, the parents (who are the paying customers) can see that they spent their money wisely, that their children are well taken care of, that they are being given good food, and so on.

Second, one of the rules of camp is that parents aren't allowed to visit, and kids aren't allowed to leave. When the counselors send photos and updates all the time, they are managing the conversation (which in any event takes place between the parents on the question of whether the children were enjoying themselves or suffering, and how were they feeling and what they were up to).

By managing the conversation, the counselors save themselves and the heads of the Scout Brigade from receiving phone calls from anxious parents, and attempts to visit the camp to see what's going on, and from general complaints and grievances.

Third, this three-day camp is the peak (and the end) of that year's Scouts activities, and immediately after camp ends, marketing starts for the next year's activities at Scouts. When parents are happy, and of course when the kids are happy as well, the chances are higher that they will continue to attend (and pay) for the following year.

So it is well worth investing in keeping the parents updated, which doesn't cost money. WhatsApp messages are free, they hardly take up any energy; for counselors of that age it's completely natural, and it doesn't take time because it's all done during activities. And, most of all, it "educates" the parents to cooperate with camp rules.

WHY DO PEOPLE REPEAT THE SAME ACTIVITY OVER AND OVER AGAIN?

Have you ever read a book more than once? It's the same with movies you love; you've probably seen some movies several times in your life.

Why? The book is the same book you have read before and the words are the same words you have read before. The movie is the same movie you have seen before.

The answer is: The movie or the book has not changed. You are the one who has!

Every time you experience something again, you experience it in a different way. This happens for two reasons:

1. You already know some of the information, so you're a lot more open to absorb new information, beyond what you absorbed the first time.

2. You arrive at the experience from a completely different level of awareness, maturity and wisdom compared to the previous time, especially if a few months or years have gone by since the last viewing or reading.

I have noticed a similar phenomenon in my recent conferences. In each of my conferences, there are a least a few dozen people who have already participated in a previous conference on the very same topic; yet they have come again and have paid for a ticket again. When I asked some of these people why they were returning to the conference for a second or third time, the answers were similar every time:

"It's a totally different experience today."

"I still laughed at the same jokes, even though I almost knew them by heart."

"I heard many things you said for the first time, even though you already said them the last time."

"I only really understood what you meant just now."

"This time I didn't just pay attention to what you were saying, I was paying attention to how you were saying it."

Conclusion: If you experienced something that you loved, there's no reason for you to do it only once. Repeat it again and again, so that you can hone your professional skills, enjoy it again, and experience it in a completely different way.

WHY DO WE ALLOW THE WAITER AT A RESTAURANT CHOOSE WHAT WE EAT?

You're probably familiar with the following situation: You arrive at a restaurant you aren't familiar with, you get the menu, you scan it quickly and then you ask the waiter, "What do you recommend?"

Sometimes we point the waiter in a general direction; for example, we might say something like, "What salads are they having at that table?" or "I feel like having meat, what's good here?" But, generally speaking, we let our waiter choose one or two options for us, and then we almost always agree to go with that suggestion.

Why do we trust someone else to decide for us what would be most enjoyable—and how much we're going to end up paying? In the restaurant, from our perspective, the waitstaff are the experts. They understand the menu a lot better than we do, see what other people order in that restaurant all day, and know (more or less) what would be right for people of our age and status. And that, in itself, is a lot more than what we know when it comes to this specific restaurant.

Because what do we expect of experts, no matter what the field, when we consult with them?

First, we want their unique perspective, how they see things. With regard to the waiter, we want to know what they think about the menu and the various dishes on it.

Second, we want to shorten our learning curve. We want to make a decision as quickly as possible, and to make the right, most worthwhile and convenient decision for ourselves. We could dive deep into the entire menu, try the "trial and error" method, maybe order and sample a few dishes, and then decide what we like best. But that will take time, cost us money, and waste our energy. Or, we can just ask the expert, listen to their professional opinion, and increase the chances that the first decision we make will be the best one for us.

Bottom line: Even if you're extremely smart and experienced, there are some fields you're not that knowledgeable about.

And in those fields where you don't have that much knowledge, in order to save time, money and energy, and in order to shorten your learning curve, you need to turn to the right expert. Just like your clients approach you, in your areas of expertise.

KEY ELEMENTS OF COMMANDMENT NO. 5

Create a growing community of relevant clients and educate them.

✓ When customers don't understand your value, you're in a price market.

✓ Your level of authority rises amazingly fast as soon as you put out professional information products; it positions you in a value market.

✓ Content is king: every product and service that you want to sell can and should be sold through high quality professional content about that particular product.

✓ A mailing lists sorts between interested customers who will pay in the end, and customers who aren't ripe.

✓ There is enormous importance to educating the market to perseverance.

✓ Turn your product or service (or yourself) into something that is a must (absolutely necessary) for your customer!

✓ Instead of customers choosing you, choose your customers.

✓ Instead of working with bad customers from your perspective, because you have no alternative, work only with good customers.

✓ Two tests in order to find out whether a customer will be suitable for you over time—the fun test and the money test.

✓ Twenty percent of customers generate 80 percent of your business' revenues. Twenty percent of our customers take up 80 percent of our time and energy.

✓ Two ways of firing customers properly, in as far as is possible—worsening of conditions and significantly increasing prices.

✓ Like attracts like: People tend to be in contact with people like them.

✓ Because the good customer probably knows a lot of other good customers, just like them, then it is the good customer you should ask for referrals.

✓ Plan your marketing properly from very beginning.

✓ Let your customers miss you a little. Longing is also part of "educating the market."

✓ Every time you experience something again, you experience it in a completely different way.

✓ We expect two things of experts, no matter what their field: we want their unique perspective, and we want to shorten our learning curve.

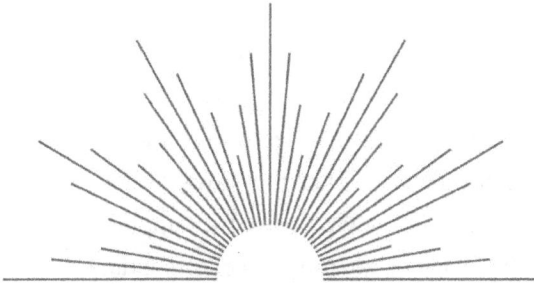

COMMANDMENT NO. 6

*Market and sell differently, and more
effectively, than your competitors.*

WHAT IS THE MAIN REASON THAT
CUSTOMERS PICK ONE SUPPLIER
OVER ANOTHER?

A few years ago, researchers in the United States
carried out a study among hundreds of large companies,
examining how they choose suppliers to do various jobs
for them and to supply them with products, and what
leads them to commence working with a particular supplier. The study looked only at cases in which companies
had turned to at least three different suppliers in the
same field; in most cases the companies had turned to
five suppliers and sometimes more.

In other words, there is a wide basis for compari-
son between suppliers.

One would have expected that in a competitive

and "saturated" market. And in a digital world where it is possible to know everything about a supplier just by visiting their website, Facebook page and through Google, that the companies would make in-depth and serious calculations. That they would take into account parameters such as what price the supplier offered, how long they have been around, recommendations received about the supplier, the supplier's experience in the field, similar companies from the same market that the supplier has worked with, and so on.

However, the number two reason that led companies to choose a supplier was surprising: The reason we chose to work with this particular supplier was that they were the first to get back to us!

In other words, when a company has a professional need or problem, it looks for a speedy reply or solution. It approaches three-to-five different suppliers (via the Contact Us field on their website, by calling and asking for a quote, and so on) and one of the main considerations taken into account when making a decision is: whoever got back to the company first with a quote and is willing to get to work straight away.

That may seem to you to be a rather superficial reason, but it also make a lot of sense. The purchasing, training, marketing, or human resources manager who approached the suppliers wants "to get the job done" and to start work on the project as soon as possible. The first supplier that gets back to them, assuming they meet the stated conditions and has a reasonable level of experience and isn't a serial killer, is good enough to get the job done and allows them to move on to the next task.

What's more, there is also a kind of proof of intent here. At the courting stage—the stage where the supplier is supposed to do everything to get the company to like them—the supplier that is the first to get back to the company is also seen as the most serious.

If you thought reason number two was surprising, wait till you hear reason number one:

"The reason we chose to work with this particular supplier was that he was the only one to get back to us!"

That doesn't sound logical. On the face of it, in a competitive market with a lot of suppliers waiting in ambush for each client, the client should get a lot of proposals, price should play a central role, and more. But once only one supplier gets back to that company, then basically there is no competition. The price the supplier asked for is most likely the price they will receive.

If it doesn't sound logical to you that a company approached five different suppliers and asks them for a quote, but only one gets back with a reply, then ask yourself: how many times have you as private clients left a note via a company's Contact Us page, or left a message on a supplier's answering machine, and nobody has gotten back to you?

How many times have you wanted to work with a specific person, because you received recommendations about them, and as a customer you have chased after them and called them several times before managing to speak to them?

Now, with a hand on your heart, how many times have you as a supplier not got back in time to customers, or not got back to them at all?

Let's assume that a company has invested a lot of money on a web campaign with Google or Facebook, with the aim of attracting customers or bringing in quality leads. But when the customer actually arrives at the company's site via the campaign and calls the company, it takes a week from the moment he left a message before anyone calls him back. And sometimes the company misses the customer altogether because the admin happened to be sick at the time, managers are overseas, the supplier is busy with a fair or something like that.

All the reasons why people don't get back to customers in time or at all can be right and justified, but the bottom line is "throwing away money for nothing."

The company will lose money twice - once on an internet campaign that won't be efficient if "circuits aren't closed" and no one actually speaks with customers who leave a message, and also because a potential job has been lost and will go to a competitor.

So what's the bottom line from your point of view?

Stop thinking and saying that "the market is saturated," "there is a lot of competition," "whoever gives the lowest price will get the job." Get into your head that the decisions made—even by huge companies—are a lot more down to earth and result from simple considerations such as your personal touch, your avail-ability, your hunger for more customers, correct inter-personal communications between the departments of your company, so that information and quality leads don't "fall between the cracks" and nobody handles it.

In this chapter I expand on diverse but simple marketing and sales methods that will maximize your conversion rate, increase your business's sales and prof-its, and will cause your customers to choose you with a high degree of certainty. Together, we'll explore a series of real-life cases, business mistakes and maneuvers, both right and wrong, made by companies and business in relation to their customers, and I target the right solu-tions and the principles that led to those solutions. I also expand on the issue of telephone sales conversa-tions with customers, specifically, how to maximize your chances of success and to sound different from your competitors and colleagues.

WHY DO MOST PEOPLE FAIL WHEN IT COMES TO ONLINE MARKETING?

I have mentored dozens of private clients involved in online marketing and I have advised some of the largest companies in the world who use online mar-keting. And I have discovered something very interest-ing: Most people who do online marketing don't really manage to make much money from it.

Some of them don't even manage to recoup their initial investment, and some have a really bad experience with the whole thing. I have always asked myself: Why, even if the product is good and the marketing method is basically a good one, do most people who engage in online marketing not fulfill their business potential?

They don't know whom to sell to, and they don't know how to sell. Some of those who participate in online marketing programs get really excited about the idea, about the dream and about the product, so they buy a small inventory and get started.

But then they find out that they do not know whom to approach. No one along the way has explained to them such crucial things as marketing strategy, market segmentation, defining your target audience, matching the message to suit the customer, and so on.

And then what do they do? They turn to their immediate environment—their family, their friends, their neighbors, people who live in their town or neighborhood, colleagues from work—only because these are the people who are most available to them. They do it even if the product is not at all relevant to a major part of this audience.

And, to top it all off, they don't even know how to sell. No one ever taught them about soft selling, telling a story, talking in terms of customer benefits, using humor, giving examples, and more. When I write "soft selling," I mean the process in which you don't sell anything at first: You simply tell the customer stories, and only after that they (hopefully) buy your product or service. I am referring not to imaginary stories but to true stories whose purpose is to support you and your products or services.

This is not a formal sales situation in which you present yourself and your products and services in a technical and serious manner. In that kind of situation, the client often becomes defensive, scrutinizing every sentence you say. In a soft sell situation, you develop a conversation with the customer, in which you gently let him or her know about the benefits of your product and services. People really like to buy things but they don't really like being sold to or being pushed into buying something. Get your message across through stories and make your customers feel that it was their decision to buy your product or service.

Since many online marketing entrepreneurs do not know this method, they follow their instincts, that is, they go for the hard sell, which is an aggressive, annoying and threatening sales technique. Not because they really like doing it, but simply because they don't know any other way. They don't know whom to sell to and don't know how to sell, and lose out twice in the process—first because they make few or no sales, and second, because they can ruin their relationships with the people who are closest to them when they try to push them aggressively into buying a product they don't really need.

Now you are probably going to say, "But some people do succeed in online marketing and make a lot of money doing it." True, some people do succeed in online marketing, but, after getting to know these people, I'll let you in on a secret: They would have succeeded in any other field as well. They have what it takes to succeed, in any field: excellent interpersonal communication skills and the ability to ignite people and motivate them to act, plus they are persuasive, and capable public speakers.

Conclusion: Success in any field (in this case, online marketing) has nothing to do with the field you are in, and everything to do with your life skills and rhetorical capabilities.

In addition, you need to sell only to a relevant audience and you must use the soft sell approach. More on this later in the chapter.

HOW YOUR COMPETITORS CAN INCREASE YOUR SALES.

In one Christian town, there was a central church and every Sunday, all the Christian townspeople would gather there for prayer services. Just before the entrance to the church were two salesmen: One of them was selling crucifixes and the other was selling Stars of David.

The churchgoers would look at the two of them and immediately buy a crucifix and go in to pray.

One day one of the townspeople took pity on the guy who was selling Stars of David, so he turned to him and said: "Listen, I don't know if you've noticed, but everyone in this town is Christian. There's not a single Jew here! There's no chance you're going to sell any Stars of David here. I suggest you move to another town and try there." The man walked away. Then the guy who was selling Stars of David turned to the crucifix salesman with a smile and said to him:

"Did you see that, Izzie, my friend and partner? He wants to teach us how to do business!"

This story contains a very important marketing principle: "oppositional marketing."

Meaning, you don't always buy a product or service because you want it and need it; very often you buy it because you identify with one of the "players" in the market, as opposed to his or her competitor.

An example of "oppositional" marketing that you are perhaps familiar with is Lionel Messi vs. Cristiano Ronaldo. The huge international popularity of these two soccer players and their highly publicized "clashes," which have mainly been created by sports commentators and marketing professionals, not by the players themselves, have resulted in their both selling a lot more shirts and advertising.

Competition exists in practically every field. Sometimes the competition is stiff, but the trick is to leverage the competition so that it works in your favor and to use it to increase your sales. Don't speak badly about your competitors; in fact, it's better if you don't mention them at all to your customers. (I also wrote about this principle in Commandment 2.) Focus on differentiating yourself from the rest of the competition and on explaining the relative advantage you have in your field of activity.

How can you tell whether your daughter is pregnant?

A true and amazing story: In June 2013, a man from Minnesota found coupons for baby products in his mailbox that were addressed to his daughter. This bothered him quite a bit, for the simple reason that his daughter was fifteen years old and was still in high school. He went to the local branch of the supermarket chain that had sent the coupons and complained to the manager about the matter. But a few days later he found out that his daughter, a high school student, really was pregnant!

How did the local supermarket know about the daughter's pregnancy before everyone else did, even her own parents? Well, that same chain of American supermarkets had issued its customers club cards and credit cards. It then used those cards to collect huge amounts of information about the shopping habits of each customer and created a personal identity card for each of them. Next it analyzed these habits to reinforce those habits and create new ones for these customers; in other words, the idea was to make their customers buy more.

In the case of the man's daughter, the supermarket chain had identified that she had bought certain products that are typically purchased by women at the start of their pregnancy such as nutritional supplements. Because parents-to-be and young parents tend to spend a lot more money compared with the average customer, the chain was quick to send her coupons suited for pregnant women, before the other chains could do so. The chain therefore knew the daughter was pregnant before her parents did, because it based its sales on her shopping habits.

How can you use this story (and not just so that you can know whether your daughter is pregnant)? Don't offer all of your products and services to all of your customers.

Categorize your customers, based on their buying and consumption habits with regard to your business (try to do this as accurately as possible) and offer each customer the product or service that is closest to what he or she prefers and likes. This is how you can significantly increase your conversion rates and, as a result, your income.

This method is also being applied to you, as a consumer: The supermarket chains, the retail clothing chains, the airlines, the travel agencies—all have subtle ways for making you feel special, and they give you the feeling that they are doing all this for you in order to make your shopping experience easier and to help you save money. It's time for you to get into the game and to offer this level of value and precision to your customers, too. They will thank you for it, and so will your bank account.

WHY DO PEOPLE THINK THAT IF YOU DON'T BUY FLOWERS AND CHOCOLATE FOR SOMEONE, YOU DON'T REALLY LOVE THAT PERSON?

Every year on February 14th, St. Valentine's Day—holiday of love—is celebrated all over the Western world. Originally, this holiday was celebrated to commemorate the deaths of three different saints, each named Valentine. According to Christian legend, during the reign of Emperor Claudius II, one particular St. Valentine secretly performed the marriage of a pair of lovers in accordance with the laws of Christianity, despite a ban by the Emperor Claudius who thought single men made better soldiers for the Roman army. He was sentenced to death. Eventually, St. Valentine came to be considered the patron of lovers, and the holiday named after him is traditionally celebrated by the exchange of messages of love between lovers, and also between friends.

I am a big fan of love, in romantic relationships and in life in general, and I am happy for every opportunity we have to celebrate something and have a good time. But as a marketing person, I look in awe every year at the change we as consumers undergo in our consumption habits and how holidays and traditions are "hijacked" by corporations and private companies for their own purposes because the original tradition on Valentine's Day was about lovers sending each other love messages such as poems.

And what happens today? The messages have become completely materialistic, and we as members of a Western society are overwhelmed with ads calling us to buy presents for our loved ones, especially chocolates, flowers, fancy greeting cards, and so forth. Of course, the very same bouquet that cost, let us say, $25 a week ago is sold before Valentine's Day for double or triple that price, because now it has been elevated to the status of a Valentine's Day bouquet—a level of sanctity that supposedly justifies the price. (Recall the discussion of wedding bouquets in Commandment 1.)

There are those who say to themselves, "I refuse to participate in this game! I love my wife/husband every day of the year and I express my love in many different ways and on many different opportunities, including through the purchase of presents every once in a while. But I am not willing to be part of the herd and to buy overpriced presents for no reason!"

What about those people? Ah. This is where the advertising industry kicks into action and uses a highly effective persuasion tool: peer pressure. For days and weeks, you are told in every possible way that, if you love someone, you have to buy them something. And, if this "attack" has not led you to buy something for someone, it means that you either have no love partner or spouse, or that you do not own a TV, a cell phone or a personal computer.

Personally, I always find it amusing to see how people adapt (yes, I do it, too, sometimes) to a certain reality that others, who have ulterior motives, have set up for them. In this case, it's the flower companies and chocolate manufacturers who have "taken ownership" of Valentine's Day.

People really love to celebrate—anything and at every opportunity—and they probably just look for a reason to buy something. In addition, peer pressure works.

WHERE DO YOU REALLY NOT WANT TO GO ON YOUR BIRTHDAY?

A few years ago, a repair shop in the United States carried out a clever marketing maneuver. For a whole year, it sent all its customers an envelope in the mail a few days before their birthday, with a coupon for an annual maintenance job on their car. With this envelope, the shop let them know that they were entitled to a 50 percent discount on their yearly car maintenance if they came into the garage with their car on their birthday and presented the coupon.

A clever campaign.

It had a personal touch.

It gave loyal customers a significant benefit.

It created a viral effect; customers probably told their friends and relatives about it.

And it motivated them to act.

Theoretically, it should have been a very successful campaign. There was only one small, problematic detail the repair shop owners overlooked: Do people really want to go to the garage on their birthday? If the coupon had been for a restaurant, a movie, or a theme park, the customers would certainly have considered using it on their birthday. But taking your car in for its annual maintenance on your birthday—really?

I can think of quite a few more interesting and fun ways to spend one's birthday and so did the garage's customers: Less than 1 percent of them used the coupon and showed up on their birthday. Some of them even came in a few days afterwards, and then, much to their surprise and disappointment, they had to pay the full price.

A better move would have been to give out this same annual maintenance coupon, but to let the customers use it either a few days before or after their birthday. The garage could have said that the coupon is good during the customer's entire birthday week or even birthday month, instead of limiting the coupon to just one day.

What is the conclusion? You always need to consider your customers' needs and interests, and you must choose your marketing plan and messages so that they match those needs and interests.

WHOSE INTERESTS DO YOU CARE ABOUT MORE, YOURS OR THE CUSTOMER'S?

One of the most inspiring companies for me when it comes to marketing, sales, customer experience, marketing content, motivating employees—and most of all service—is The Walt Disney Company. The company has successfully operated amusement parks since 1955, and since then has been growing and expanding despite the fact that this is one of the most dangerous and challenging fields in business.

One of the less known stories about Walt Disney, the creator, planner and all-powerful boss of the parks until his death in 1966, deals with the famous Magic Tower at the mythical park in Los Angeles, which to this day is one of the symbols of "Disneyland." One day, while Walt Disney was making a tour of the park, a gardener came up to him and told him there was a problem. "What's the problem?" Walt Disney asked. The gardener explained that they had planted a very large and beautiful flower bed in the middle of the park and visitors would keep treading on it again and again to have their photo taken from a good angle in front of the tower.

The gardener asked Disney's permission to build a fence around the flower bed to prevent people stepping on the flowers and having their picture taken there.

Walt Disney told him: "On the contrary! If our guests want to have their photo taken from there, we will let them do it!" He ordered the stunned gardener to create a path through the flower bed , removing some of the flowers he had just planted, and to create a balcony opposite the tower, which would be a good spot to have a photo taken with the tower in the background.

The conversation, which I heard about personally

from a well-known Disney researcher in the United States, sums up for me Walt Disney's different, and important, way of thinking.

The gardener thought about the park's interests. He didn't want to leave his comfort zone, he didn't want to have to do double the work, and he didn't want to see the beautiful flowers damaged.

Walt Disney thought about the customers' interests. He understood that if so many people insisted on taking a photo precisely at that spot, and were prepared to step on a flower bed to do so, they were sending a very specific message to the company and they should be listened to. So instead of spending money on a fence to protect the flowers, Disney spent money on a path and a balcony -to please the customers.

From a historic perspective, this was a brilliant decision, not just in terms of service but also in terms of sales because photos with the Magic Tower in the background have become the park's trademark, and visitors shared those photos everywhere, even before the age of the social networks. By doing so, they became enthusiastic ambassadors for the park and created more sales.

The lesson of the story is: If you want to succeed in business and in sales, you have to listen to your customers, and to see what motivates them, what moves them, and most importantly, what bothers them. You have to fix that and sell accordingly, even if that requires from you more hard work, creative thinking and getting out of your comfort zone.

WHAT THE DUTY-FREE SHOPS IN THE
AIRPORT ARE REALLY SELLING YOU.

Anyone who has flown internationally and has spent time in airports anywhere around the world has probably noticed an interesting phenomenon: All around the world, the same things are sold in airports.

There are some items and products that you will never find in any airport, and then there are other items and products that are always available in any airport: chocolates; perfume, aftershave, cologne and other fine toiletries; wine and whiskey; flowers; toys; children's games; books; and so forth.

Why are these products and not others sold in airports? The answer is related not to the products themselves but to the reason we buy them.

Studies have shown that the number one emotion people experience when they get back from spending time abroad (and they mainly experience that emotion when they are in the airport after they have returned from their trip overseas) is: guilt.

Think about it: Let us say, you're a couple and you have little kids or teenagers. You left them back home on their own or with their grandparents, and you two set off for a romantic holiday. On the way back, wouldn't you feel the need to make it up to them? To compensate them? And what about your parents who were on babysitting duty? Of course you would.

Or, let us say, you are a professional who has gone on a business trip. You left your spouse at home, with or without the children. You have not seen them in a few days. Besides, you had the opportunity to break your routine, while they had to deal with her own exhausting routine. Wouldn't you feel guilty? Of course, you would.

And then the duty-free shops at the airport come to your rescue, offering you just the right presents you need to buy when you want to make up to someone: Top-quality alcohol and chocolates, boutique perfumes, luxury jewelry items and games for the kids, and much more.

And contrary to the myth that everything's cheaper at the duty-free shop, in many cases, the products sold in airports around the world are actually more expensive than they are outside the airport.

We continue to buy things at the duty-free shop, however, because of our need—of the reason behind the purchase. When we feel guilty, we're willing to pay more.

Therefore, if you want to sell more to your customers and charge higher prices for your products and services, think about what's motivating them, and what their emotional reason for buying from you is.

DO YOU WANT TO BUY LAND ON THE MOON?

One of the most original and successful business initiatives I have ever heard of was the brainchild of an American entrepreneur by the name of Dennis Hope. In the 1970s, he registered the moon and all the stars in the solar system in his name (with the exception of Planet Earth).

Hope took advantage of a loophole in land registry laws that stated that any American citizen could register under their name any plot of land that was not registered under someone else's name, and if no one objected to registration of the plot, the land would be registered under their name—so he registered the moon under his name.

Since the 1980s, Hope has been marketing land on the moon and planets through the Lunar Embassy®. On the face of it, all this looks like a cheap marketing gimmick by a pretty weird and somewhat delusional guy, but the amazing fact is that by 2020, Hope had sold millions of acres of land on the moon (at a price of around $280 an acre out of a total of around 10 billion acres of surface area of the moon.

In a best-case scenario, it will take many, many years from now until it will be possible to settle on the moon. No one knows what the legal validity of these land purchases will be. Each buyer receives an ownership certificate and a map of the area they purchased, but there is a major dispute among legal experts and NASA over the legality of the sales. None of the purchasers is familiar with the moon, none of them has ever been to the moon. So why did they make the purchase? Just as with every product or service, the real question is, what did people *really* buy when they purchased land on the moon?

Here are a few possible answers:

» A future investment for the kids and grandchildren. From answers provided by many customers, it appears that they don't believe they themselves will be able to cash in their purchase, but "perhaps my son or grandchild will be able to sell the land in the future at a profit of thousands of percent, when plans to settle the moon are finally fulfilled."

» An investment that shows the originality and long-term thinking of the investor. People that purchased land on the moon send a message to themselves and to their environment that they think differently and see things that other people don't see, that they take risks where others don't. Thus, for example, buyers who were aware of the legal complications and the lack of clarity regarding an investment on the moon, said that when the time comes, "they wouldn't be surprised if NASA preferred to compensate them, if only just to avoid having to settle the matter in court." That is the reason why in December 2006, there was a rush of investments in land on the moon when NASA published plans to set up a manned base there in 2020.

People who buy land on the moon feel international; they send a message to themselves and their environment that they are more sophisticated, that they invest abroad (in this case very far abroad), and so on. No one purchases land on the moon and keeps the information to themselves. On the contrary, they rush to tell everyone.

What do all three reasons that I mentioned have in common? They all fill needs, and address the "pain" and problems of the purchasers. Land on the moon is just a solution to these problems and a response to these needs.

When you sell a product or a service, the real question you need to ask yourself is what am I *really* offering my customers? Why do people *really* buy my products and services? If you understand that, you will be able to significantly increase your sales and revenues. That may sound easy and obvious, but from my experience, people find it hard to define to themselves and to others what they are really selling, and they find it even harder to explain to customers the needs and problems that their products and services solve.

HOW MUCH WOULD YOU PAY TO HAVE SOMEONE TAKE YOU FOR A WALK IN THE PARK?

Let's say a huge guy with a long, thick beard approaches you, in the street or at home, and presents himself as a "People Walker." Just like a dog walker, he offers to take you for a walk in the park, for the sum of seven dollars per mile. In other words, he will walk alongside you, talk to you, and of course, listen to you, and you will pay him for his time at a per mile rate.

Sound absurd? Amusing? Meet Chuck McCarthy.

McCarthy, an unemployed actor from Los Angeles looking for a way to make some money, came up with the idea of taking people for a walk in the park, and charging them per mile. The idea may sound too absurd to be a success, and certainly for the business model to succeed over the long term. After all, why should people walk with him and not with their friends? Why should they pay him by the mile, when they can go to the park and walk by themselves, for free, at their own leisure?

What made the difference were the ads Chuck prepared and posted around town (as well as posting on Facebook) in which he wrote things like:

"Need motivation to walk?"

"Scared to walk alone at night?"

"Don't like walking alone at all?"

"Don't want people to see you walking alone and just assume you have no friends?"

"Don't like listening to music or podcasts but can't walk alone in silence, forced to face thoughts of the unknown future, or your own insignificance in the ever expanding universe?"

The results were amazing. Chuck received hundreds of emails from lonely, curious and adventurous people who wanted to walk with him. He began taking them on walks, and after not too long, he recruited another five "people walkers" to work with him around LA.

It's quite simply an amazing story, but then again, perhaps it isn't. The principle that Chuck used (whether he was aware of it or not) is, again, one of the most brilliant and basic principles of marketing: "sell the problem before you sell the solution."

If you were to be offered the solution straight-off—go to the park with a complete stranger and pay them for something you can get for free—you would reject the idea with contempt. But if someone was to talk to you and sell you your problems, needs and pains—loneliness and boredom, lack of motivation to engage in sporting activity, being scared of the dark in the park, the need to confess something, fear of what people will say if they see you walking on your own—you would be curious, you would take an interest and you would want to hear more.

Now that we have your attention, (thanks to selling you the problem, need or pain) we sell you our product or service (in this case a walk in the park with a stranger with payment per mile) as a solution for the problem or answer to a need or medication for pain. In that way, you can sell any product or service, as weird or absurd as it may be.

More to the point, you can sell the product or service that you are offering.

Here's another example. There are a lot of reasons to go to lectures and workshops, including the experience, the fun, unique knowledge, networking, breaking routine, meeting friends or colleagues, meeting the lecturer personally and hearing the content directly from them.

After two decades of giving lectures and workshops, and polls and studies that I have conducted, I have heard a diverse range of reasons that customers give for coming to workshops. The absolute majority are among the reasons I gave above, but I have also heard other reasons, some of them quite unique and "strange": for the refreshments, to find a date, to "escape" from home and come back when the kids are already asleep, and much more. The strangest reason I have heard from a customer is coming to a workshop to get a certificate.

A true story: in 2008, a customer called to inquire about a workshop and spoke to one of my salespeople. The first question he asked was, "Do you award a certificate to participants after the workshop?" The truth is that up till then we had never awarded a certificate to participants in our workshops, but it sounded like a good idea.

We told him that we were preparing certificates and would award them to participants. A short conversation with the customer revealed that he was an obsessive collector of certificates. He was very well educated and intelligent, but what motivated him primarily to register for lectures, courses, and workshops was his need for another certificate for his collection.

In other words, the same workshop, the same lecturer, the same content, the same price, but without a certificate—no deal.

Once he understood that he would get a certificate at the end, he asked the saleswoman, "What does the certificate say?"

We had no idea what the certificate would say; we hadn't even thought about it yet. So we asked him, "What would you like the certificate to say?" He replied, "It's important to me that it states that I can persuade anyone, any time and any place. . ."

When I heard that, I said to myself, "good idea!" A cute slogan, easy on the tongue, practical and with a twist of humor. I went along with it.

To this day, hundreds of workshops later, thanks to that client, everyone who completes one of my workshops gets a personal certificate signed by me, which ends with the words "can persuade anyone, any time, any place!" It's obvious to me that most participants don't come for the certificate, but it's a nice touch and a fitting end to a workshop.

We sold the customer their specific need (the certificate) and so he bought the product (the workshop).

The best sales scenario for a sales conversation either by phone or face-to-face is to listen to the customer, to hear them and to understand their problems and needs, and then to say just one thing: "I've got the perfect solution for you!"

You have to listen to a customer regardless of whether they approach you or you approach them to understand them. You have to ask straightforward questions, ones that guide the customer, that encourage them to talk. You have to truly understand what bothers the customer and what they really need. Only after we have registered everything, after we have understood the customer and identified their problems and needs, show them how our product or service is the solution to their problem, the answer to their needs, or the bandage for their pain.

It doesn't matter what you are selling or offering—cooking workshops or jeep rides, real estate or SEO services—because that isn't what you are really selling. They are "just" a solution.

You have to understand that what you are really selling or offering to the customers are things like peace of mind, realizing their dreams, good feelings, quality of life, the opportunity to share something with their friends, economic freedom, the ability to leave their mark, and so on—and that is something you will only understand when you truly listen to your customer.

The need or problem or pain changes for every individual customer, and everyone comes to you for completely different reasons.

WHAT IS THE BEST WAY TO GET PEOPLE TO PAY YOU MONEY?

In November 2012, I gave a workshop to businesspeople in Barcelona. In a prior conversation with the CEO of a large travel company who helped to promote the workshop, he revealed an astonishing piece of data. He told me that when people book flights abroad and hotels, they haggle and argue about the price as if their life depended upon it, and that even an offer that is $10 cheaper from another website or agency will cause them to book their trip elsewhere. Those same people, when they arrive at the duty-free shop in the airport will spend unplanned amounts of money that considerably exceed what they may have saved on their travel package.

To give me an extreme example, he described the following case which he and his staff come across every day: When people fly to London, most of them head for the city's central airport, Heathrow. But there is another smaller airport that some of the charter flights offer and which also lets you fly to London: London Luton Airport. A flight to London that lands in Luton costs $100 less than a flight to London that lands in Heathrow. But there is a catch. Luton is 28 miles from London and is a very small town. Thus, when you leave the airport and you want to get to the center of London, the cheapest cab during the day will cost you £100.

Even though the travel agency that offers flights to Heathrow explains this point to people over and over again, many of them still go to another agency and book a flight that is $100 cheaper. They do so despite the fact that, by the time they arrive in London, they have already paid more than the $100 they had saved.

Since this is not logical behavior, the question is: Why? Why do people act in this financially illogical way?

When people are booking a flight, they are still in their usual routine. However, when they land in

England, they are already outside of their routine, they are on vacation. Based on many studies, it has been found that people spend a lot more money when they are outside of their routine.

When people are at home or in their office and they call a travel agency, they calculate their actions, they plan their moves, they remember all their daily tasks and expenses, and they are busy. That is why they fight for every dollar, and the chances of their spending unplanned sums of money or exceeding their budget are very small.

But when they function outside of their daily routine, they feel much freer, more relaxed; they are happy, optimistic, generous and kind. That is when they are prepared to spend a lot more money, and they will not think about their bank account as much as when they function within their regular schedule.

Think about it: Where do you really feel the way I described? Mainly when you are not working by your regular routine—when you are on vacation in your home country or overseas; when you are attending a lecture or conference; when you are at a party or participating in a workshop; when you are visiting a casino or when you are on a cruise or an excursion. Therefore, if you want to maximize your income from customers, take them out of their daily routine! Or, at least, make them feel as if you are releasing them from their daily grind. Get them out of their office or work environment, or their home, and invite them to come to your office or to some "neutral" place.

Prepare for the meeting, presentation or lecture ahead of time and create an atmosphere that is conducive to a successful encounter by choosing the right food, the signage, the training material, the seating arrangements, and so forth. Customers who are out of their regular environment will be more prepared for changes and will spend more money.

It is at casinos where this has been developed into an art. When we go into a casino, there are no windows, there are no clocks on the walls, there is a round-the-clock buffet featuring the same food all day long. The casino owners do that to get you into a different zone, where you feel like you've left your routine and regular schedule behind, and then you will spend more money. If a casino had windows, and I were to go in with the sun high in the sky and suddenly I would see that it's getting dark, then as a customer I would say to myself, "Wow, I've been here a long time! My family is waiting for me for dinner and it's time to go." If I had eaten breakfast at the casino and suddenly I noticed they are serving lunch, I would know that a lot of time has gone by and feel uncomfortable.

The casinos want you to feel comfortable so they erase your sense of time. But the icing on the cake at casinos is tokens. When you go into a casino, what's the first thing you do? Change your cash for casino chips.

On the face of it, this looks like a very short, simple and meaningless action, but it is by no means meaningless. With tokens in hand, you feel (subconsciously) that you are playing a game. You don't feel that you are losing real money that you worked hard for, just tokens. If people were to gamble with 20- and 50- and 100-dollar bills they would gamble a lot less, realizing it's not Monopoly money.

Want to sell more of your products and services? Get your customers outside of their comfort zone and out of their routine. Make them feel good about themselves. Create a break in their routine. This can be done anywhere, anytime, all year round.

WHY HAVE BIKINI-CLAD MODELS BEEN USED TO SELL CARS ON TV?

For the same reason that the entrance to an expensive clothing store for women is perfumed.

The smell of perfume releases endorphins, just the sight of a bikini-clad model will release endorphins for certain audience members. Both cause a buyer to feel good, to feel positive about the buying experience. The same applies when we are offered tastings in the supermarket, when a bakery or delicatessen diffuses a smell of bread or pastry, and so on.

Every time a customer feels good, or feels a connection to you, they will buy more from you.

WHY DOES ABUNDANCE CONFUSE US?

You have arrived at a large parking lot with wide spaces and the parking spots clearly marked (in white lines). Now imagine two situations:

» Situation #1 - The parking lot is almost completely empty, with only three or four parked cars.

» Situation #2 - The parking lot is almost completely full, with only three or four empty spots.

In which of the two situations will you park faster? On the face of it, the answer should be Situation #1. If the parking lot is almost completely empty, you can park wherever you want, including pulling over at this very moment. But the correct answer is Situation #2. Because if the parking lot is almost completely full, and there are only a few spots remaining, there is no room for deliberation and we don't have time to think about where we will park.

If we can park wherever we want, then we start to think about it.

"Where is the best spot to exit the parking lot later?"

"Where is the closest spot to get to where I am going?" and so on.

Abundance confuses us. It is the possibility to choose whatever we want that causes us to deliberate and not to decide.

In Commandment 3, I talked at length about one of the most effective, efficient and important principles in marketing and persuasion—people obey road signs—and I gave a few examples and implications.

Here's another one. Studies of our shopping habits at the supermarket revealed a surprising conclusion. The greater the abundance of similar products or the choice of nearly-identical products, the less people buy.

For example, in Option 1, there are two flavors of jam on the jam shelf, let's say cherry and strawberry. In Option 2, there are twenty flavors on the jam shelf. With which option did people buy more? On the face of it, the answer should be Option 2, but the correct, surprising answer is Option 1.

If I want jam and there are only two flavors on the shelf, the decision is pretty simple; I ask myself, "Which flavor do I like more—cherry or strawberry?" and then I buy one of them.

But if I am standing in front of a shelf with twenty flavors and I have to choose, I will become confused. "Which flavor do I prefer?"

The customer deliberates, thinks, hesitates, consults, and bottom line may buy less.

What does it mean that "people obey road signs"? It means that you have a much higher chance of selling to people and persuading them if you manage the conversation with them at a sales meeting and don't let the customer manage you; if you give the customer one focused offer, not a whole range of possibilities and prices; if you package your knowledge in a clear fashion during a lecture or presentation and don't talk in an unfocused way and expect the customer or the audience to understand themselves what you meant; and if you define to the customer what you as experts in your field recommend they do.

WHAT ACTIONS ARE CRITICAL TO TAKE BEFORE MAKING A SALES CALL?

Customers often come to me to build a sales scenario for their telephone sales calls, or to write a landing or sales page for their service. I have noticed an interesting phenomenon: Most people that turn to me, be they from small businesses, or medium and mega businesses, come to meetings unfocused.

On the one hand, they want results now and fast, and on the other, they don't know how to explain elementary and essential things for marketing writing and transmitting messages, such as who exactly is their target audience—and saying things like "hi-tech companies," "mothers," or "small businesses" is not a sufficient answer. They also fail to explain their precise product or service (and offering a range of possibilities to the customer is not a good option; we have already learned that abundance confuses. And then they don't articulate what problems their product or service solve (and saying things like "health" or "overcoming any difficulty" is not an answer).

I sit with them, encourage them to talk, I try to get essential information for the article they want me to write, or the sales conversation they want me to build. Most of the time, I discover something interesting: They have no patience. Most of the time, they don't understand why I'm asking all these questions, why it's taking so long and why we have to talk about strategic issues, when they don't have time and need to launch a campaign.

I explain the following to them: **Without strategy, there is no tactical discipline.**

Without understanding who an internet campaign is aimed at, or what problems you are solving for the customer, then you are wasting money on online ads, Facebook campaigns and sales centers, because the ads will not be focused and your conversion rate will be low.

In a game of soccer, twenty-two players play for ninety minutes, with one ball. Namely, each player, even the best player, the one who every attack goes through, in practice touches the ball for just a few minutes every game—two or three minutes on average. So a player who is worth millions and has trained all week touches the ball for a total of two minutes during a ninety-minute game. That's it.

What should we focus on to discover whether a player is good or not—on the two minutes they touched the ball, or on the other eighty-eight minutes?

The correct answer is on the other eighty-eight. Good players need to be able to know how to manage themselves throughout those minutes, so that in the two minutes they have the ball, they'll be efficient. They need to know how to sustain strength during the game and when to charge forward and sprint; they need to know where to place themselves on the field to get the ball positioned; they need to know how to read their team's next few moves ahead, and what to do in every situation.

None of that is directly connected to talent, but rather to hard work. Perseverance. Understanding of the game. Strategic planning. Cooperation with the team. So successful soccer coaches judge players by their behavior off the ball.

In the same way, the approach of "let's start selling already" without any focus, without strategic understanding of the sales process the customer should go through, without an organized sales script and the right messages, without determining the target audience, without coordinating with the other teams in the sales chain is **wrong**.

Strategic planning in sales, including defining the ideal customer, which I wrote about at length in Commandment 5, is critical in order to carry out truly successful campaigns, and in order to achieve a high conversion rate.

HOW DO YOU KNOW A CUSTOMER IS INTERESTED IN WHAT YOU ARE OFFERING THEM?

One of the most important things in marketing and sales is an elevator pitch, a short conversation under a minute aimed at introducing yourself and your operations, your product or service to someone who doesn't know you. It can be useful at a conference, a meeting, at a lecture, or in negotiations.

Most people mistakenly believe that the goal of the elevator pitch is to relate everything you can about yourself. In other words, "to overload" the other party with information, and to take advantage of the fact "they cannot escape"—just like during your conversation in an elevator. That of course is an error, assuming that you want to see a continuation of the conversation and gain that person's cooperation, and not create a situation where the moment the elevator doors open, they run away screaming, or where they take your business card and throw it in to the first garbage can they see.

The real goal of an elevator pitch is to get the other party interested. To get them to want to continue the conversation with you once your thirty seconds to a minute are over, or to want to set up a further meeting with you.

They show their interest by asking you a question. That sounds obvious, but the truth is that people like to talk, and they like to listen a lot less (especially if time is limited) and so we often "shoot off" a lot of information, and we aren't available to listen to the needs of the person on the other side of the conversation.

If we were the only ones to talk and the other side barely said a word, that's not good! When we have finished saying our first few sentences, it's important that that other party ask a question. By doing so, they give us approval to keep on talking about ourselves.

People often won't tell you that they aren't interested. They will listen to you politely and then tell you "send me an email." And that's another way of saying, "Allow me to brush you off politely."

When they ask for a further piece of information that you didn't mention, you've piqued their curiosity. The goal is to say a few sentences that will tempt the other side into conversation, and will make them interested and cause them to continue the conversation with you. That ensures you that the conversation will be longer, that it will be pleasant for the other party, and a high degree of possibility that the conversation will promote your interests and help you reach the goal of your conversation with that person.

TO WHAT EXTENT DOES YOUR CLOSE ENVIRONMENT KNOW EXACTLY WHAT IT IS YOU REALLY DO?

Here's a small exercise. I've used it to test hundreds of clients, from managers of big companies to owners of small businesses, and every one of them got an "F."

Ask people in your close environment what it is that you do, or what products and services you sell. I'm talking about your closest personal environment like your best friends, neighbors, parents at your kid's school, brothers and sisters, and your parents.

Just ask them. "What is it I do?" or "What do I sell?"

Most likely, the answers will range from "I don't know" and "I have no idea," to more general answers like

"Something in real estate," "IT," "You have a registered patent," "Drug company," "Therapy," "Attorney," "Toys," and so on.

How do I know those will be the answers? Because that's how all my customers who I asked responded.

Why is it bad that those are the answers? It says two things:

1. You don't know how to explain well enough what it is you do.

2. You will never see a dollar from your close environment.

They may respect you and think you are nice, but they will never turn to you as customers and they will never generate connections and work for you, even though they can. Not because they don't want to; they just don't have the ability because you haven't provided them with it.

One of my customers, who has dozens of assets of his own in Europe and the United States, also buys assets from around the world for his clients. I sent him to ask people close to him what it is he does. He was sure *everyone* in his close environment knew exactly what he does; their responses surprised him.

Some of them had no idea what he does. Most of them knew, but what they knew was limited to "real estate guy" or "deals in real estate."

Why isn't that good enough? They don't know

exactly what he does and will never turn to him as clients. Their characterizations suggest he could be a contractor, realtor, renovator, entrepreneur, or architect.

I asked him what kind of clients he is looking for, and he replied, "I'm interested in anyone who has $200,000 to $600,000 to invest immediately."

Quite a few people in his close environment meet that definition. Those people also know other similar people (like attracts like—remember Commandment 5?) and could also bring them along as clients. But they won't do that. Ever. Not because they don't like or respect him. They do. They just don't know what exactly he does, and who to refer to him. They also don't know whether he can help them.

In fact, it's reasonable to assume—and I proved it to him in his case—that if they were to want to invest their money, they would go to someone else that they don't know, and not to him, their friend, neighbor and brother!

They are losing value, and you are losing money. How can you change that? Define to yourself and your environment what exactly it is you do, and primarily who can be referred to you.

Create a great "elevator pitch" and know to leverage every event—personal, business and professional - to create leads and revenue.

DO YOU SPEND TOO MUCH TIME TALKING TO YOUR CLIENTS?

One of the services that we provide to companies and organizations we consult for is listening to recordings of our customers' telephone sales calls. We receive recordings from our contacts at the company, listen to them, and provide them with an improved script for whoever sent us the recording.

One of the phenomena that I see again and again, one that repeats itself in a very troubling manner, is that the calls are too long. People conduct "infinite" telephone sales calls with customers. Some go for more than half an hour.

For those of you reading now and thinking to themselves that a half-an-hour call with a new customer is not a long time, and perhaps also conduct similarly long calls, you have a serious problem. The longer you spend talking to a customer, the more the chances of selling to them declines.

That is contrary to a lot of people's instinct and logic, which says the opposite, that is, the longer you spend talking with a customer, the more they are likely to buy from you. In practice, a telephone sales call that is too long has many disadvantages that reduce conversion rates.

> » The longer the conversation, the more likely
> you will make mistakes. You may say something
> "out of order," note a minor detail or technical

issue that will scare the customer, reveal a personal opinion that does not sit well with the customer, state a fact that could cause the customer "to pull back" in the conversation and not make a purchase right now, and so on. We are all human and we all make mistakes. In a long conversation with a new customer who we aren't yet familiar with and who doesn't yet know you, and is currently sitting on the fence and deliberating whether to buy from you or from other suppliers, every sentence, example or figure you state could be critical.

Longer conversation time = more potential mistakes you may make.

» The longer the conversation, the more the customer will think you are their friend.

I'm in favor of developing a long-term relationship with customers, and I have wonderful relationships with most people I have worked with and currently work with, but in order for the customer to make a purchase, a certain "distance" has to be maintained between them and the salesperson. Why? Because if the customer thinks you are their friend, they will expect a discount, free consultation, exceptional requests which, if you agree to, the deal will no longer be worthwhile. After all, we don't pay friends, right? With friends, we usually exchange "favors" and help each other, right?

Too much time in conversation with a customer breeds familiarity and sometimes gets personal (about things that aren't relevant to the sales process), and then the customer gets the wrong impression about you. Worse yet they may think you aren't busy and don't have other customers! And then the chances of you closing a deal will definitely decline. Remember the realtor and old man in Commandment 2?)

More conversation time = a potential customer who thinks you are their friend, and the chances they will buy from you will decline.

» Long conversations will exhaust you. Let's say you spoke with a customer for forty minutes, and at the end they say to you that they "have to think about it." That's really disappointing because you have just invested forty minutes of your time at the expense of other clients or other tasks in that customer, with the expectation that they would close a deal at the end of the conversation and, to your surprise, no deal was closed. Now you are tired, moody, and all you want to do is to go home or go to sleep. But you can't because you have a lot more calls to make. And more customers to proposition. You still have to get through the rest of the workday. In other words, the annoying customer not only took 40 minutes from your life, but also drained a lot of your energy and attention, and "screwed up" the rest of your day.

In order to be a successful entrepreneur, salesperson or manager, you have to make a lot of calls and to carry out a lot of tasks. If every call took you twenty to forty minutes, the effect would be fewer calls in a day, many fewer deals closed, and a lot less revenue.

More conversation time = less sales conversations, less conversions and more customers who will exhaust you and make you consider switching professions.

WHEN DOES AN OVERENTHUSIASTIC SALESMAN CAUSE DAMAGE AND MISS OUT ON THE DEAL?

One of the stories that I remember best from my law studies (it that took place in the 1980s, and I read about in the early 2000s) was about a prosecutor who managed to lose a criminal case in the United States, even though all the evidence, and the law, were in his favor.

The case involved a young man who had broken into a house and stolen jewelry. Following a police investigation, he was caught, and the jewelry was found in his apartment. A case that at first glance seems very easy to prove: there was evidence against him, the jewelry was found in his possession. But one thing wasn't taken into account—the human factor.

The trial took place in front of a jury, and a public defender was appointed for the young man. The public defender saw from the start that there wasn't much of a chance of winning the case, and decided to call the young man's elderly mother to the stand so she could tell the court he'd been at home on the night of the break in thereby providing him with an alibi.

The mother quickly turned out to be doing more damage than good; she didn't provide a convincing alibi, and she also said things during her interrogation like, "It's true that my son may have broken the law from time to time, but he's a good boy." The defense attorney understood that nothing useful would come from her, and ended his interrogation.

Then came the cross examination. At this stage in the proceedings, there was no need for a cross examination. The elderly mother had already done enough damage to her son's case and the prosecuting attorney could have waived his right to a cross examination. But the prosecutor insisted and commenced with an aggressive interrogation. In sales language, that is known as overkill.

The prosecutor spoke in a very callous way to the poor and elderly mother, shouted at her often and made fun of her, saying she was bringing up a criminal. At one point during the cross examination the mother started crying. Tears ran down her face and her glasses fell to the floor. The prosecutor, who was already "in his stride" approached her, stepped on her glasses by mistake and broke them.

At the end of the trial, the jury found the young man not guilty. Despite the fact that all the evidence was against him and despite the fact that he had clearly committed the crime, the jury hated the prosecutor so much that they wanted to decide against him.

This story is told in law school to prove the point that a "non-professional" jury cannot be relied upon from a legal point of view, and that professional judges are preferable.

But what I took from this story is the critical error made by the prosecutor, that is, overkill. Everything was in the prosecutor's favor, and had he waived his right to cross examination, he would have won the case. By insisting on continuing with his game plan and being too aggressive without any need, he killed his own win.

That's a classic mistake made by over-enthusiastic and inexperienced attorneys, and also by over-enthusiastic and inexperienced salespeople. Let's imagine a scenario where I'm at an electronics store and am interested in buying a TV. I've come from home prepared with the model I'm looking for, I see it in the store and say to the salesperson, "That's the TV I want!"

What should the salesperson do? Close the deal. Have me sign the paperwork, take my credit card.

It's true that the sales rep could tell me about additional and complementary products. First they have to catch me as an enthusiastic customer, and make sure the deal is closed.

An overenthusiastic or inexperienced salesperson won't do that. Because it seems to them too easy, or too short, or doesn't go according to the sales script they were taught. So the salesperson continues to try to sell to me (even though I have already told them that I want to make a purchase), and here we have potential for overkill.

In reality, even with all the expected resistance when you are selling something, sometimes a customer arrives ripe and ready to buy, and doesn't need selling to. All they want is for the purchase process to be completed. In this case, selling just disappoints the customer and spoils their desire to make a purchase; in other words, it kills the deal.

In sales and persuasion, you have to pay attention—not to cross boundaries, not to try too hard, not to sell to a customer who doesn't need selling to, and to maintain the right balance between a personal touch and paying attention to the customer, and between being too aggressive and overdoing a hard sell.

WHAT DO YOU ANSWER A CUSTOMER WHO SAYS, "I NEED TO THINK ABOUT IT?"

One of the most annoying phrases in sales conversations is, "I need to think about it."

You are in the middle of a sales conversation over the phone, by video on your computer, or at a face to face meeting. You have encouraged the customer and you have understood their needs and problems; you have presented your product or service to them as an answer to their needs, and as a solution to the customer's problems, you have explained the benefit they will gain by using your product or service. At the end of the conversation you have given them a quote.

On the face of it, you have done everything right. And then you hear, "I have to think about it." The customer didn't show too much resistance, they understood the value they would receive, and heard everything they needed to hear, but at the end of the conversation with you—decided not to decide.

That isn't real resistance. The customer isn't going to lock themselves up in a cabin in the wilderness for three days to think about your offer. It's just a polite way of brushing you off and choosing a prominent human characteristic, that is, putting things off.

Here's my recommendation for a good answer. Before you read it, I would like to stress that there is no miracle formula, or magic phrase that the moment you say it, every customer will change their mind. In sales, we work on as high a "conversion rate" as possible, and the following phrase when you say it will increase the chances that the customer will change their mind, either during the conversation or shortly afterward.

The phrase is, "No problem. Just take into account that—" There are several possibilities with which you can complete the sentence, depending on the conversation that came before:

"Take into account that if your event is next month, you will need at least two weeks to prepare, so you will need to decide quickly."

"Take into account that my diary is filling up quickly and if you want to meet next week, I'll need an answer by tomorrow."

"Take into account that prices in the market are going up all the time."

"Take into account that the product you inquired about is really hot right now and demand is high, so I'm not sure there will be any left."

"Take into account that the government is due to pass a bill that will change the rules of the game and the terms we discussed won't be relevant any longer."

What did we achieve with the phrase, "take into account?"

> » We were the ones to get the last word in, and we left the customer with food for thought. This is infinitely better than the alternative, which is mumbling weakly and in a defeatist tone saying, "Okay." By using the phrase "take into account,"

we have the last word with the customer and we are also drumming in important messages from our point of view.

» We have used a key tool in marketing, and the most important tool for dealing with "people who put things off"—the "scarcity effect." When a customer says to you, "I need to think about it," the underlying assumption behind what they said is, "I have time to think about it, there's no need to rush." And as far as the customer is concerned, down the road, the terms will stay the same terms and you will be just as available. Using phrases such as those I have used here, we make it clear to the customer that this is not an assumption they can be certain about. Perhaps you will be just as available in two weeks' time, perhaps the price will remain the same in another two months, perhaps the customer won't "lose" anything if they hesitate. But then again, perhaps not. Perhaps there will be price changes and the customer will pay more if they wait too long. By using the words "take into account," you have created doubt regarding the customer's assumption, and this doubt is sometimes enough to change the customer's mind in the short term.

Adopt a habit: at the end of every conversation in which the customer hasn't closed a deal, you have the last word and make your last sentence begin with "take into account that."

WHY SHOULD YOU NEVER GIVE A CUSTOMER A PRICE RANGE?

Let's assume that a customer asks you how much your product or service costs. Let's assume also that the price is not fixed and is dependent on a number of factors (such as the number of participants, location, delivery, assembly, type of product and so on). One of the most common mistakes businesspeople make at this stage is to give the customer a price range, "Our workshop costs between $3,000 to $5,000, depending on (factors)," "Building a website will cost you between $3,000 to $10,000 depending on (factors)."

Customers have what is known as selective hearing, so this approach works against you.

If, for example, you said that constructing a website will cost between $5,000 to $15,000, when what you meant to say was that a basic site without all the upgrades will cost $5,000, and a more advanced site with all the upgrades and an online shop will cost $15,000, what will the customer hear? The customer will hear $5,000. They will want to receive all the upgrades and all the extras, but to pay only around $5,000. Later the customer will argue and bargain and say to you, "But you told me it was $5,000!" They want all the upgrades and extras on the $5,000 website.

You can prevent that. First, don't give a price range.

The customer will always hear the price that is convenient for them.

Let's say I am selling consultancy services and my customer asks, "How long is a meeting?" and I answer, "Between an hour-and-a-half to two hours." What will the customer hear? Of course they will hear "two hours." If the meeting lasts only an hour and fifty minutes, the customer will be angry with me and will complain, and feel that I "owe" them ten minutes.

But if I tell the customer that a meeting lasts an hour-and-a-half, and in practice I spend an hour and thirty-five minutes with them, the customer will be happy because they received a few more minutes than expected.

Second, if you have a few price options, start with the highest price. For example, we could say, "A website with all the upgrades and extras, including an online shop, will cost $15,000." By doing that, you have set in the customer's mind the highest price; this is known in marketing as *anchoring*.

If a customer argues and bargains, we can say to them, "You can get the website without all the extras, in a basic version, and that will cost you just $5,000." At this stage, if the customer opts for the most "basic" version—statistically, most people don't want the most basic option and will choose a better website—they will be thankful for the low price they received.

Third, if you have several offers that differ from each other in content and in price, explain each offer separately, without drawing a connection between them: "There is an hour-and-a-half long meeting, in which we will do such and such," and then, "There is a possibility to hold a three-hour-long meeting during which we will do such and such."

In other words, present them as two separate products or services and not as the same product or service with different range of prices. One small sentence that makes all the difference between a satisfied client who values what you are doing for them, and a customer who is not satisfied, who pays you less and respects you less.

WHAT DO YOU DO WHEN YOU ARE HAVING A "BAD DAY" AND DON'T FEEL UP TO TALKING TO CUSTOMERS?

It happens to all of us. Even if you haven't prepared your schedule in advance, you no doubt have a lot of tasks for tomorrow. Some of those tasks include conversations with customers. These can be sales calls with potential customers, retention and services conversations for existing clients, ongoing work conversations with customers, or coaching conversations with trainees, to name a few.

Maybe you get up in the morning and you just don't feel up to talking to anyone because you had an argument with your partner or are simply exhausted. Even most energetic, lively, and enterprising people have bad days and low spirits once in a while.

What do you do?

What about all the lists of tasks you have waiting?

What about the customers you promised to get back to today?

What about the leads that arrived through the Contact Us page on your website that you need to get back to and sell to?

Sorry to disappoint you, but there is no decisive and absolute solution to this issue. There is no winning formula that suits everyone. But as someone who lives and works (out of choice) at a very high pace, manages his time strictly, does a lot of things at the same time and meets *many* people in a week, here's what I do when I'm having a bad day, or just a few hours in which I don't feel like doing anything:

First of all, I just "go with the flow." Because it doesn't happen a lot, I have learned with the years to listen more to my body, and especially to my instincts. When I can see that I'm not focused at the moment or I don't feel like talking to customers, I just let go and I just don't do so for the next few hours. When I am focused, my productivity is extremely high. I can write a sub-chapter like this in a few hours, I can write a sales script for a company or a lecture for a client in a couple of days' work, and I can write a whole book in a few weeks.

When I'm not focused, and I don't feel like it, I can sit at home all day next to a computer or a pen and paper, staring at them while they stare back at me, and the whole day can go by without writing anything. Then I'll be frustrated I didn't write anything and be angry with myself.

On good days, I can talk to a few people at the same time and give them all a good feeling. I can talk on the phone or lecture for hours on end, and I can give consultations for twelve hours straight. But if once in a while I'm not at my best, then it's better that I don't talk to customers if I don't have to.

POSITIVE ENERGY IS CONTAGIOUS; NEGATIVE ENERGY, INFECTIOUS.

A sales conversation, for example, won't succeed and the customer won't make a purchase if I'm gbroadcasting some form of negativity to the other party.

What does go with the flow really mean, then? It means I'll just do something else instead. I'll go for a run or a walk to clear my mind. I'll go and rest for an hour, or do some task that doesn't require any real thought, like washing the dishes at home, or filing papers at the office. Usually, when I let go and flow with my bad feelings and just do something I like instead of forcing myself to do something I don't feel like doing, the bad feeling passes quickly, and is replaced with a good feeling.

What happens if I have no choice, like an appointment on the schedule tat can't be changed? In cases like that, my way to do those tasks and enjoy them even to whatever extend possible is to change the internal narrative running through my head.

Let me give you an example. I have a lot of days when I lecture two or three times a day to different audiences and in different places around the world, or when I hold ten to twelve hours straight of consultancy, or a series of meetings one after the other on the same day. Sometimes, toward the end of the day, I find myself exhausted but my schedule for the day is not yet over.

This is a point where you find yourself at a mental junction, and the way to cross it is to change the negative internal story that is running through your head into a positive internal narrative.

Let's say that I am driving to my third lecture of the day, and I am feeling worn out and exhausted. The internal stories that are taking over me right now can sound something like, "What a bummer, I really don't have the strength for this lecture!" "What was I thinking to myself when I booked this lecture? "I hope no one turns up," and the like. When I do that though, I bring myself down, and the result can be that my lecture that night won't be as good as it should be. The audience will feel that I'm not in a good mood and not enjoying myself and then they won't enjoy themselves either. People will start to disrupt the presentation and they will leave unsatisfied.

So instead of that pessimistic scenario, here is an alternative "reality creation." I'm still tired. I still want to drive home instead of to the lecture. I still don't have the strength. But now, I force myself to think positive internal stories such as,

"Be thankful that you have three lectures in a day! A lot of people would be very happy to swap with you!"

"I worked for years to reach the situation where my calendar is full. That's what I always wanted!"

"A lot of people took a babysitter, bought tickets, and are paying right now for gas and parking, just to come and hear you lecture. You can't take that for granted. You have to give them your best."

If that sounds like a cliché to you and too spiritual, here's a much more down-to-earth, positive internal narrative: "Let's go, one more lecture and this long day is done."

"Another two hours and you are back home to see the game," or "to see the kids," or "to see my wife," or "to have a good dinner."

So, positive thoughts create a different, better reality for the same tasks that I have to do in any case. Change the internal narrative in your head to a story that is more empowering and beneficial, and your reality will look completely different.

WHY DO MOST START-UPS, WORLD-WIDE, END UP SHUTTING DOWN?

The life cycle of most start-up companies is as follows:

» First comes an idea. Work commences on the idea. During the initial stage the founders work out of Grandma's basement (or they rent an office if they have a little capital). At the same time, they start to raise money from investors, or they turn to a venture capital fund, or they bring money from home.

» They hire programmers, designers and engineers to develop the newest and the best product, service or application that will create a good "user experience" for the end-client.

» They succeed in raising some money from investors or funds. Excited about raising money, they go out and hire more developers, engineers, programmers and designers. They rent offices big enough for everyone.

» They hold a lot of lunch and dinner meetings with colleagues, the team, and possible collaborators. They develop a version of the product, the site and/or the application. And then another version. And then another one, which is better and has less bugs.

» Then the money raised from investors starts to run out.

» At some point, someone at the company asks, "What about sales and marketing?" But they are immediately interrupted by someone who explains to them that before you start marketing, you must have a really good product to sell, so they continue with development.

» In the meantime, the money from the first round of fundraising is finished. So they try to raise more money from additional investors, that is, the second round.

» They manage to raise more money.

» They continue doing the same as before: paying high salaries to the best developers and programmers on the market, and paying high office and administration expenses, and so on. At some point, even if they have put some money aside for marketing when the product is ready, that money also goes to fund "current" expenses.

» Or they don't manage to raise more money. And then they shut down. Or, first, they burn through their personal savings.

» Even if they do manage to raise more money, at some point, a rival company develops a similar product to theirs, and then they invest all the remaining funds in something that will be even better than their competitors' product.

» In the end, in a best case scenario, they have completed development of a product that is not bad at all, that even has a market of potential customers, they have invested years of crazy work in it, without taking a salary, and eating only pizzas and drinking Coke during work hours.

» But they have no money left for marketing and

sales, they have no budget for advertising, PR, internet campaigns, or other promotion. Worse yet, they don't have any salespeople on their team. They didn't hire any, and they didn't even think about it.

» All the programmers, designers and engineers are very nice and professional, really, and they are very loyal to the company, but they have no idea about marketing and sales.

This is the stage at which most start-ups collapse altogether: with a good product, lots of good intentions, but without paying customers and revenues for the company.

Now comes, as a rough generalization, the life cycle of start-ups that have made it around the world:

» First comes an idea. The founders check the feasibility of the idea with potential customers and potential investors. If the responses are positive, they start to work on the idea.

» Parallel to development of the website, app or product (and even before), they hire salespeople and set up a marketing department for the company, to start selling the product, which has not yet been completed, and perhaps doesn't yet exist, all around the world.

» Successes start to accumulate; there are some paying customers that the salespeople have brought in, traffic on the website, a good number of users on the app, a mailing list and a constantly growing database of potential customers, and more.

» With these successes they build a winning presentation that leans on *social evidence*, which I will expand upon in Commandment 10, and with that presentation, they go to investors, funds, and others.

» Only this time, armed with an attitude of, "It would be nice if you invest in us, but we'll get along just fine without you."

» If they invest, then the company "expands" activities like crazy. If they don't invest, the company can get along just fine without them.

Why will be company be fine without the added investment? Because the company has marketing and sales. The product has been developed, in advance, in line with what the customers want and need (and are willing to pay for), and not the other way around—where they first develop a product and then see if it has a market or if someone is willing to pay for it.

It's called *marketing before product launch*; it's the hottest trend in the world of business over the past decade.

Here are a few examples:

Instead of working for months on the content of a presentation—and only after I have the "perfect" lecture do I start to try to understand where the audience will come from—first I spend a few months filling the lecture hall. Only when the hall is full do I prepare the lecture in full.

Firs, invite customers to pre-order on eBay or some other platform, and only when the customer has ordered and paid, you take the thirty days you have to complete the product and supply it. (Note: Publishers do this all the time. A book may not be available for months, but a page goes up on myriad online sites and makes the book available for pre-order. The publisher can then ascertain receptivity in the marketplace.) Or, find an external supplier who has the product and make sure it gets sent to your customer. This is called *drop shipping*.

And *crowd funding* is what some successful start-ups do today instead of going to professional investors. They directly approach the general public instead of turning to the veteran financing funds, not only raising money, but also building a community of loyal customers.

Crowd funding bypasses venture capital funds, banks, publishing houses, and music labels.

In all of the above examples, marketing and sales are put at the forefront and are treated as a critical component in the company's life.

In this chapter I spoke extensively about creative marketing and sales, and in the next chapter I address sharpening your marketing messages, with marketing writing, and with motivating your audience to action through the use of content.

KEY ELEMENTS OF COMMANDMENT NO. 6

Market and sell differently.

✓ Decisions, even those made by mega companies, are the result of your personal touch, your availability, your hunger for more customers and correct interpersonal communications between the departments of your company.

✓ Success in any field has nothing to do with the field you are in, and everything to do with your life skills and persuasive speaking capabilities.

✓ Don't speak badly about your competitors; in fact, it's better if you don't mention them at all to your customers.

✓ Don't offer all of your products and services to all of your customers. Categorize your customers, and offer each customer the product or service that is closest to what he or she prefers and likes.

✓ You always need to consider your customers' needs and interests, and you must choose your marketing plan and messages so that they match those needs and interests.

✓ When we feel guilty, we're willing to pay more. Think about what's motivating your clients, and what their emotional reason for buying from you is.

✓ Once you have a customer's attention, (by selling the problem, need, or pain), sell them your product or service as a solution to their problem, as a response to a need, or as a cure for their pain.

✓ People spend a lot more money when not working within their regular routine.

✓ The better a customer feels, the more they will buy from you.

✓ Strategic sales planning, including defining the ideal customer, is critical to conduct successful campaigns and to create a higher conversion rate.

✓ The real aim of an elevator pitch is to awaken the interest of the other party and get them to want to continue talking with you later.

✓ Define—to yourself and to your environment— what exactly it is that you do, and primarily who can be referred to you.

✓ The longer you talk with a customer, the less chance you have of making a sale.

✓ Don't sell to a customer who doesn't need to be sold to.

✓ At the end of every sales conversation in which the customer doesn't bite, make sure to have the last word, and your last sentence should begin with, "Take into account that. . ."

✓ Don't give a range of prices to a customer.

✓ If there are things you really have to do, but you don't feel like doing and they can't be put off, change the internal narrative running through your head.

✓ Marketing before product launch means the product is a response to what the customer wants, needs, and has already committed to paying for.

Put people through a persuasion process with marketing communications.

HOW TO WRITE BRILLIANT HEADLINES THAT PEOPLE WILL WANT TO READ.

One of the big trends in the business world right now is upping your game in marketing writing. Posts, newsletters, op-eds, articles, flyers, sales pages, landing pages—all need to be written today with a greater marketing and sales orientation. The goal is to motivate customers to action through content.

Which headlines cause more internet users or readers to open your mail, to stop and read your post, and to dive into your article or text? I have been researching the subjects of marketing writing and call to action since 2004, and, among other things, I've conducted statistical checks of my mailing lists and publications, and

those of my customers through A/B Testing. In every email and post that I publish on my mailing list—if you aren't on it yet, then go to drpersuasion.com and register now—I write two different headlines for the same content, an A headline and a B headline.

I send each of the headlines to two focus groups, and after a period of a few hours to a few days, I check to see which group had a higher percentage of people who opened the emails. In other words, which headline motivated to action more users to open the email? Then I send the mail with the best headline to the rest of mailing list.

Here are three insights from my A/B Testing over the years:

FIRST INSIGHT:

People prefer specific, practical tools over general headlines.

Example 1:
Headline A - "Why should you never give a customer a price range?"
Headline B - "Why do customers always hear what is convenient for them to hear?"
Headline A won and led a lot more users to open the email.

Example 2:
Headline A - "How to get your customers to feel a more intimate connection to you, with one simple action"

Headline B - "Why is it more worthwhile to send your customers a WhatsApp message and not a regular text message?"
Headline B won; it motivated far more users to action.

It is more specific for the user, and breaks down a specific situation clearly.

SECOND INSIGHT:

People are by nature risk haters more than risk lovers and therefore most always prefer information on how not to get hurt, over wanting to read about how to be more successful. (All economic theories are based on this and usually refer to this concept as risk aversion and risk tolerance.)

Example:
Headline A - "How to prevent your customers from being disappointed in you"
Headline B - "How to get your customers to appreciate you more"

Which headline do you think won? Headline A.
People want, first and foremost, not to damage what they already have, namely, not to disappoint people.

THIRD INSIGHT:

People prefer information that they perceive as niche—personal and more suitable for them than nonspecific information, which they perceive

as generally enriching (even if the conclusions are identical and they can learn a lot more from the more general case).

> Example 1:
> Headline A - "How do you get customers to spend a lot more money than they had planned on?"
> Headline B - "What do a backpacker, a new parent, and a new army recruit have in common?"
> People first look at headlines for "the bottom line."

> In this case, Headline A won.

> Example 2:
> Headline A - "How do you get a one-off customer to become a repeat customer who will stay with you for eternity?"
> Headline B - "What do a home printer and an electric shaver have in common?"
> Headline B is interesting and intriguing, but Headline A won.

People are interested first of all in themselves and their own immediate interests.

Those were a few insights that will improve your email open-rate percentage, the number of shares you get on social networks, the number of entries to your website, the number of views of your videos and the number of leads going to your company. As a result, your revenues will grow.

In this chapter, I offer you tools and tips on proper marketing writing that is interesting, and, more than anything, convincing and motivates to action.

WHAT'S THE WORD THAT WILL MAKE THE LARGEST NUMBER OF PEOPLE WANT TO HEAR AND READ ABOUT YOU?

Every few years, various studies check which words affect us the most, make us listen more attentively, buy more, show up more often, vote more often and speak more openly.

One word in the last decade that came in first place on the Attention Index List was "secret."

"I have a secret to tell you," "The secrets of (name it) revealed," "The secrets that will make you succeed, earn more, have a better love life."

Why do people love hearing secrets so much? In this day and age, we all live with a sense that there's something we need to know but still do not know; this is based on studies and surveys. There are certain fields in which we feel strong, confident and professional, and in which we (seemingly) know all the secrets. But there are also fields where we feel we need a boost.

For example, in romantic relationships, "My relationship is good, all in all, but there's this couple we meet every now and then. They've been together for twenty years, yet they still hold hands and seem to be completely in love with each other. What's their secret?"

Or self-management, "I basically manage my time well, I'm focused and efficient, but there's this woman who sits next to me in the office. She gets a lot more done in less time than I do. How does she do it? What's her secret?"

Or in business and finances, "I make good money, very good money even, but there's this guy who makes a lot more than me. He always looks happy and everything seems to come easy to him in business. How does he achieve such results with practically no effort? What's his secret?"

Almost no one in this generation thinks, "My life is perfect and there is no area in which I need to improve myself." If there are some people who think they are perfect, then in this competitive, digital, marketing-oriented age, they will receive plenty of messages and see plenty of articles and ads about all the things they have not managed to do yet, places they have not been to and things they have not yet achieved.

We tend to always want more. (Which is, by the way, another word on the Attention Index List!) However, in order to get "more," we need to know the right "secrets."

Do you want people to listen to you more? Buy more from you? Then reveal your professional secrets to them. I am intentionally using the word "reveal," not "teach." "Reveal" (also on the list) is closely associated with the word "secret," while we tend to associate the word "teach" with school. (And who wants to go back to school and sit in a classroom again?)

Tell them things they don't know in your field of expertise. Highlight the benefits they'll get from using your products or services, and explain how through working with you they will get "more"—improve their quality of life, increase their income, get the most out of themselves and their employees, and on and on.

WHY YOUR CUSTOMERS WILL BUY MORE WHEN YOU SHOW EMOTION.

There are three ways to write an email to a customer. The first way is formal, matter-of-fact wording.

"Dear Rudi,
Please see the quote I've attached
as requested.

I await your authorization,
Matt."

That's how most people in the business and work worlds write emails—without any personal touch, without any specific reference to the recipient, other than his name, and without any courteous words.

The second way is a more genial, polite and "casual" wording.

"Hi Rudi,
How are you doing?
Following up on our conversation, here's the

price quote you asked for.
Please approve.

With thanks and all the best,
|Matt"

Still matter of fact, but more genial, more polite, and most importantly, a wording that enables you to write even unpleasant things and still stay "friends."

For example, if you have interviewed someone for a position and have decided they aren't suitable, you can:

Simply not get back to them—a rather disgusting way of doing things if you ask me, and not at all service-oriented, but that's how a lot of businesses in the world behave.

Write something in the style of the first example:

"Dear Rudi,
After carefully reviewing your application,
we have decided that you are not suitable for
our company.
Human Resources."

Or, you could write something in the style of the second example:

"Dear Rudi,
How are you? Thanks for interviewing with
us.
After reviewing your application, we have
decided not to use your services.

We reserve the right to get back to you in the future, and wish you success.
Best regards,
Matt, Human Resources."

The response is the same response—negative. Rudi didn't get the job, and yet, with the second version, Rudi will feel a lot better and will be a better ambassador for the company, and there's a chance the sides will collaborate in the future.

Then comes the third way of writing emails to customers.

"Hey Rudi,
How are you doing?
It was great talking to you and getting to know you.
Following up on our pleasant conversation, please see the attached quote for me to carry out a workshop for your company, with the aim of improving the sales, marketing and persuasion capabilities of your managers and staff, and to do team building for the company's various departments.
I'd be happy if you could approve the quote as soon as possible.
Looking forward to collaborating with you!
Yours,
Matt."

It offers a personal touch, and is service oriented, with a specific mention of the topics raised in the telephone conversation, meeting or email correspondence with the customer.

Almost no one writes like that. But precisely because of that, when someone does write in that style, using positive, happy, and personal words, such as "our pleasant conversation," "it was great meeting you," and "looking forward to working together, customers will remember them more, will want to work with them more and will respond with the same positive tone.

A few years ago, I was in a meeting with one of my publishers, a particularly happy and optimistic guy, and he showed me an email that he had been sent by a purchase manager at a large company. She wanted to order a large number of books for her employees as a gift for the holidays.

She drafted a frighteningly laconic email, something like:

> Dear George,
> Please send me a quote for 100 copies of the book *Creative Marketing* by Dr. Yaniv Zaid.
> Anne

That's it.
He responded with a particularly warm email:

> Hi Anne,
> How are you?

I was very excited to read your email!
We are very happy that your company has
selected the book *Creative Marketing* as a gift
for your managers and staff. We are certain
that they will enjoy it and derive a lot of value
from it.
I'm happy to send you a price quote of
_____ and am looking forward to
sending you some copies signed by Dr.
Yaniv Zaid."

I have to admit that even I, with all my optimism,
joy of life, and use of positive language, told him that, in
my opinion, it was over the top.

"Why did you write 'I was excited'?" I asked him.
"That could suggest to their purchase department that
we are hardly selling any books, when the truth is exactly
the opposite and the book is very successful. 'I was very
excited' sounds like flattery and is too emotional."

But then he showed me her return email. (She is a
purchase manager at a large company, who has no personal acquaintance with George or me.)

She began her email as follows: "We are also very
excited! And happy to collaborate with you. . ."

At that moment, I, too, learned an important
lesson. People treat you the way you treat them. Everyone, even when formal and conservative, is happy to
receive a positive and personal letter, and will often

respond in kind. There are no limits to positive attitudes or positive words.

The third way, beyond the fact that it brings people and businesses closer, differentiates you from the rest of your market and leads people to remember you favorably—and increases sales!.

Be nice, generous and optimistic.

Give customers personal attention every time you are in dialogue with them, be it by email, by telephone or face-to-face. I'll talk more about the personal touch in Commandment 9.

WHY WE WATCH MOVIES WHEN WE ALREADY KNOW HOW THEY WILL END.

When you watch a romantic movie, especially if it is a Hollywood classic, you already know how it will end, right? Let's take, for example, the movie *When Harry Met Sally*. A man and a woman meet at different stages in their respective lives, and one can sense chemistry and sexual tension between them. One time he is in a relationship, another time she is in a relationship, and things do not seem to work out for them as far as the possibility of a relationship is concerned. Is it not completely obvious to you that, by the end of the movie, the "conditions will ripen" and they'll become a couple and live happily ever after? Yes, as we watch the movie, we can already guess that's what's going to happen.

Another example: war and action movies like *Rocky, Rambo, The Expendables, Star Wars* and others.

Isn't it clear to us, as we watch the movie, that, by the end of the film, the "good guys" will come out on top, Rambo will return from the Vietnamese jungle with all the prisoners of war and Luke Skywalker will win the final battle against Darth Vader? Of course it is.

So why do we watch the whole movie? Because of the journey. We are interested in the final outcome, but the journey to that final outcome is no less interesting. A good screenwriter, a good author and a good presenter focus on the way they tell the story, which is just as important to the listener, reader, or web surfer as the final result.

When you tell a story—and it can be during a work meeting, a business presentation or even when you are talking to a friend—the small details are the most important, and they are what make the story. Yet, for some reason, people tend to leave out and skip over the small details and go straight to the end of the story. And that's a lot less fun to hear, a lot less interesting for the listener and, mainly, a lot less persuasive.

A few years ago, I had a consultation meeting with two principals of a boarding school. They came into my office and immediately one of them said to me, "Last night, one of our boys came back drunk in the middle of the night, made a lot of noise, woke everyone up and it took us a long time to calm him down." During the meeting, the other one repeated the same story, but told it differently, "Last night, at 2 in the morning, we suddenly heard yelling from the seniors' dormitory. We ran upstairs and saw that one of the boys had come back from a night on the town. He was drunk, and he had woken up all of his roommates—they sleep four in a room. He was cursing, throwing things around, and he didn't have a clue where he was. We tried to control him but it was tough. Finally, we dragged him outside, but he kept screaming and cursing all the way down the hall; he woke up the entire floor. We took him to the garden, and he started throwing up on the lawn. He was shivering and we covered him with a blanket. Half-an-hour later we took him back to his room, laid him down on his bed and sat with him until he fell asleep."

The same story, told in two different ways. Now ask yourself: Which story was clearer and easier to understand? Which story got you more emotionally involved and had you identifying with the characters in this drama more? Which story was more interesting to listen to?

The second one because of the way it was told. The second storyteller made sure to include key details. In the way the second story was told, we could imagine, even though we may have never run a boarding school, what it felt like to drag a drunken teenage boy along a dormitory corridor and take him outside to the garden in the middle of the night.

A good persuader is a storyteller who knows how to present things in an interesting and original way. When you tell someone a story or present people with an idea, do not skip over the details and do not try to save time.

Be generous with the information, put an emphasis on the details; that way the other side will understand your messages a lot better.

HOW DOES BARACK OBAMA, EVEN THOUGH HE WAS THE PRESIDENT OF THE UNITED STATES AND THE BUSIEST PERSON IN THE WORLD, GIVE PERSONAL ATTENTION TO MILLIONS OF PEOPLE?

Many people think that Barack Obama's popularity as President of the United States was based on the fact that he is a great public speaker. However, a large part of his popularity during both his terms in office (and a reason he was elected twice as President of the United States) can be attributed to his fantastic use of distribution lists and viral marketing.

Yes, even Barack Obama, who has millions of followers around the world, gives his community of online followers personal attention. To be more exact, what appears to be personal attention. (Studies show that in terms of how the customer feels, this is the same thing.)

And how do I know? Because I was on Obama's email list between 2010 and 2014 (not because I could vote for him, but because I wanted to learn from him) and I myself received a lot of inspiration from many of the things he did online.

Here is one email I received from Obama in 2012, around the time of the presidential elections, when he was running for his second term in office:

"Hi guys, How are you doing? I'm really swamped these days. I'm traveling a lot and meeting a lot of people..." (In other words, this "ordinary" person is telling us what he is going through these days, as if he is a friend sitting in our living room, grumbling about the tough day he had at work. People love this, and mainly they love to be told things they do not know.)

"Next week we're going to meet our friends in Virginia..." (This was a prestigious fundraising event that cost $1,000 per person, but Obama does not talk about the money. Instead, he describes it as a meeting where he is going to "hang out with some people." It should be mentioned here that, out of his millions of readers and followers, only a few tens of thousands live in the Virginia area. Therefore, the event would only have been relevant to them, but he made a point of letting his whole list know about this meeting.)

"Michelle and I are looking forward to meeting with you." (He is talking about an event with hundreds or thousands of people. Almost none of them will get to speak with Obama, or even get close to his podium. However, the President makes it sound as if each guest will be able to talk to him personally for half an hour.)

Toward the end of the email, the sentence I remember most of all is, "Should be fun!"

(The President of the United States, the leader of the free world, is writing a note to his voters and is, in fact, saying, "Come over, it should be fun!")

I could keep analyzing this approach even further, but here is a question: If Obama, a sitting President, can let himself be so personal and chummy with his voters, doesn't that mean that you, too, can afford to give personal attention, or the appearance of personal attention, to those around you?

Of course you can.

HOW SHOULD YOU WRITE TO YOUR CUSTOMERS ABOUT A DISCOUNT YOU ARE GIVING THEM—IN PERCENTAGES OR ABSOLUTE NUMBERS?

Say you are offering your customers a discount on one of your products, services or activities. What's the best way to present the discount? In percentages ("a 15 percent discount"), or in absolute numbers ("$150 off")?

The answer is complex, and many studies have been done about this subject around the world because it greatly affects your conversion rates, your income and the way your customers will treat you—and also whether they will appreciate the discount and take it seriously.

After reading many studies on this issue and in light of my many years of experience as well as my customers' experience, here is the bottom line: It depends.

On what? On the price of the product or service being discounted. If the product price is relatively low—up to $100—the discount sounds a lot better if it is presented as a percentage.

If the product price is over $100, it is better to present the discount in absolute numbers. This is a small piece of data that most people do not think about, but it could be very significant for your income.

WHY IS IT IMPORTANT TO MAKE SPELLING MISTAKES ON EMAILS SENT TO MAILING LISTS?

In 2009, I took part in a big marketing conference in Dallas, Texas, held by two of the top marketers in the United States, Bill Glazer and Dan Kennedy. The conference was entitled "The Money Making Super Conference 2009."

Some 1,200 people from around the world took part in a four-day conference packed with lectures by the best lecturers and top marketing people from the United States. In addition to the lectures I give around the world, I make sure to participate in an overseas international conference in my professional fields at least once a year, in order to learn about innovative marketing tools and to network with colleagues from around the globe.

In one of the sessions at the conference, Bill
Glazer, one of the top experts on marketing writing in
the world, gave the audience tools to write marketing
materials such as emails, flyers, and letters to customers
in a way that would increase their conversion rate. As he
was speaking, a woman in the huge audience got up and
shouted in his direction, "I have to tell you something
about your emails!"

Surprised, Glazer gave her permission to speak and
she said, "I'm a professor of linguistics, and I have to tell
you that you have a lot of spelling mistakes and gram-
matical errors in your emails. I've been reading you for
years, and every time I'm surprised that someone of your
standing allows themselves to write in common language and once in a while to make linguistic mistakes!"
Obviously, it's clear that the woman wasn't asking the
question in order to correct Glazer—after all, she could
have kept her thoughts to herself or just taken him aside
to let him know. She was asking the questions in order
to market herself and to broadcast she was a professor
of linguistics.

I was surprised by her question, but was also happy
that she asked. I leaned back in my chair, and thought
to myself, "Well. Finally, I'm in the audience and not
on stage. Finally, I have the opportunity to see someone else dealing with an interruption from the audience, and seeing how they answer the question in front
of everyone!"

Bill Glazer smiled, and his answer surprised

everyone, even me. He replied, "I would like to tell you that you are our ideal customer!"

She was in shock, and didn't understand what he was getting at, and neither did the audience. And then he added, "You read all my emails. Word for word! That's wonderful. When you write marketing content, you want as many people as possible to read you, and to read your email in full, so that they go through the entire sales or persuasion process that I, the writer, want them to go through.

"So while it's true that you specifically read my emails in order to spot my errors, nevertheless, you read every last word! And that's fantastic.

"And anyway," added Bill Glazer, (putting the final nail in her coffin) "You're here, aren't you? You have come to the conference! You have paid us! You have listened to our lectures! Why?"

"Because of the emails," muttered the woman and sat down. His point had been understood.

I remember the situation to this day as a formative event in my life as a lecturer: The moment Bill Glazer took a "problematic" question from someone who was trying to undermine his authority in front of his audience, and used that question to build authority, and along the way, also taught the audience something about marketing writing.

Authenticity is important.

Of course it is desirable and recommended to write without a single spelling mistake—and that should be your goal as writers. But you should also be aiming for a message that is simple like in Facebook posts, Twitter tweets, text messages and so on. When the message is right, and your writing shows empathy and a real desire to help your readers improve their skills, and when you give added value in your writing, your readers will forgive you for a few innocent spelling or grammar mistakes, or for using slang expressions. And that won't harm your conversion rates or the goals of your text.

IS IT WORTH NOTING EXACTLY WHICH AGE GROUPS YOUR PRODUCTS AND SERVICES ARE SUITABLE FOR?

One day, when my younger son Yoav was seven years old, he saw a board game in a toy shop with "Suitable for ages 4 to 99" written on the front of the box. He asked me an innocent but amusing question, "Dad, does this mean that when I'm a 100 years old this game won't be suitable for me any longer?"

When it says suitable for ages 4-99, what it really means is that the game is suitable for everyone, but I would recommend making it clearer to customers (and of course to yourselves), which ages your product and services is most suitable for.

The gimmick of writing "recommended ages" is very efficient from a marketing perspective. Once I define a specific age, or more precisely, a range of ages that is relevant for me, then on the face of it would seem I am narrowing my target audience, leaving a lot of people out of range, but in fact I am increasing my conversion rate—in practice more people buy.

Two important things are very clear to whoever reads the age range. First, it or is not suitable and beneficial for them. Second, it is very clear to them , whether they are the right age or not, whom they can refer to me. That's how I get new customers.

Two examples to illustrate:

» When I wrote my children's book, in all my ads I wrote, "If you have children or grandchildren ages two to seven, this book is for you!" That really increased sales. Adding "grandchildren" expanded the target audience.

» A customer of mine organizes dating tours for singles all around the world. As soon as he started to give a more accurate profile of status and ages, and to advertise "A group will be going to Greece for a week, aimed at singles ages 25 to 35," then on the face of it, he seemed to be narrowing his potential customers, but in fact, registration was strong and the tour sold out very quickly. It was very clear to people for whom the activities were designed, whether or not they were suitable, and also to whom they could pass on the information. In such a case, it is of course also important that you are credible and true to your promises. My customer insisted on not allowing anyone outside of the

25-35 age group to join the tour, even if they were really close in age. That may have surprised and angered a few people who were left out, but over time it was the right step to take, because people understood that he kept his promises, the groups remain homogenous and people felt more comfortable signing up when they knew they wouldn't be surprised during the trip by participants who were too old or too young.

Focus yourself. Define to yourself the age groups you wish to reach. (Recall the discussion of choosing your ideal customer in Commandment 5.) Spell out that age range when you are advertising your products and services.

WHY LAWYERS ARE BAD FOR BUSINESS.

A few years ago I provided consultancy services to a business client who was organizing a customer conference for the first time in her life. She wanted to bring a videographer to the conference to document it. She received a recommendation for a particular videographer, spoke with him, and received a quote. She then sent it to me to look over and give my opinion before she closed with him.

I read his quote (two pages) and saw that it included a lot of things that he wouldn't do:

"The price does not include preparatory work;"

"The price does not include filming testimonies during breaks;"

"The price does not include materials and hard disks;"

"The price does not include editing the shoot;"

"The videographer will leave immediately after the event."

"Listen," I said to my client," I don't know the videographer, but looking at the quote, it isn't at all clear to me what he will do. I can mostly see what he won't do, and at least some of the things that he isn't planning on doing are precisely the things that are very important to do, such as shooting participant testimonies."

At the end of the day, after receiving an additional recommendation and speaking to him again, she did close a deal with him. On the day of the event, the videographer turned up—nice guy, very professional, did a great job, arrived before, stayed later, shot participant testimonies, was polite and obliging and did everything she asked for.

After the conference I couldn't resist myself and said to him, "In person, you leave the opposite impression of your quote. Because of your quote, which was anti-marketing, you almost missed out on the job."

He replied, "I had a lawyer write up my customer agreements."

I want to reveal something to you. I am making a very gross generalization here, but I myself am a lawyer so I have permission: Legal education that lawyers receive is, by its very nature , anti-business and anti-marketing. The way lawyers draft agreements is usually done in a way that doesn't promote business, but puts obstacles in the way of business and creates suspicion and lack of trust between the parties, and even generates resistance that didn't previously exist.

Lawyers want to protect their clients—which is a good thing—and therefore they put into the agreement a lot of clauses specifying what will happen if all sorts of bad things materialize—which is not such a good thing. I have seen too many cases where the parties reached an understanding and wanted to cooperate on a business level, and even on a personal level, but when lawyers were brought into the picture, negotiations ran into trouble and in the end the deal blew up. By virtue of their job, lawyers are liable to make things complicated and to insist on seeing doom and gloom in the name of protecting their client at the very time when the sides are at peak motivation and optimism.

By the way, the most successful lawyers in this respect are those who are entrepreneurs and business people themselves, and therefore prefer not to make things complicated.

The quote given by the videographer at the beginning of the story was on the face of it perfectly logical; he only wanted to make clear to the customer what his services include and what they don't. But the result was a price quote that was anti-marketing, and that scared potential customers and damaged the videographer's good name, especially when someone who doesn't know him is reading it.

Contracts, work orders and quotes are also part of the persuasion process. Just as during a telephone call you are required to by persuasive and to market, the same goes for written material that you send after a meeting or call. True, you have to protect your interests and to make things that are important to you clear, but you can write anything in a more marketable and positive, and less legalistic way, because people who aren't lawyers don't like complex formulations with negative aspects.

Words have enormous power, especially when they are written out on paper. The emails that you write and the written materials that you send are still part of the persuasion process.

WHAT'S THE NUMBER 1 PROBLEM PEOPLE HAVE WITH MARKETING WRITING?

A lot of people get writer's block when they want to write any type of content. Not just a book, but also a blog, marketing content for a website or pamphlet, an academic paper, an article, a professional guide, and so forth. Sometimes they even freeze trying to write posts for social media. People get stuck, they forget their vocabulary, and in the best case scenario, if they ever do write anything, it takes them a long time to get going again. In the worst case scenario, the experience can discourage them from writing anything ever again in the future.

Based on many years of experience with my clients

and their writer's blocks, I have discovered that the Number 1 problem that creates writer's block is that they try to be too sophisticated! People use simple language every day, they give advice or lecture about their material in a very clear and coherent way, but when it comes to putting the information in writing, they suddenly try to be Harlan Coben or John Grisham and write in a "literary" and sophisticated way.

What is the solution for writing marketing texts quickly and effectively? The Number 1 rule in my opinion for good marketing writing—not necessarily book or article writing—is write like you talk. When you write marketing copy, imagine you're having a conversation about this topic with someone, and just write those words exactly as you would say them.

Another option I always recommend to lecturers is that they should record themselves and transcribe the material. Then they will also have prepared, written marketing material.

If I am talking and I say, for example, "Take this story, for example," that's exactly how I should write. In contrast, if I try to be sophisticated and write "Let us examine this example, which illustrates. . ." it will bore and irritate the readers, because almost no one speaks like that.

So just use simple language, and write the way you speak in real life.

KEY ELEMENTS OF COMMANDMENT NO. 7

Rules of marketing writing:

✓ People prefer specific practical tools over headlines they perceive as general.

✓ Most people are, by nature, more risk haters than pleasure lovers.

✓ People prefer information that they perceive as niche, personal and more suitable for them, over general information.

✓ We all live with a sense that there's something we need to know but still do not know. Tell your clients things they don't know from within your field of expertise.

✓ Use positive, happy, and personal words.

✓ The small details are the most important, and they are what make the story.

✓ Be personal and chummy and give personal attention, or the appearance of personal attention, to those around you.

✓ If the product price is relatively low—up to $100—the discount sounds a lot better if it is presented as a percentage. If the product price is over $100, it is better to present the discount in absolute numbers.

✓ Authenticity is important. When you are writing, show a sense that you care and a real desire to interest and improve your readers.

✓ Define a specific age or a range of ages that is relevant for your product or service.

✓ Contracts, work orders, and price quotes are also part of the persuasion process. Write then in a marketable and positive, and non-legalistic, way.

✓ Write like you talk when you write marketing copy.

COMMANDMENT NO. 8

Make as many people as possible talk you up as much as possible (and say good things).

WHAT'S THE CONNECTION BETWEEN THE CORONAVIRUS AND YOUR MARKETING CAMPAIGNS AND WHAT CAN YOU LEARN FROM HOW IT SPREADS?

Welcome to the best viral marketing campaign of 2020—the coronavirus (COVID-19).

The coronavirus apparently emerged at the beginning of December 2019 in the town of Wuhan, China. The virus was new and we knew almost nothing about it, and the scariest thing was that there was no vaccine against it.

The consensus among the scientific community is that it began in a local market in Wuhan (where, among other things, reptiles and wild mammals are sold) from

a combination of bats and snakes sold there, and then underwent adaptations in order to infect humans as well.

After sequencing of the genetic code of the new virus, researchers discovered that it belongs to the family of coronaviruses, which includes Severe Acute Respiratory Syndrome (SARS).

The name corona is given to these viruses because of their form which, when observed under an electronic microscope, resembles a crown.

Now back to marketing.

In the year since the virus erupted, even though the whole world fought it, the virus just kept spreading and infected over 80 million people around the world and killed over 2 million.

Why does this virus spread so efficiently? Because all it has to do is to infect one person (or a few people), and from there, humans do its work for it.

The virus doesn't jump from one person to the next, but stays with the o carrier and duplicates itself in the newly infected person, who then becomes a new carrier. Thus, it is the best "viral marketer" of 2020. The word "viral" in that context comes from the spread of information by word of mouth, from person to person, just like the spread of a virus.

Let's say I see *Fast and Furious 9.* The next day I enthusiastically tell a friend about the movie, and that he just has to see it. The friend goes home and tells his wife what I told him. The wife says, "Great. Let's go to the movie with another couple!" The four of them go and they really enjoy it. The next day their friends go to their workplaces and tell their colleagues about the movie. And that's how information about the movie spreads, and more and more people will buy tickets to see it. All thanks to me.

What's interesting about the viral spread of information about the movie is, first of all, I only told one friend about the movie, and that, in weeks or months, led dozens of people to go and see the movie.

Second, I still have the information, and I could without any effort continue to enthusiastically tell others about the movie, and lead hundreds and perhaps even thousands of people (depending on how popular I am) to see the movie.

Third, no one asked me to do it. The managers of the movie theater and the creators of the movie don't know me, they don't pay me a referral commission for every person that buys a ticket through me. There is no real way to stop information if enough people are willing to share it of their own accord.

If we go back to the original coronavirus, then as long as there was no efficient cure and vaccination, the most efficient way of stopping the spread of the virus was simple: prevent people from meeting. That's why most countries closed their borders, cancelled mass events and asked people (or forced them) to stay at home.

Do you want to be the best viral marketers of the coming years? Do you want as many people as possible to talk about you for a long time? Let's now explore how to achieve that.

WHY PARENTS TAKE SUCH PRIDE IN THEIR CHILDREN'S ACHIEVEMENTS.

One of the most important rules of viral marketing is: People will talk about you and tell their friends about you if the information about you will create the impression that your ambassadors are interesting, sophisticated, talented individuals. In other words, when they will be talking about you, they will not only be marketing you but they will also—and primarily—be enhancing their own image, perhaps without even being aware of it. Thus, they will be promoting themselves while you can enjoy the free marketing and the positive buzz that is being created around you and around your products or services.

To demonstrate this point, I will give you an example we are all familiar with: parents who talk proudly about their children's achievements.

Think of the following situation: A proud mother is talking to her neighbor. She tells her, "My son just graduated from law school with honors and he's been hired by one of the leading law firms in the country." By the way, our children are "always" outstanding, talented and gifted individuals. And parents are not the only ones who say so; their teachers, coaches or other mothers in the kindergarten also agree.

The mother in this little anecdote is in fact

marketing her son: She is talking about him with pride, she is enhancing his image and is telling others about his accomplishments. Why?

Her neighbor is not a member of the legal community and cannot possibly help this woman's son find work or help him in any other way. Moreover, the son is not part of this conversation; he is completely unaware that his mother is talking about him and therefore he will not even thank her for this "commercial."

Then why does this law graduate's mother feel the need to talk about him? Because it says something about her. Even if she was not at all involved in her son's legal studies, the very fact that her son has succeeded in his field says something about her in both her and her neighbor's subconscious. Here is solid proof that she has been a good mother, that she has educated her son properly, that she has enabled him to excel in his studies and succeed in his career path. Thus, his success is also hers.

Do you want your customers to say good things about you even when you are not in their immediate vicinity, even when you are unaware that they are advertising you and your products or services? Then you must make them feel special whenever they mention you.

How do you do that?

In February 2014, after a lecture I had delivered at a conference for businesswomen, one of the participants walked up to me and said, "We don't know each other and I don't think you're aware of this, but you changed my life!" I don't tend to take that kind of statement for granted. I immediately became intrigued and I asked her how and why I had changed her life. And she told me, "I'm a lecturer, and in the past, whenever I would give a lecture, I would suffer from severe stage fright, which would paralyze me and ruin my lecture, even if I had shown up as prepared as I possibly could be. A few years ago, I heard one of your lectures in a different forum, and you said one sentence that really got to me. You said, 'A lecture is just a conversation, a conversation with many people at the same time.' And that changed my entire perspective. Since then, every time I start to get nervous before a lecture and whenever I feel a wave of heat slowly creeping up from my lower back to my upper back, I just take a deep breath and remind myself of what you said!"

I was very happy to hear what she said. My wish, like that of any mentor, lecturer, author, business owner or entrepreneur who has passion for their work, is to make people think about me and talk about me as much as possible, and become my ambassadors, with minimal effort and minimal costs.

That woman's story is a classic example of one of the most important principles of viral marketing: If you give people something that is really useful to them—a practical tool they can work with—they will think about you every time they use that valuable tool and they will give you (in their subconscious) the credit for their success over and over again.

William Buckley was once asked, "What book would you take with you to a desert island?" He answered: "A book on how to build ships."

Think about that in connection with the story I have just shared with you. That woman had heard my lecture and, at the time, I must have said hundreds of sentences and given hundreds of tips. Yet only one of those sentences impressed her as extremely practical from her point of view. She heard it at the right time (for her); it touched her and made the whole lecture worthwhile for her. From that moment on, she began acting differently.

What happens in reality (in her subconscious) every time she takes a deep breath before a lecture and reminds herself, "A lecture is just a conversation?" She thinks of me on some level.

She gives me credit for the tip. And she tells other lecturers about me when they ask her for advice. This is how she became my ambassador, without my even being aware of it, and without my being aware of her and the influence I had on her.

Do you want your customers to have a high professional opinion of you and to also create a wonderful reputation for you (for free) throughout the entire market? Then give them tips that they will find useful and of practical value and which they can work with. They will thank you for this and will remember you forever.

WHAT DO AN EVENT PHOTOGRAPHER, A BUSINESS CONSULTANT, AND A SOCCER REFEREE ALL HAVE IN COMMON?

You are not supposed to notice any of these three in the course of the activity they are involved in.

Good event photographers are professionals who take the most authentic and meaningful photos that will include all the relevant people at an event without stealing the show. Good referees are those who can go through an entire soccer game with their name hardly being mentioned and without their being shown or talked about at all while the game is in progress. The players are the focus, they are the ones the audience came to see, and they are the stars whom the camera is meant to concentrate on. And business consultants? Good consultants do not make their client develop too much of a dependence on them. The job of business consultants is to teach their clients "how to fish" and not provide them with a supply of fish. In other words, good business consultants supply their clients with long-term tools such as managerial or marketing tools so that the client will know how to apply them later on, even when the consultant is not present or involved.

Many times clients ask me to come with them to their business meetings, to tell them exactly what to say, or dictate to them what they should write. My instinct is to do exactly that, and sometimes I do so, if the clients insist and if it is really important to them. But contrary to what my instinct tells me, I understand that it is important for my clients not only to copy what I say but also —and primarily—important that they themselves understand the logic and the principles behind what was said, so that they can stand on their own two feet before their own clients and their own audiences.

It might be in your short-term best interests (and in the beginning, your best financial interests as well) to make your clients need you for every move, conversation or deal. However, in the long run, your best interests are to teach your clients how to conduct themselves in their particular business context and to reveal to them the secret of every move they must make. If you follow this approach, then they will think of you and be your loyal ambassadors every time they make those moves. What is more, those clients will always come back to you—because they choose to, not because they have to.

WHAT IS THE MOST IMPORTANT THING PEOPLE WHO TALK TO YOU NEED TO KNOW ABOUT YOU?

You meet with a client, a colleague, a supplier or just someone you happen to start talking to at an event and you network. You have spoken with this person for a minute or two, or for even less than a minute.

Here is an important question that must be asked in connection with such meetings: What is the most important thing that person needs to know about you?

When I ask this question in workshops, I get a range of replies: "What I do," "What I deal in," "What products or services I sell," "What benefits they will receive if they buy from me," "What they will get out of working with me." These are all good answers, and they are definitely in the right direction. However, if you read Commandment 6, you know that the most correct and accurate answer, in my opinion, to this question is this: whom they can refer to me.

As I mentioned before, for many of us, if we were to ask the people around us who are close to us what exactly it is that we do, they will simply answer, "I don't know." Or perhaps they might know something general about our occupation, such as "Something in real estate."

You might have customers who have bought a product or service from you, who were very pleased and who complimented you. Perhaps they have even come back and bought some more. Nevertheless, they have never referred any customers or people they know to you.

This means that they do not know exactly what you do. They might have a general idea, however, in reality, they do not know who to refer to you, when to refer them to you, and/or how to refer them to you.

That's bad news for you. It means that, at this very moment, there are many people out there who love you and want nothing but the best for you; that there are paying customers who were happy with you; and that all of them could be your active ambassadors, could talk about you a lot more and send work to you, but do not do so. As a result, you are missing out on many possible opportunities to sell your products and services. You can be a lot more successful, on both the business and personal levels, if you use the following "intangible assets,"

your customers

your reputation

your community

and turn them into "tangible" financial assets.

Based on my experience since 2003 working with hundreds of companies and organizations and with thousands of self-employed people and entrepreneurs, I have come to the conclusion that one of the greatest challenges people face, if not the greatest challenge of all, is how to translate compliments from customers into income.

Even people who are held in high esteem professionally, who are content experts providing excellent service, have a hard time understanding the gap between the compliments they receive and their actual income. And this is because they have not utilized these intangible assets, and have not turned them into tangible ones.

WHAT'S A BETTER GIFT CHOICE FOR YOUR EMPLOYEES: A WEEKEND AT A HOTEL, GIFT VOUCHERS, OR CASH?

You've decided to give your staff, or specific employees who have excelled, a gift to express your appreciation and to strengthen the motivation and commitment of your employees. You have a budget of $500 for each employee, and you have three options:

» Give them cash such as five $100 bills for each
employee, or a one-off payment of $500 on top
of their salaries.

» Give the employees $500 dollars in
gift vouchers.

» Give each employee a hotel vacation, maybe
an overnight midweek stay with their partner,
worth $500.

All three options will cost you as an employer
exactly the same.

Which one would you prefer?

Which one would the employees prefer?

On the face of it, most employers would prefer to
give cash as the simplest and most immediate option,
saving organizational work.

On the face of it, most employees would also prefer
cash.

But the results of studies conducted over the years
show a surprising finding: the favorite option—both of
employers and employees—is a night in a hotel.

The second preference for both sides is a gift
voucher, while the least favored option is cash or a direct
bank transfer.

Why? Because personal attention is the most
important thing for all of us. For employees, personal
attention such as a compliment, public praise, or a
recommendation always beats work conditions like a
room with a view or a cell phone at the expense of the

employer, and work conditions always beat cash. That's great for the employer as well because the employee will really appreciate the gift.

If you give employees cash, it disappears quickly and they won't even remember that they even received anything from you. If the money comes in through the employee's salary, they won't even feel it, and they will have to pay tax on it. If you give employees gift vouchers, they will also disappear quickly, especially during the holiday season.

But a hotel? That's another story. First of all, the employees will probably book the hotel a month ahead. Then they will tell the whole world that they got a hotel vacation from work—no one keeps that kind of information to themselves—and then they document every moment in the hotel and upload it to Facebook, Instagram, and all the rest of the social networks. (And they don't forget to mention again that the vacation was paid for by their employer.) Then they return with memories and experiences and tell all the other employees, customers and suppliers, and they will also remember the hotel for the next couple of months.

So if you need to spend $500 on each of your employees, would you rather they forget the gift after two days, or to buy yourself an ambassador and a grateful employee for the next three months? The ambassador will do viral marketing for you, giving your company positive advertising in their immediate and far circles, without you even having had to expressly ask them to do so.

WHAT IS THE PART IN A CHILDREN'S PLAY THAT KIDS LOVE THE MOST?

A few years ago, I went with my sons to see the children's play *Aladdin* in our neighborhood shopping mall. For those who do not remember the story, Aladdin comes out of a cave with a lamp, his wishes come true with the help of the Genie in the lamp; he becomes a prince, marries the princess, and the two embark on a future where they will seemingly live happily ever after in Aladdin's palace. At this point, the evil sorcerer, who has been frustrated by everything that has happened to Aladdin, plans to steal the lamp from him. One day he disguises himself as a poor old man, comes to Aladdin's home and asks to swap the new lamp he has brought with the old lamp in Aladdin's possession. The princess, who does not know the story of the lamp, agrees to swap lamps, and then the evil sorcerer gains control of the magic lamp and makes Aladdin go back to being a pauper.

Back to the play. When the sorcerer tries to convince the princess to give him the "old" magic lamp—he is dressed as a poor man, but even the children in the audience know his real identity—the princess suddenly turns to the audience, and asks the kids:

"Children, what do you think, should I give him the lamp?"

At first the kids are shocked that they have suddenly become a part of the play, and then they yell: No! Don't give him the lamp!"

The princess and the sorcerer ignore the children, and the sorcerer "explains" to the princess, "They actually mean 'yes.' They want you to give me the lamp!"

The kids scream wildly to the princess, "No! Don't give him the lamp!"

The princess and the sorcerer repeat this routine a few times. Each time the princess "innocently" asks the children, "So you want me to give him the lamp?" the kids really go crazy and scream back, "No!!" There was a three-year-old boy sitting next to us who went almost blue in the face and screamed over and over again—he was taking all this completely seriously—"Don't give him the lamp! He wants to take over the world!!" It was really amusing to see this small boy in action.

What is my point? That is the part the kids loved the most in this show. When I heard the kids and the parents talking after the show, that was the part the kids remembered the most.

Why? Because they had participated in it. They had played an active role (or so they thought), and therefore their experience during that segment of the play was the most powerful in their eyes.

And that is what I have been teaching my clients for many years now: Do you want your audience to have a good time? Do you want them to tell others about you? Then don't just give them knowledge, give them an experience. Give them a chance to participate and feel active. There are many ways to do this such as simulations, examples and demonstrations, questions and answers, and humor. The main thing is that the audience must feel part of your presentation. Activate your customers, and the chances of their closing deals with you and talking about you will be greater.

WHY IT'S *REALLY* IMPORTANT TO FLATTER CUSTOMERS, COMPETITORS AND COLLEAGUES.

One of the principles that I have adhered to since I set up my company in the beginning of the 2000s, is to praise and give credit to customers and colleagues. Colleagues are otherwise known as competitors. I don't use this word, however, because I believe in creative thinking and not competitive thinking, and I believe in abundance and in there being plenty of room in the market for everyone.

Giving praise to customers and colleagues, and taking delight in their achievements is known in Hebrew as *firgun*, a unique word that explains part of Israeli culture.

If I read an email by a colleague that I liked, I will promptly write them a complimentary response, comment, or commendation. After all, I know just what a pleasure it is to receive a compliment, comment or feedback after sending a successful email.

If someone has asked me to give a recommendation

or a testimony about a colleague or a customer at a conference of theirs that I was invited to, I will happily give a testimony or recommendation, make a video, or give an interview. One of the most important marketing tools for marketing your next conference is taking testimonies from your current conference and using them for future marketing.

What if I've seen a clip or a post that I like put up by a customer or colleague on Facebook? I'll give it a "like" straight away, and in most cases, I'll respond with a post of my own.

Let's say a customer or a colleague has written a book and wants me to write a blurb on the back cover, or to write opening remarks to be published as an introduction to the book. I'll happily comply. Of course I will read the book or at least part of it first and I will write only my opinion, in the most marketable way possible, in order to help the author. It's challenging to market a book, especially your first one, and recommendations by an "authority" in the field are key in promotion.

All these actions require a lot of time and energy from me, but I warmly recommend that you give as much praise and credit as you can, at every opportunity. This is a classic win-win situation in which each side benefits.

First of all, at the mental level, this creates positive energy and good karma; the universe "sees" the help you provide to your surroundings and rewards you in a thousand other ways, some of them in the short term and some in the long term. A more practical message is simply to get you to feel a lot better and to be happy and at one with yourselves.

Second, it strengthens your connection with colleagues, customers and your environment. I'm a big believer in the principle of "growing with customers, suppliers and colleagues, and helping them grow."

The more that people around you grow and thrive, the more you will too. The more my customers succeed in business, or if they write a successful book as a result of my mentorship or a consultancy process that they have undergone with me, the more I will profit in all sorts of ways, even if I don't have a stake in the company's growth or royalties from the customer's book.

The customers will go on to do another mentorship program, they will give me a testimony as a satisfied customer, portray me as a success story, refer me to other successful people just like them (like attracts like—remember Commandment 5?), will talk about me everywhere and will give me credit.

I know just how hard and challenging it is to set up a business, expand a company, break out overseas, write a book, be a professional authority, and serve the community. That's why I identify with the requests, and with the writers, and do everything I can in order to help them. People also enjoy working more with people who give them praise and credit and take pleasure in their accomplishments (*firgun*), and are far happier recommending people who do so.

Third, from a marketing perspective as well, *firgun* is good for you! For example, hundreds of my clients have published business books following my consultancy, mentorship programs, or workshops. I wrote a warm recommendation for many of them that appeared on the cover and/or in the beginning of the book. In the majority of cases, I read the book, or at least most of it, before writing a professional recommendation. Sometimes, I don't have time to read the book, in which case I will write a recommendation for the writer only. Many of my colleagues have asked me over the years, "Aren't you afraid of putting your name on a book and being identified with it? What will happen if the book fails? You will be identified with failure! What happens if someone buys the book at your recommendations and is disappointed in it? They will be angry with you!"

It's true, and it could happen, but this is what I say to them every time, "I want to give *firgun* to the author regardless." (On the assumption of course that I believe in the content.)

If the book succeeds, then I have received free publication and marketing, because thousands or maybe tens of thousands of copies of the book will be distributed and sold around the world, with my recommendation.

Many people who don't know me are exposed to my name as a result of the recommendation and some will join my community at some point.

If the book is a failure? If only a few hundred copies are sold, most of them to the author's family and friends? Then my recommendation has changed very little as almost no one has been exposed to the book.

So the possible reward here is far greater than the risk.

Give as much *firgun* as you can, all the time, to as many people as you can. *Firgun* is the cheapest and most easily available managerial and marketing tool around. If I had one dollar and I gave it to you, I am down a dollar, and I can't give it to anyone else. But if I gave you a recommendation, compliment or praise, I can do it again and again without any limits.

If you have given someone *firgun*, if you have helped them and given them a recommendation, they will give you *firgun* back. They will talk about you, they will help you when you need them and they will recommend you over and over again.

HOW TO GET A JUDO BELT IN LESS THAN TWO MONTHS.

When my son Noam was seven, he took an exam in his judo class and got his first belt. The class took place in the afternoons at his school and until then he had a white belt, which is the color everyone gets when they start to learn judo. Parents and siblings were invited to the graduation ceremony. There were refreshments, the kids were examined on the exercises they needed to know, and the teacher—the former national champion—handed out their new belts with the parents excitedly taking photos.

A long time ago, when I was Noam's age, I, too, was in a judo class. I had to go through two years of judo lessons before getting my first belt, a yellow belt. So when we were told that there was a certification ceremony for Noam for graduating to the next level, I was curious and I asked his teacher how he got a yellow belt so quickly.

The teacher's answer surprised me, "It's not a yellow belt," he told me, "it's a white-purple belt. The rules of judo have been changed and now you get a new belt every six months; a white-purple belt after six months, a purple belt after a year, a purple-yellow belt after a year-and-a-half, and a yellow belt after two years."

I look for the marketing angle in everything, and this time it really stood out. This was genius marketing!

What happens now, when you get a new belt every six months during your first two years, and you don't have to wait two years in order to go up a level for the first time?

First of all, you create for the kids an experience of success, and that causes them to try harder because they have something to aspire to, to show greater desire to reach their target and to succeed as a result of receiving compliments and being empowered by graduating to the next level. They also like the class more because they feel they are making progress.

I looked into the matter and found that before new belts were awarded every six months, the dropout rate for kids in judo was very high. Most of the kids that started judo in grades one and two didn't complete two years and never got a new belt. (I didn't survive two years, either, and to this day I have a white belt.) Once they switched the system to a belt every six months, a lot more kids stuck with the class, including kids who joined up after the year had begun, and in practice received a belt after less than two months in the class.

Second, it's an opportunity to charge the parents more money. As parents, we paid for the new belt and the refreshments at the ceremony—a payment that is in addition to the ongoing cost of the class. Of course we were happy to pay and had no complaints, but from a business marketing perspective, instead of charging the parents an extra payment once every two years, a "sales event" is created here once every six months. And the parents (the customers) pay happily and are even pleased to pay because that means their kid is successful!

Third, cutting the time between belts creates viral marketing and free advertising for the class, and makes the parents active ambassadors for the judo class, without them even being aware of it. When a parent goes to their kid's exam, competition, graduation, or ceremony, they tell other parents, friends, family, neighbors, and colleagues. When a parent takes a photo of their kid with their new belt, they show that photo on social media, at family dinners, and when they meet with friends.

As I noted before, they do this because they are, in fact, marketing themselves. What the parents are doing, indirectly, is saying, "Look what a good parent I am, look how I invest in my kid, attend their events, encourage them to succeed." But what the parent is actually marketing is the judo class. They are showing how the judo class is fun and rewarding, and how much the kids are enjoying themselves. That's good for everyone—a classic win-win situation.

Give value to your customers and they will pay you more, and happily. Empower your customers and make them feel good about themselves, and they will stay with you. Give them an experience and get them out of their normal routine, and they will become active ambassadors for you.

HOW DO YOU GET PARTICIPANTS IN A WORKSHOP TO REMEMBER WHAT YOU TAUGHT THEM?

A few years ago, I read a study that shocked me: Some 90 percent of people who take part in lectures or workshops forget about 90 percent of the content that they heard or learned in that workshop or lecture, within a week, at most from the end of the activity.

Why is that a very worrisome finding for every consultant and presenter? Because at the end of the day, when people hold workshops or give lectures and transmit content to others, they have an agenda, both from a marketing perspective and an ideological perspective.

The ideological perspective is to influence the audience and to teach new content. Anyone transmitting content to an audience wants that audience to understand and take in the material. If we are talking about an idea or an opinion (say a political panel) - we want the audience to adopt that idea or opinion. If we are talking about a change in habits such as adopting a healthy lifestyle, we want the audience to adopt new habits. If we are talking about new explanations and a new way of looking at reality, we want the audience to remember the new data it has heard and studied.

So if people forget almost everything within a short time, then that is a little wide of the goal. But there is also a marketing agenda.

Every lecturer or consultant, at the end of the day, wants the participants in their activities to buy their products and services, and to invite them for further activities. And they want for the audience to talk about them. If people very quickly forget what you taught them, that hurts their ability to talk about you, and to invite you for further activities.

In short, both for your ideological agenda and your marketing agenda, you have to make participants in your workshops apply what you have taught them.

How? There are two main types of workshops:

1. An intensive workshop that runs for a few days straight, morning to afternoon or evening or night. The participants clear their schedule and come for a few concentrated days of programs, simulations, and insights.

2. A process-oriented workshop that is spread
   out over a period of a few weeks or months,
   in which meetings are held periodically. In a
   process-oriented workshop, people apply and
   remember what they learned to a much greater
   degree.

The reason is that, in an intensive workshop, people
receive much greater amounts of content at one time.
These workshops are usually accompanied by various
gimmicks such as dancing, loud music, energy drinks
in order to keep people awake and energetic throughout the day. The participants are on a high, studying,
practicing, writing down a lot of information, receiving
a sugar rush and so on, and on the face of it everything
is okay. But after a few days of breaking routine they
return home, go back to the office, and then they have
a lot of tasks to do from the time they were absent, and
have to return to routine very quickly. After a few days
back in their regular routine, they already don't remember—and aren't implementing—almost anything they
learned. It's like when we come back from a pampering
vacation and by the end of our first day back at work, we
have forgotten that we were on vacation.

A process-oriented workshop on the other hand,
enables the right dose of absorption and assimilation
of content. Meetings take place, let's say, once a week.
New materials are learned, and then there is a whole
week in which participants can apply and practice until
the next meeting. If there are questions, problems or

deliberations, they can be raised with the group or with the lecturer, at the next meeting, or between meetings. If you forget some of the material, the next meeting will refresh your memory.

The chances that you will remember the material, see how things work in your everyday real life, that they are suitable for you, and that you will be ambassadors for the content and the lecturers, are much higher.

WHY DO DAYCARE AND PRESCHOOL TEACHERS SEND YOU PICTURES OF YOUR KIDS IN THE MIDDLE OF THE SCHOOL DAY?

If you want proof of the revolution that has taken place in the digital age, just take a look at the education system. As someone who has been consulting with schools from a business and marketing perspective for the past two decades, I can say that what is happening today in schools when it comes to marketing, persuasion and call-to-action is nothing less than amazing.

Some twenty to twenty-five years ago, the word "marketing" in an academic environment was considered almost rude, and schools saw themselves as "educators," refusing to market themselves. At best, communication with parents took place at parent-teacher days and occasional conversations with specific parents, usually in the event of problems. Today, schools and teaching staff invest an enormous amount of time and energy in persuading parents to register for schools, and no less importantly, in customer retention—in marketing schools activities all year round.

I have two boys in the education system. As a parent, I am therefore the school's customer. The following are just a few examples of what I have received from the kindergarten teacher, schoolteacher and school principal over the year:

» An email almost every day from the teacher to all the parents in the class that details everything done in the class that day and the homework the kids have been given.

» An email from the principal to all the parents in the school once a week, listing all the special activities conducted at the school that week, including many events that the school initiates, such as "health week," "entrepreneurial skills week," "road safety week," and more.

» I am also bombarded with photos from those events, including, of course, constant updates from the school's website and Facebook page.

» For me, though, the peak, from a marketing perspective is live updates sent via parents' WhatsApp groups, both at kindergarten and at school. Once every so often, the teachers sends photos of the kids playing or doing special activities such as making a cake or perhaps a trip outside of school to the parents' WhatsApp group. From a technological point of view, it's very simple. The teacher photographs the kids several times during the activity, selects a few of the best photos and uploads them to the group. Within seconds, dozens of parents see the photos via live broadcast. It only takes the teacher a few seconds to do this, but from a marketing perspective, it's a revolution.

Today's technology enables marketing, persuasion and motivation-to-action at levels that we couldn't have imagined in the past. I talked about this in Commandment 5, in connection with photos from my son's summer camp.

What is the special marketing effect of photos sent to parents during a regular day when the kids are at school and the parents are at home or at work?

First of all, it calms the parents. You've left your kid at kindergarten in the morning, they cried a little and didn't want you to go, or just wanted you to stay a little longer; you couldn't stay because you were in a hurry to get to work, but when you left the kindergarten you were suffering from pangs of consciousness or guilty feelings, and the final image flashing in your mind is that your kid is "miserable" that you are leaving. A couple of hours later, you get a photo of the kid all smiling and happy during some activity, and your heart widens. You are relieved.

Second, it helps the kindergarten and schoolteachers. Some parents drive the kindergarten teacher crazy, calling incessantly to check that everything is okay, maybe calling the teacher in the evening, and asking for a "report" when they pick their kid up. With one photo sent during the day, the kindergarten teacher gets most of the parents to refrain from bugging them.

Third, it strengthens the relationship between the parent and their kids. If I see my child making a cake, looking for ants in the courtyard or dancing in costume, I have something to talk with them about in the afternoon. From experience I can tell you that my kids are surprised every time anew when I pick them up from kindergarten and from school, and I know what they have been up to and talk with them about it.

Who gets the credit (consciously or subconsciously) for the strengthening relationship with my kids and for my conversation with them after kindergarten? Of course, it's the teacher.

It also helps the teacher if there is a foul-up or a problem, because then everything they did for my kid will stand in their favor.

Fourth, it creates very strong viral marketing. If in the middle of your workday or in the middle of a meeting you receive a photo of your kid smiling during some activity. After your heart widens and you smile, what do you do next? You show the photos to everyone who is around you at that moment. Why? Once again, you are doing it (subconsciously) in order to market yourself. What you are saying about yourself or broadcasting to the other party? "I am a caring and involved parent," and "I may be here, but I'm thinking about my kid all the time."

Subconsciously, the viral marketing that the kindergarten teacher has created also causes you to talk more about the kindergarten or school—good things only of course.

A real revolution.

Correct use of technology, with the right messages, can, in one moment, make dozens, hundreds, thousands, tens of thousands of people into your active ambassadors, who are talking about you and marketing you at this very moment, without a commission, without any pay, without you having even asked, and without them even knowing.

WHAT DO SUCCESSFUL PEOPLE HIDE?

In this age of personal branding, when huge corporations as well as small- and medium-sized businesses place their owners, CEOs, and top executives at the forefront and brand them as experts in their field (we addressed this in Commandment 2), one of the most common mistakes they make is to present that person as Superman or Superwoman.

That is, they are mistaken when they present their owners, CEOs, or top executives as "geniuses," "prodigies," "brilliant individuals in their field," people who have the "magic touch," people who have a "unique talent," and so on. This sort of presentation seems like a great idea in the short term, and the media really loves such headlines, but the truth is that, in the long run, it is damaging from a marketing standpoint.

While there are some people who look up to such experts, most customers cannot really relate to them and cannot identify with them or with the corporation's service and product.

If that expert is Superman or Superwoman and has "superpowers," which I as a customer do not have and will never have, then I can always say, "Well, it's no wonder they're successful; they what it takes."

My argument is that in order to brand yourself correctly as an expert and as a quality service and product provider, you need to brand yourself as Bruce Wayne/ Batman. In other words, you should present yourself as a normal, regular person, who is just like your customers and who is successful not because of some "God-given gift" or because of "superpowers," but because of your diligence, perseverance, your basic talent which you have refined, your constant desire to take the initiative, your optimism and your capacity for hard work.

Successful people tend to emphasize their natural talents and to hide their acquired traits, namely, perseverance, diligence, a capacity for hard work and the ability to maximize their personal abilities.

The result: Their customers see only the success and then they become envious. They begin to harbor animosity, they gossip, they find excuses to justify themselves, or they just look up to these successful people—which is also not good in terms of marketing in the long run.

And they don't see the *lab hours*, that is, the hard work behind the scenes.

A few years ago, I came back from a conference in London and I was happy to discover that my previous book, *Persuade and Influence Any Audience*, had appeared in the latest weekend newspapers on the bestsellers list. I received a large number of supportive messages congratulating me, and many people asked me "how I did it." The book is good (I am not objective), it is written in an interesting way and it appeals to a wide audience; however, it made the bestsellers list not just because of my talent as a writer but also because of some very mundane actions that had been carried out beforehand, notably marketing moves to promote the book, such as pushing it in bookstores and on other platforms. I worked with a robust, skillful, and dedicated team, costing quite a bit of money, on which I had to expend considerable energy and maintenance tim, but which took the steps needed to promote the book. In the end the book sold very well.

Such success never comes without perseverance, diligence and initiative. This is difficult for customers to see, when they think you are Batman rather Bruce Wayne, an ordinary person who sets his goals and priorities, who works hard and properly to maximize his abilities, and who therefore arrives at extraordinary achievements.

So contrary to what your instinct might tell you,

you have no real reason in the long run for wanting your customers to admire you and think that you are "larger than life." Your marketing success will be far greater if they think highly of you and want to be just like you (and if they think and understand that they, too, can do it).

DO YOU FEEL LIKE YOU MARKET A LOT, BUT AREN'T SEEING ENOUGH RESULTS?

A lot of people experience frustrations with their internet marketing. They relate to their Facebook, LinkedIn, Twitter, YouTube and Instagram pages as a means and not as a goal. In other words, they expect these platforms to bring them customers and results; they market on these platforms and make a call to action at the end of (almost) every post, email or video clip, but, from their perspective, they aren't getting a lot of results—and sometimes none at all.

Let's say you put up a post on your company's business page, with top-quality content that you are very happy with. You've made a call to action at the end. You expected a lot of responses and even automatic purchases, and yet, there are no purchases. There are almost no responses.

The content that you counted on so much didn't create the expected buzz. The video clip that you thought would light up the network didn't become viral. Frustrating, a downer, annoying, and most of all, this result brings down your motivation to create more content. You think to yourself, "I'm writing content that is high quality and relevant and there aren't enough responses, views, clicks and impressions, so why continue?" And this is where doubt usually creeps in:"Perhaps the content I posted isn't good enough," "Perhaps this audience isn't relevant," "Perhaps the subject isn't interesting enough," or "Maybe this marketing method isn't working."

To all the doubters, the skeptics, the dejected, and the hopeful marketers, I have some good news for you.

First, marketing is a long-term process. Marketing is building up a community of customers who follow you over time and with whom you create a close relationship and trust.

Marketing isn't just one action, but a series of actions, over a variety of channels. There isn't just one platform that is the only one from which you can bring customers.

There is no one post, video clip or email that is strong enough, that only it will bring you customers over the next year. You have to create a lot of content, over time, over many different marketing channels and on several web platforms, in order to create consistent results over time.

Second, the key to marketing is persistence. In marketing, the saying goes, "one drop, another drop, and yet another drop, in the end creates a sea."

When you hit a rock a 100 times and on the 100th time it breaks or cracks, that doesn't happen only because of the 100th blow, but because of all the 99 blows that came previously.

To state that in internet terms, when you have suddenly created marketing content that sets the network alight and gets a lot of exposure, responses and sales, it isn't because of one specific piece of content, but primarily thanks to all the content you published previously, the vast experience you have gained, including errors and failures, and the community you have built around yourself over months and years.

Third, there is an interesting phenomenon that has been taking place over the past decade when it comes to marketing on social networks called *marketing in the dark*. We are active on social networks, we create content and relate only to tangible results, but we don't really see the deep currents that are created by our marketing.

Let's say that we published a video on Facebook or YouTube with high-quality content that ends with a call to action for your product, service or activity (as you've added a link under the video to register or make a purchase). The video gets 1,000 views within a few days. On the face of it, that's fantastic.

In practice, however, there are no purchases, there are hardly any clicks and there are very few responses. You are very disappointed, and rightly so, and you don't understand why you have a lot of views but no one has registered. But even at moments like this, and precisely at moments like this, it is important to remember that 1,000 people viewed your content, and that is fantastic!

You don't know who these people are, you don't know what key positions they hold in the business world, and you don't know how ripe they are to make a purchase or how much money they have.

You also don't currently know which of these people won't make a purchase now, but will come back to make a purchase in a few months as a result of the video or will approach you a week later by email and will offer you a job, a deal, a collaboration or an interview in the media.

As someone who throughout their entire adult life has appeared before audiences and filled halls (a Sisyphean task), I would not take figures like that lightly. A thousand views of a video, is, let's say, equivalent to filling five halls of two hundred people each! That's a lot of people; it isn't at all a figure to be taken for granted.

Without a doubt, if 1,000 people have just viewed your video, even if none of them has made a purchase, something good will come out of it for you down the line. Statistically, it is impossible that not one of those 1,000 people won't meet you somewhere in your professional future or buy something from you in the coming years.

It has happened to me countless times that customers have come to me (directly, via the Contact Us field on one of my websites, or through one of my employees), closed a deal and made a purchase and said to me something like, "About eight years ago I was at your conference, I have all your books at home," and "I read the guide to the internet that you wrote five years ago and it had a really big impact on me." In real time, five, eight and ten years ago, I didn't see results and I didn't know the people who viewed my content. But one day they grew ripe, and then deep currents swept them back and they returned as paying customers.

Persistence, remember? In the end it happens.

Don't despair, continue marketing and creating good, quality content that will make as many people as possible read what you write, watch what you create and become your active ambassadors, talking about you again and again. In that way, you will educate your market to buy from you—in the short and long term.

KEY ELEMENTS OF COMMANDMENT NO. 8

Make as many people as possible talk about you as much as possible.

√ People will talk about you and tell their friends about you if the information about you will create the impression that your ambassadors are interesting, sophisticated, talented individuals. Make them feel special whenever they mention you.

√ Give your clients tips that they will find useful and of practical value and which they can work with.

√ The job of business consultants is to teach their clients how to fish and not provide them with a supply of fish. Teach your clients how to conduct

themselves in their particular business context
and reveal to them the "secret" of every move they
must make.

✓ People need to know whom they can refer to you,
in order to be your active ambassadors.

✓ Use your customers, your reputation and
your community and turn them into tangible
financial assets.

✓ Personal attention beats conditions, and conditions
beat cash.

✓ Don't just give your audience knowledge, give
them an experience. Give them a chance to
participate and feel active.

✓ Give praise and credit as much as you can to as
many people as you can.

✓ In order to brand yourself correctly as an expert
and as a quality service and product provider, you
need to brand yourself as Batman, an ordinary
person (Bruce Wayne) who works hard and
properly to maximize his or her abilities, and who
therefore arrives at extraordinary achievements,
as opposed to Superman, who is imbued
with superpowers.

Provide personal attention, making people feel comfortable, even if they've just met you.

HOW CAN YOU REMEMBER THE NAMES OF PEOPLE YOU HAVEN'T MET OR SPOKEN WITH IN YEARS?

Personal attention is one of the keys to persuading people. According to studies, the most important thing to all of us is to feel important, honorable, memorable, respected, and/or like a celebrity.

When you meet people that you remember but they don't remember you, or when you know someone's name but they don't know yours, it's very disappointing and dampens your desire to do business with that person, to vote for them, to invest in their project or to buy something from them.

On the other hand, it's more difficult today than ever to remember names and faces, or to remember

telephone numbers. The digital age has harmed our memories because our computers and phones "remember" everything for us.

I want to share a few tips and tools for this to remember people.

A few years ago I gave a lecture at an accountants' convention. One of the participants, "Brian," came up to me after the lecture and inquired about my presenting to his firm. He gave me his business card and purchased a book at the booth. The lecture at his firm didn't work out in the end and we had no further contact apart from the fact that he is on my mailing list and once in a while reads my emails and posts. But I had done a little something extra. After conversation I had with him at the convention, I kept his name in the Contacts list on my phone, and also wrote down the context. I wrote "Brian accountants' convention lecture at his firm." A little long, not run-of-the-mill, takes a few seconds each time to input, requires a moment's concentration, but worth every moment.

Fast forward five years, the phone rings, and what I see on the screen is "Brian accountants' convention lecture at his firm." I press send and say, "Hey Brian. How are you doing?"

The response is always the same response: a few seconds of silence and (positive) shock and then with great enthusiasm, "Wow, I can't believe you remembered!" or "Well done for remembering!" or "You wrote me down in your Contacts? Nice."

What usually comes next is a second statement (a little more hesitant) that says, "You surely don't remember when we spoke," or "where we met" or "what we spoke about?"

And then I say, "Of course I remember. We spoke a few years ago at an accountants' convention. You came up to me after the lecture, purchased a book and we spoke about doing a lecture at your firm."

Even the most cynical of them simply "melts" and the response is really positive, usually along the lines of, "How did you remember!" "What a phenomenal memory, unbelievable!" "Absolutely incredible! You really are the king of the personal touch!"

It doesn't matter what the person wanted when they called - to ask a question, to consult with you, to book the lecture at his firm right now that he inquired about five years ago—the conversation starts from a completely different place! I have increased my chances that the conversation will end with a deal. As a result, Brian will become a far more passionate ambassador for me.

I simply like people, I care about people, and it is important to me to give people attention. That's why I devote attention to the small details that create big results. I also use technology like the Contacts list on my mobile phone in my favor. Because I made that little extra effort at the end of a conversation a few years ago and wrote down the context, as soon as I see the number, it doesn't matter how much time has gone by, I can still remember everything about that person.

WHY YOU MUSTN'T TURN YOUR CUSTOMERS INTO YOUR FRIENDS.

Your car breaks down at two in the morning on the way home from a night out. You are in the middle of nowhere, you are really upset, you call a good friend to come and help you start the car or change a tire or just to take you home. The friend turns up and saves the day.

And then, the next day, they send you an invoice in the mail.

Doesn't sound right, does it? You called up a good friend, your expectation was they would do it for free. In fact, there shouldn't be a conversation about money. After all, you would have done the same favor for them.

But if you were in that same situation and you called a pick-up truck to tow your car to the garage, or you called a pro to come and jump start your car, then it would be perfectly clear to you that you have to pay for that service. Not only will you have to pay for it, but you will probably pay a much higher price, because now it's a night-time rate. Not only do you have to pay, but you must pay immediately, not tomorrow and not next week.

In the first situation, it is clear to us that we don't have to pay—even if the friend is a professional. We would even be insulted and hurt if the friend wants money. In the second situation, it is obvious to us that we have to pay. We would even be surprised if we weren't charged then and there, and if we weren't charged a high price.

Money and friends don't go well together.

In Commandment 6, I spoke about how from a business perspective, you mustn't make your customers your friends. Let me tell you another secret: as a business, as a company, as experts or as tradespeople, you have to make money!

That's the significance of a business as opposed to a non-profit or a hobby.

That money comes from paying customers. So if those customers were your "friends," it would be difficult for them to pay you money, and it would be difficult for you to charge them money.

I heard two stories from customers I was giving consultancy and mentorship services to.

The first story I heard was from a lawyer who told me that he "no longer represents relatives" because he had done so a number of times and saw that he was investing his time and energy (and money) to represent them and to do the best job he could, as for any other client, and even giving them more hours than he usually would, and talking with them more than he would with a regular client. At first, he didn't take money to represent them, and then, when he did ask for money, he felt bad and he asked for a significantly lower fee than he would normally charge, and even told them that he would accept installments for a long time.

During this time his frustration and bitterness grew, and that of course had an impact on his relations with his family, which of course affected the time and attention he gave (and could give) to his other clients (and then his firm was hit and revenues declined). The most absurd thing was that his relatives weren't happy with the service either, they didn't appreciate the low rates he gave them and the high availability, and they even had complaints. From their side as well, relationships were affected.

The more a customer pays, the happier they are. They will appreciate you more, they will talk about you more, and will argue with you less. That may not sound logical and may be in contrast to all the theories that claim you should reduce prices to grow and bring in customers. But that's how it is in life and in business.

The second story is that of a financial planner who lived in a small community and some of his neighbors were also his customers. The financial planner is a serious guy, who is professional and experienced. He takes a fee for each consultancy session, just as he should and just as I taught him;if he gives value from the first moment, then the customer should be paying him from the first moment.

That works great with all his customers, except for his neighbors in the community.

Some of them have a habit of stopping him at church, on his morning run, or at the supermarket, and asking him a few professional questions. Some of them drop by his house for "coffee," and then sit with him and his wife and ask him professional questions.

On the face of it, he's just giving "friendly" service,

right? In fact, he is destroying his business, his reputation, his time management and his authority.

I'm all for being available, for personal attention, great service and pleasant conversation, but it is also important to place limits on customers, just like one places limits on children. A customer who pops by your house every time he needs to ask a question without paying is not a good customer for your business.

They don't pay, they take up your time, which comes at the expense of other customers, and worst of all, they don't appreciate you. They take it for granted, and even if they do recommend you to other people, they will tell them how to "milk" this professional for free, just like they did.

What's the conclusion from these two stories? First of all, customers shouldn't be your friends. It's important to have a good connection with your customers, but if you cross the boundaries and make them friends, the chances of your closing a deal with them or selling to them will decrease.

From your side, it isn't acceptable or doesn't feel right to ask for money from "friends," and from their side, if they ask for something from you, they will expect to receive it without paying, or paying a lot less.

It's also important to "place limits" on customers. Most of you make the mistake from time to time of giving "too much" service and making your customers your friends. That wastes your time, drains your energy, and comes at the expense of your other customers, and at the expense of your own personal time, and worst of all the customers may not even appreciate it.

That hurts your sales and your revenues.

Personal attention—yes. Friendship—no. It is important to put limits in the right places on your customers. It is important for you to define in advance a time for each conversation, meeting or presentation with customers and stick to it. It is important that you give customers the message that you have other customers and other issues to deal with, and it is important to maintain a certain distance from customers and to give them great service nonetheless.

Set clear limits between personal and business affairs. Either you consciously and in advance give free service to friends and family (I don't recommend it) or you treat them exactly like you would any other regular customer: They will pay the same price, and will discuss professional affairs with you only during work hours, will meet with you only at the office and will receive the same terms and conditions as other customers. That may sound difficult and unpleasant, but it is necessary for you, your business and your family and friends.

WHAT IS IT THAT YOUR CUSTOMERS WANT TO HEAR MOST? AND WHY YOU MUSTN'T SAY IT TO THEM UNDER ANY CIRCUMSTANCES.

With the development of the global experts industry, I noticed an interesting phenomenon connected to marketing promises that many mentors, coaches and therapists give to customers.

I read more and more marketing promises to customers in Internet sales pages of various products, in emails that I receive and in text messages sent to my mobile phone, which go something like, "Sign up for my activity, and your revenues will double!" or "Buy my Internet course and make millions!" Promises along these lines aren't good, and don't serve either side, not the customer, and not the consultant or coach.

What's the reason that people even make marketing promises like these to customers? Why do they promise quantifiable results or various figures, without even knowing the customer? Because most customers are basically looking for a magic wand—maximum results with minimum costs and minimum effort, time and energy. Entrepreneurs, managers and business owners are always looking for the magic formula that will let them make a lot of money without making an effort, to get great results without almost any investment, to be experts in a specific field without wasting years studying and gaining experience, and so on.

All of us would like to lose weight or be well-built, without having to do a lot of sport and only eating healthy food. We would all like to be very rich, without having to take risks or to invest money. We would all like to have loads of customers and for our phones to ring non-stop, but without having to market ourselves, to sell, to be active on social networks, and so on. That's why marketing promises exist.

And that's why, as I noted in Commandment 7, the words "secret" and "more" were the most popular words in advertising around the world, over the past decade. Commonly, we all want more, and all of us want to discover the secrets behind each success. But the fact that customers look for a magic wand and are willing to hear bombastic promises doesn't mean that we should be making them.

What's the difference between legitimate marketing promises and those that aren't? A legitimate marketing promise is one that is dependent on the person making the promise being able to stand behind it. A marketing promise that isn't legitimate is one that doesn't depend on the person making the promise, and deceives the customer, knowingly or not. For example, there is a fundamental difference between the marketing promise, "Come to my activity, and if you implement even a little of what you discover there, your revenues will increase," (it's potentially legitimate) and the slogan "Come to my activity and your revenues will double" (not legitimate).

The latter promises a quantifiable result that is out of my control. Whether revenues will increase with certainty or not, and if they will double definitively is not up to me. That is up to my customers, and in turn their customers.

You can't guarantee something like that. Worse, that doesn't serve the customer. Because customers have selective hearing; in other words, they hear from the seller what is convenient for them to hear. They will come to you because of your exaggerated promises, but then, in practice, the nature of your promises means you have transferred responsibility from them to yourself.

The customer attends your workshop, and says to you something like, "What's going on? The workshop is half over, I've come to several sessions, and my revenues haven't yet doubled!"

Of course they didn't double, and they didn't even increase, because the customer hasn't done anything outside of the classroom, right?

Your promise was, "Come to the workshop and your revenues will double." And that's why they came. You can offer marketing promises to a customer, but only those that you are prepared to be responsible for.

WHY IT'S IMPORTANT THAT YOUR CUSTOMERS AREN'T HUNGRY WHEN THEY MEET WITH YOU.

In Commandment 5, I wrote about my visit to Las Vegas (aka "Sin City"), which is also in my view "the city of the call to action."

Every tool in the book, every trick known to man in the field of sales, marketing and persuasion is used there, big time: from the slot machines that await arrivals in the airport as soon as they get off the plane to the "mazes" inside the casino (it's difficult to find your way out of the casino, and that's why we stay there longer) and the fact that you can change money for chips at any station to play or gamble, but to change the chips back to cash, you must walk a distance to special counters.

One of the things that really caught my attention is the fact that the casinos offer customers free food and drink. In some of the hotels they also give free drinks to companions sitting with the gamblers. On the face of it, that is a waste of money for the hotel, but that's small change compared with the hotel's real goal, that is, that people don't stop gambling for a moment. If you sit the Blackjack table, or the poker or roulette table, and an hour later you get hungry or thirsty, you'll get up from your table to go and buy something to eat. But if you are given free food and drinks, you will not leave your table; you will keep on gambling and spending money and you will even lose your sense of time and stay to gamble more and longer than you had planned.

Food and drink also cause something else: they make the customer calmer and happier. As noted in Commandment 3, when someone eats and drinks, they release endorphins in their brain (happiness hormones) and they feel much more relaxed, positive and optimistic. Exactly what the casino wants you to feel when you are gambling.

If you want to influence people, to persuade them, and to motivate them to action, you should create a situation where they feel comfortable, happy and more positive.

WHY DON'T WE REALLY LIKE TO CHANGE SUPPLIERS AND SERVICE PROVIDERS?

You are sitting in a restaurant, having just finished a good meal. You have time, and you are enjoying yourself. You feel like having a desert and a hot drink. You ask the server for a dessert menu, and he says, "Sorry, we don't have desserts." Since you would still like to have a dessert, you pay the bill, get up, leave and go to another restaurant in the area that does serve dessert.

That's a downer, right? Here's something that's even more of a drag. Let's say that restaurant does have dessert, and you don't know it. You even assume in advance that there are no desserts there, and don't even ask the server. So you pay, leave, drive, look for another place, when all that time you could have stayed seated, and enjoyed the rest of the meal—at the same place.

That is already a drag, not just for you, but for the restaurant, which sells desserts, but you didn't buy there from them, but rather from the competition.

I am reminded of this example again and again, when I advise clients who have a wide range of services and products, but their customers are only exposed to a small number of them.

Here are a few examples:

> » A law office that provides legal services in many fields, but their clients are familiar only with their real estate department. The clients don't know that the firm has a damages department,

an international department or a family law department, and so they turn to another law office when they need legal advice that isn't connected to real estate.

» Food chains that have an abundance of different food products, but customers buy specific products only each time, and aren't exposed at all to the array of products at the branch or the chain or to discounts or new products.

» Business consultancy companies that also provide financial consultancy or organizational consultancy, but their clients aren't aware of this. Then an absurd situation arises where a client, who trusts his business consultant, goes and looks for another organizational consultant when he needs one, instead of receiving organizational consultancy from the same consultant whom he already knows well and wis familiar with his company.

» Digital companies that do promotions and advertising on Facebook, Instagram and Google, among other platforms. But the customer who used them in the past for a specific Google campaign doesn't even know that they can also promote him on Facebook and goes to another company to do a Facebook campaign.

The point is clear: Everyone stumbles here—small business owners, medium-sized companies, and giant multinational firms. The thing is, if we go back to the example of the restaurant, that not only companies and businesses lose out from the fact that their regular customers, who have already purchased from them in the past, went and bought from someone else, when they could have stayed with them. The customers lose as well.

Even though we live in an age of abundance and plentiful opportunities, in the digital and technological age that makes the whole search-check-and-compare process a lot easier, and in an age where on the face of it, "the customer is king" and holds the power, customers don't really like changing suppliers. Most people don't really like to check, interview, compare and search. Most people want long-term relationships with their suppliers. Most people don't change their repair shop, accountant, cosmetician, dentist, insurance agents or family doctor that they know and love, even if a long time has passed.

It's difficult to find a supplier, service provider or consultant that we really trust. If we have found one we trust, it's even more difficult to switch to someone else. Something really dramatic has to occur for that to happen, or that we think that supplier is simply not relevant to what we need in addition to the service we're also receiving from him.

Most people would be happy if their supplier and service provider were a One Stop Shop. In other words, that their supplier provide them with everything they need in that field, without them having to make an effort and go to someone else; that

» the restaurant where I go and enjoy the main course, they will also have great desserts;
» the law office that handles my business affairs will also take care of me if I get divorced;
» my Facebook agency will also run a successful Google campaign for me; and
» my mortgage adviser will also give me advice on family financial planning.

If people are looking for a One Stop Shop, then be the one that provides them with an all-inclusive experience, even if that means you have to create a range of additional products and services in your field; even if it means telling your clients all the time about additional products and services that you have that they don't know about; even if that means educating your clients to turn to you with every problem or question they have in the field. And even if that means working with subcontractors or referring your clients to colleagues for a commission.

There are a lot of possible economic and business models in the field.

YOU WERE OFFERED SOMETHING TO DRINK AT A MEETING. WILL YOU ACCEPT?

You arrive at a business meeting with a client, colleague or vendor. You walk into their office and they ask you, "Would you like something to drink?" What will you answer? "Yes" or "No"?

It's a situation we all run into many times in life but never stop to think about the right answer. Research studies show that most people answer "No" to the offer of a drink. Not because they're not thirsty, but for other important, marketing-related reasons.

Here are some answers people give as to why they refuse such an offer:

"I don't feel comfortable being served."

"I want to be efficient and focused instead of wasting time on having coffee and chatting."

"It automatically puts me in an inferior position in the other person's eyes because I already need something."

The truth is that the right answer should be "Yes." Accept a beverage when it is offered. it's polite, it facilitates some background conversation with the other person, it's good for him or her to get used to doing something for you, and this way, you won't be thirsty and you can refresh yourself so you can be at your best during the meeting. People tend to think on a "macro" level about persuasion and sales, but their interpersonal communication usually succeeds or fails on petty matters. For example, don't turn down a person you don't know who has just offered you something.

The response or meaning is not always obvious. Sometimes it's in the other person's subconscious.

You answered "Yes," and now we move on to the next question: hot or cold? Studies show that most people who have answered the first question positively, ask for a cold drink like a glass of water when the real answer should be a hot drink!

Why? Because a hot drink "buys" you at least fifteen minutes of conversation until the coffee cools off a bit, and until you finish drinking it. If a person offers you a hot drink and you say, "No, it's okay, just a glass of water will be fine," you've actually (unintentionally) cut your meeting time short.

By the way, note that when you arrive for a meeting with someone who's impatient or wants the meeting to be brief, you won't even be offered a beverage at all, and, in extreme cases, you won't even be asked to take a seat!.

Thus, in order to ensure that the meeting will be meaningful and high-quality, you should accept an offer to drink something, you should ask for a hot drink and, most importantly, you should ask the person you're with to join you in having that cup of coffee or tea. It shows that person you care about his or her welfare and that will strengthen the trust and mutuality between you. These are small details that can yield wonderful results. So next time you're asked, "Would you like something to drink?" the ideal answer you should give is: "Yes, thank you, something hot, please, and I hope you will join me."

WHEN IS IT WRONG TO ANSWER YOUR CELL PHONE?

What do the two following situations have in common?

> **First situation:**
> You're in a lecture when all of a sudden, your cell phone rings. You answer, hiding your mouth, as if no one in the audience will hear you this way), walk through the entire row you were sitting in and exit the hall to continue the conversation. As soon as you finish, you return to the room.

> **Second situation:**
> You're with the kids at the park in the afternoon, when suddenly your cell phone rings. You respond, of course, and start talking to work colleagues or friends, even moving away from the kids a little, so they can't hear what you're talking about. All the while, your four-year-old is climbing on a playground installation that reads "Children under 7 with parental supervision only."

Do you know what these two situations have in common? You're not really present in either of them.

You're not really listening to the lecture, but, on the other hand, you're not really listening to your work colleague, even though you answered the call. You're not really giving your children quality time, and yet you're not really engaged in the conversation, because you're keeping an eye on the kids.

I see it around me all the time, as a speaker and a consultant, as well as a father. You may say, "What can I do?" "These are the constraints of the modern age." Okay, but imagine the following situation: You're in a meeting with an important client, who's about to close a huge deal with you and is explaining her business needs to you, when suddenly, your phone rings. You answer it and then you walk out of the room to take the call, only to return a few minutes later as if nothing had happened. Do you actually think your client won't mind that you got up and left in the middle of her presentation? That's how your kids feel when you answer every call on your cell phone while "spending quality time" with them, even if they don't say so explicitly. And that's how the lecturer felt now when you shut him out, completely ignoring the other people in the room who were listening to him.

Be present!

In every situation you're in—a conversation, a meeting, a lecture, time with family—be fully attentive to the person before you, to what is happening, and enjoy the situation. If the lecture bores you, then just leave and don't come back.

If it's important for you to be at work, stay at work. Don't try to be at work and at the playground; it simply won't work (you're only human) and you'll only miss out on things and fail to motivate people.

WHY DID THE HOTEL HOUSEKEEPER SMILE AT ME?

In May of 2013, I was in the United States with a colleague as part of some professional training. After staying in a certain hotel for a few days, we vacated our room and were on the way to the hotel lobby to check out, on our way to our next destination. As we were walking down the hall with our luggage, we saw a housekeeper who was cleaning another room on the same floor.

She smiled at us and said, "See you again. Enjoy your trip and thank you for staying with us!" We smiled back, thanked her too and complimented the hotel.

For the next few hours, her smile and words echoed in my head, and I couldn't stop thinking, "What excellent service that hotel has!"

It was part of a large chain of hotels, the housekeeper had no direct contact with us, we did not come to her with any type of request, we had just happened to see her and still she smiled, wished us well and expressed her gratitude.

What she said might sound to you like a small and insignificant sentence, but here is what was hugely important about it: (1) she made us leave the hotel smiling, with a better buying experience as customers; (2)

she showed us that even a junior-level employee in the system feels responsible for taking care of the hotel's guests; and (3) she empowered herself. The moment she smiled at us, we smiled back at her, we talked to her and we paid attention to her.

Now be honest, how many times have you walked past junior-level service providers anywhere—in a restaurant, a movie theater, an event venue, an airport—and they were just "invisible" to you? It happens to almost all of us, and not because we're mean. We just don't "see" them.

But by addressing us, that chambermaid first of all made us see her! And that was good for her, too: Her importance and value increased in our eyes, but also, and mainly, in her own eyes.

In general, every time I'm in the United States, I'm pleasantly surprised with the level of service demonstrated by the most junior level hotel, restaurant and function hall staff members. You expect these workers to do their job quietly and efficiently and not take too much of an interest in the guests. Businesses in the United States place service above everything else, and all service providers, even those at the most junior level usually see their job as a profession and take pride in it.

Studies have shown that in the U.S., a very high percentage of junior-level service providers hold on to their job for many years and treat it as a profession for all intents and purposes. In Europe too, and especially in countries such as Italy and Spain, you can find a similar phenomenon (for example, most waiters in Europe are over forty years old). When you consider your job to be a profession for all intents and purposes, you treat what you do with respect, and you see yourself as part of the organization in the long term.

Even if you're just starting out, treat every step and position you hold on your way to success as your most important job at that moment, consider every stage you go through in life to be critical to your success even if you're already looking forward to your next role, and make every person you come in contact with, in any context, feel good and empowered.

HOW WAS BILL CLINTON ELECTED PRESIDENT OF THE UNITED STATES?

Bill Clinton, the former President of the United States, had a special gift.

His story begins in the 1960s, when, as a sixteen-year-old high school student, he visited the White House, met with the President of the United States at the time, John Fitzgerald Kennedy. He decided there and then that he wanted to be the President of the United States one day.

In the following decades, he prepared an index card for each person that he met, as part of his political life and in general. On this index card, he would write who the person was, his spouse's name, what he did for a living, where he knew him from, and so on. In this way, wooden boxes accumulated on his desk, containing index cards organized in alphabetical order.

In the early 1990s, when he was running for the presidency, he followed a regular habit: Before every election meeting, he would go over the index cards with his team and see whom he was about to meet there.

Then, at the meeting in front of everyone, when he saw one of his political supporters, he'd casually say something like, "Hey George! How are you? How's your wife Suzie? And how was fishing this year?" How did he know all these details, even though he hadn't seen George in years? It was all written on the index card. It may sound like a completely commonplace and banal habit, but the effect it had every time on George or John or Mary or Betty, was astounding.

Beyond the fact that these people would be very moved by having been addressed personally by Bill Clinton (creation of an emotional experience) and would tell everyone they knew the next day about Clinton's gesture (viral marketing) they would also do another "little" thing—they would vote for Clinton in the upcoming elections!

And they would also drive other people to vote for Clinton in those elections.

This is called motivating people to act. Bill Clinton excelled at it.

WHY IS IT IMPORTANT THAT YOU WRITE AND SPEAK CLEARLY WHEN COMMUNICATING?

A few years ago, I gave a lecture at a big conference, in which the audience was made up mostly of life coaches. I usually arrive early and hear the lecture before mine and stay to hear the one afterward and that's what I did this time as well. The speaker after me spoke about a certain matter, and then suddenly gave an example and asked the audience a question, "Let's say you are with your kid in the park, he is four years old and he falls, takes a knock, starts crying. What does he need from you most right now?"

The audience started to shout out enthusiastically answers like "Containment!" "Empowerment!" "Recognition!" The lecturer seemed surprised and stunned. (It seemed like only at the moment did he realize that he had an audience of coaches.) With a gesture of his hands, he quieted them down and said to them, "Hang on guys, I don't think you understood. we're talking about a four-year-old kid! He doesn't know what empowerment and containment are. All he needs from you right now is contact—a hug! And a kiss!"

Now it was the audience's turn to be surprised and stunned.

When I looked at the situation from the sidelines, amused, I again understood the reason why many people don't succeed in persuading their environment that they are right, even if they are right, or, they don't succeed in selling to clients their products and services, even if these products and services are excellent and suitable for the customer.

They talk or write in a language that is too high-brow with a lot of professional words that many people don't understand.

The other side perceives that as arrogance or contempt or maybe even detachment from reality (choose your own feeling here). All of us, no matter our age, education or experience, want to be spoken to clearly, in day-to-day language, in a simple manner that we don't have to make an effort to understand and not in highbrow professional language, especially if you belong to another profession. Most of us are swamped all day in professional material, endless articles and books in our fields, and are exposed to an enormous amount of information. Sometimes, with so much information and insights, we complicate our messages, and aren't able to explain to someone else in simple language what it is we do, what they need, why our opinion is right, what solution we are offering, and so on. We try to be sophisticated and to seem smart, and end up leaving the audience or customer floundering. I talked about this extensively in Commandment 7 in the context of marketing writing, and I explained why you should "write like you speak."

When the coaches were asked an innocent question at the professional conference they were attending, they started to shoot out answers with the professional tools they'd previously learned. And the speaker who had come from a different field was surprised and didn't anticipate those answers. They were trying so hard to be sophisticated that they didn't give the simple answer that begged to be given.

You need to make sure you're on the same page as the people you're communicating with. You need to be clear, but you also need to be sure you're starting from the same place.

HOW TO GET CUSTOMERS (AND PEOPLE IN GENERAL) TO SMILE AND TO ALWAYS FEEL GOOD AROUND YOU.

One of the most important things in connecting with people is to use positive and empowering language. The words we use have enormous influence on the subconscious of the other party of the conversation whether it be a customer, supplier, employee, colleague, friend, child, relative. We aren't aware of it (that's why it's called subconscious), but the way we choose our words and our way of speaking, along with our tone and expression, is a critical part of the process of influence and persuasion.

One of my biggest models of inspiration when it comes to this is Disney. I wrote in Commandment 6 about how Disney is an extremely profitable and successful company, even though the field it operates in, amusement parks, is a very dangerous field from a business point of view, and most parks in the world either close or go bankrupt. Disney has a lot of secrets and reasons for its long-term success. One of the main reasons is the communications of all park workers, without exception, with customers and among themselves.

The Disney Company has made experience and joy its unspoken motto: to create for the customer a strong positive experience at its parks, but more than anything, a happy experience. It wants people to come to its parks with a smile, and to leave at the end of the day with a smile.

As part of this vision, Disney has developed its own language—what I call the Language of Disney. The aim of this jargon, which all employees are instructed to use, is to create a positive language and positive thinking among employees and guests.

Here are a few examples:

» Employees are called Cast Members.
» Customers are called guests.
» Visitor groups are called Audience.
» The uniforms that employees wear are called Costumes.
» The price lists at shops and kiosks are presented as Investments.

And there are dozens of other examples. Everything to create a positive and empowering atmosphere, both for employees and guests.

"What does it matter what words you use?" you may be thinking. "How much of a difference can it make?" Huge! It has significance in our subconscious and is therefore stronger than our conscious mind.

Let's take for example a very common phrase, "no problem." Imagine that you are in a shop, a park, a restaurant or in your office, and a customer comes up to you and asks, "Can you get me this in that size?" or "Can I get extra ketchup?" or "Could you please explain something to me?" And without even thinking, you say, "no problem."

Why should that be a problem? Where's the problem here?

Why plant in the customer's mind that a trivial and innocent request they made might be construed as a "problem"?

At Disney that wouldn't happen. If you asked for something from one of the park employees, the answer would be, "My pleasure" or "Absolutely" not, "No problem!" And if there was something they weren't sure about, the answer wouldn't be, "I don't know," rather "Let me find out for you!" Everything is in the positive and with a smile. The most important thing at Disney is that the customers are always happy. When a customer asks an employee, "Excuse me, what time does the park close?" the employees are instructed to reply, "The park is open until eight thirty."

Did you notice the positive terminology? Not when the park closes, but when it is open until. A significant difference in the customer experience, a significant differentiation in the Disney park experience as compared to other amusement parks.

You can give customers bad news—there is a delay, they need to wait, the inventory has run out—and they will take it well and in a relatively calm manner if you make sure to pay attention to the little things that create big results such as a smile, patience, a compliment, praise, empowerment, and personal attention.

A more satisfied customer is

» a customer that buys more;
» visit you more often;
» argue less;
» tell more people about you;
» will be a good ambassador for you; and
» do viral marketing for you more efficiently that any salesperson you'll employ.

HOW CAN YOU PREVENT YOUR CUSTOMERS FROM BEING DISAPPOINTED IN YOU?

Let's assume that you are parents. You want to spoil your kids, and you give them chocolate every day. Every day, they get chocolate from you. One day, you decide that this week they've had too much chocolate and you tell them, "No chocolate today."

What happens?

From that moment the kids go wild, get annoyed, cry, are angry and/or shout. They think and perhaps even tell you that you are the worst parents in the world, and they are going to have you arrested.

What's going on here? You spoiled them all the time, and for once you simply decided not to. What happened is that the kids got used to things being too good, and started to take chocolate for granted and as part of their daily routine. And then, one time, they didn't get chocolate, and that was all that was needed for them to take it hard, and "forget" all the treats they got all the time—which they didn't appreciate enough, because they took it for granted. So now you are "guilty of neglect and abuse.

Imagine another parental situation. Your kids don't get chocolate all week, and then, once or twice a week, you spoil them with a piece of chocolate.

What happens now when you give them chocolate? You're the best parents in the world. You are champions, even though in fact you gave the kids far less chocolate than in the first scenario.

We appreciate it when they get something that is extraordinary or rare and will always look down at, or appreciate less, the things that come easily, without any effort, or what we receive all the time.

That's true for children, and that's true for customers as well. If you made a mistake and you promised to be available to provide a service to a customer 24/7, that customer will take advantage of that and call you regularly throughout the day, including late at night and weekends. You will bite your lip—you promised!—and each time the customer calls, you'll give up on your leisure time, or your time with your family. You'll give the customer the best service even at hours when none of your competitors are working and wouldn't even pick up the phone.

And then, one time, you are at a family event, the customer calls and you don't get back to them the same day. You call them the next day, first thing in the and what does the customer say? "Where were you yesterday?" "Why didn't you answer?" The customer is angry with you and complains because you have made them used to too much good and you haven't set them limits for them. You gave them chocolate all the time.

Not only does the customer not appreciate the great service you give them, but they are also disappointed in you after the one and only time that you didn't get back to them immediately.

Now let's say that you didn't commit to the customer to be available all the time. You and the customer assume that communication will be during standard work hours. One time the customer has a problem, needs urgent advice, some professional treatment or technical assistance, and "dares" to call you late at night or at the weekend. You answer, give them fast and efficient service and solve their problem.

What does the customer think of you now? That you are a king. World championship service. They will thank you ten times over and will tell others about you a hundred times. You made them feel special and gave them a really good customer experience. You set clear limits, but in their moment of distress you bent the rules in their favor. They don't take it for granted that you will answer at that time of night, and even less so that you will really take care of them at those hours.

You want your customers to appreciate you, to get a "wow" feeling! Give them perks, services or discounts beyond what you initially promised them, and they will worship you.

Want your customers to be disappointed in you? Promise them too much, and then try just once not to live up to your word.

KEY ELEMENTS OF COMMANDMENT NO. 9

Provide personal attention and make people feel comfortable with you.

✓ Keep the details of everyone you talk and meet with, and write down the context.

✓ Don't make customers your friends. It's important to place limits on customers in the right way.

✓ It is permissible to make marketing promises to customers, verbally and in writing, but only when these are in your field of responsibility, when you have control of them, and you can stand behind them.

✓ When people eat and drink, they feel much more relaxed, optimistic and positive.

✓ Most people want long-term relationships with their suppliers and want them to be a One Stop Shop—give them the all-inclusive experience.

✓ You should accept a drink when it is offered, and ask the person you're with to join you in having that cup of coffee or tea.

✓ In every situation you're in be fully attentive to the person before you.

✓ Consider your job to be a profession for all intents and purposes.

✓ We all want to be spoken to clearly, in day-to-day language, in a simple fashion, so we don't have to make an effort to understand.

✓ Little things that create big results: a smile, patients, compliments, praise, empowerment and personal attention.

✓ Everyone appreciates getting something extraordinary or rare, and will look down on (or appreciate less) the things that come easily to them, without any effort, or that they receive all the time.

COMMANDMENT NO. 10

Create confidence and trust in you, even if people don't know you.

WHAT DO YOU DO WHEN YOU ARE STARTING SOMETHING NEW WITHOUT ANY PREVIOUS EXPERIENCE, AND YOU WANT TO SUCCEED?

One of the biggest marketing challenges for both self-employed and salaried employees is to market a new product or service, or to do something that is different than what you have done before. Perhaps you have started a new managerial role and need to establish authority and professionalism in the eyes of employees who do not know you. Perhaps you have decided to become independent at the age of forty-five after twenty years of working as a salaried employee, and all of a sudden, you need to market yourself and tell people about yourself, without having the backing of a large company that you represent. Perhaps you are marketing

a new product that your company is launching, or you are in a new field that your company has entered, and so on.

The big obstacle here is the fact that you see yourself as "new" and "inexperienced" in the field, and then your "inner narrative" starts to work on you:

"Who will want my new product?" "Am I really worth it?"

"Will the new employees and customers respect me?"

"After all, I don't yet have experience in the field or any customers in the field!"

"The new product hasn't even sold anything yet!"

If you see yourself as "new," and that's the message you put out to the world, the market will also see you as new, and won't want to gamble on you.

Customers are attracted to proven success and people are, by nature, risk-averse, so they will always prefer what they are familiar with and trust in—or what they see as familiar and trustworthy—over taking a risk and buying a new product or service before everyone else.

What do you do?

In this chapter I talk about a powerful marketing tool: *social proof*.

What this refers to is proof that you bring about things you have already done and achieved, that "testify" about you objectively, including:

» your resume and previous jobs you worked in;

» your degrees and your formal and informal education;
» your past achievements, and recommendations written about you by previous customers and employers;
» the honors you received and the awards you won;
» your international experience or your specific specialization; and
» high-profile past customers or customers that are well-known in the field.

You have to understand that when you take on a new role or launch a new product, you are not really starting from scratch. You can always take credit for your previous successes and the previous roles you have carried out. You can tell people about your previous successes and roles, and you can bring proof and evidence such as letters of recommendation, photos, articles written about you, and the number of views for a video that you produced.

For example, you see a commercial for a new movie that has hit theaters, or you watch a trailer for the movie. The movie is new, it only just hit theaters, you have no idea if it is good or not and you don't want to take a risk, to "waste" a night out and be disappointed. The following sentence is written in to the commercial: "From the producers who brought you *Unforgiven*" or, "From the three-time Oscar-winning director Ang Lee."

Why does that information matter? Because now you say to yourself, "If it's the same director and I really liked *Unforgiven*, then for sure, I'm really going to like the new movie, too." Or, "I don't know the director, but if he's already won three Oscars, that's a sign that he's good."

That's the way it works. You will tend to choose this film, talk about it and value the director more.

Each of you has many social proofs—achievements and stations that you have gone through in life—that will definitely help you succeed at your next stop. Most of you don't take advantage of them and don't tell people about your previous successes. From a marketing standpoint, that's like coming to a gunfight with a knife.

You need to be armed with objective information about yourself, such as your resumé, academic degrees, seniority, specific training, customer testimonials, success stories, awards, military rank, famous people in the field you have worked with, and more, and out of all that to present the relevant information when you market yourself as part of a presentation, job interview, lecture or sales meeting.

What if you are only eighteen and have almost no social proof? Everyone has social proofs, from every age and every stage of life. You just use the information you have up to that moment. For example, when a high school graduate wants to get a place at a law school, what data should they display? Their high school grades and SAT score. In sophomore or junior year, they start to look for an internship and interview at law offices. What should they show now? Grades from the first two years at college. That's what the law firm is interested in. The high school grades are no longer relevant. Then go up another stage. The student has graduated law school, has done an internship, passed the bar exam with flying colors, and now is looking for a job as a salaried attorney at a law office. The proof then becomes a written opinion of them from their internship, and grades on the bar exam. At that point, law school grades are already less significant.

At every stage of life, you should present information about yourself relevant to the position or offer or client based on your achievements so far.

Social proof is like marketing ammunition; you need to have evidence from each stage and to come to meetings "armed," using whatever is appropriate for each stage of life and each position.

WHO'S THE FIRST PERSON TO TIP THE BARTENDER EVERY NIGHT?

Some bars have tip jar, placed in a visible spot on the counter, and you are expected to throw a few dollars in it after you've been served or have bought a drink, even if it's not explicitly stated. The jar is never empty.

Who was the first person to put money in the jar each night? The bartender. As soon as the bartenders place the jar on the counter, they pull out a few dollars from their pocket and place them in the jar.

This is where social proof comes in. The principle behind social proof is that people believe if others do something, they should and can do it too. The more people do that thing, the more it convinces others to do it. If the jar was empty when the evening started, customers would be more reluctant to tip the bartender. But if there's already money in the jar, even if I appear to be the first customer of the night, I'll gladly put some money in the jar.

Social proof is a very persuasive tool. If you want your clients to be more persuadable, present them with actions and examples of other clients.

THERE ARE TWO RESTAURANTS, ONE IS FULL AND THE OTHER IS EMPTY. YOU ARE STARVING. WHERE WILL YOU GO TO EAT?

In April 2014, I was in Greece with my wife. We arrived at our destination and debated as to which of two restaurants located next door to each other we should patronize that evening.

One of them was full of people, with a long line outside and a waiting list that was being deftly handled by a hostess; the other was almost totally empty. And we were "starving."

Should be go to the empty restaurant, where they would welcome us with open arms and the food would be served in a matter of minutes? Or the full one, where we would have to wait outside for about fifteen minutes, and, after entering the restaurant, wait a long time for the waiter or waitress to come to our table and then for the food to be served?

We were tempted to go to the empty restaurant. We were hungry, and it would make abundant sense to choose the place where we would be served the fastest. But this is where this simple and brilliant marketing principle—social proof—kicks into action. If many people around us think something, we will tend to think the same thing.

When we see a restaurant that is full, with a line of people waiting outside, we assume that, if so many people are eating inside and waiting outside, this must be a good restaurant and that it is worth waiting for and standing in line in order to eat there. When we see an empty restaurant, we assume that it is simply not a good restaurant.

Although this might be totally flawed logic, this thought crops up in our subconscious and it causes us to make various business, consumer and marketing decisions each and every day.

What did we do? We waited and went to eat at the full restaurant. And that's probably also what you would have done.

Do you want customers to prefer you over others and do you want people to talk about you more than they talk about others? Then you must create some social evidence about yourself and/or your business.

HOW TO INCREASE YOUR CHANCES OF RAISING MONEY FROM INVESTORS FOR YOUR STARTUP.

A key principle in economics is called *rational indifference,* that is, people make cost-versus-benefit considerations for themselves in every situation, and sometimes choose to be indifferent, to not intervene or make an effort to change a situation—even if they are harmed by or dissatisfied with that situation.

If tomorrow morning, for example, all the banks in a particular country were to decide to raise their fees by 1 percent and the news is published in the media and all bank customers know about it, the likelihood is that the majority of bank customers, even though they will grumble and complain when hearing the news, will do absolutely nothing. Being disturbed by the move was not enough to motivate them to action.

Although they have been harmed, the damage is minor, and it's not worth it for them on a cost-benefit calculation to fight their bank, sign petitions, go out and protest, cancel their account and look for alternatives, and so on. Consumers typically—subconsciously and without any coordination—wait for others to express their disapproval and change the situation, but in practice everyone waits for someone else, and nobody does anything.

Since none of the consumers will do anything, each for their own reasons, in practice, the banks will manage to make a move that will increase their profits by hundreds of millions of dollars all at once, without lifting a finger, and at the same time causing harm to the public. (Which is, by the way, the reason that the option exists to file a class action suit that will protect the rights of the "indifferent" majority.)

That's our economics and law lesson, over for today, now let's get down to business.

How does rational indifference impact marketing and persuasion?

If I want to convince a group of people, I have to give each of them a sense that all the others have already signed on and are waiting just for them, or that there is something going down here that is definitely going to work out and I am offering each and every one of them an opportunity to be a part of it.

That's the only way to succeed.

Let's say I have a start-up and I need to raise money from investors. I need a million dollars and meet with 1ten investors, with the aim of raising $100,000 from each of them. If I tell each of them separately something like "After our meeting, I am meeting with another nine investors and asking each of them for $100,000 to get it off the ground," what will happen?

Each of them—separately, without any coordination—will tell me: "No problem. I'd be happy to invest. When you have nine signed agreements with all the other nine investors, come back to me and I'll give you the money." No one will want to be the first to invest before the others in order not to risk their money—rational indifference. The start-up won't manage to raise money to get off the ground.

However, the picture changes if I show the venture to each investor individually and tell them things are perceived as certain and safe: "The launch is planned for six months from now. We did a feasibility study and it has great market potential. If you invest $100,000, you'll hold 10 percent of the company, and I am offering you the chance to be a part of this success." In this scenario, I sketched it as something that is not dependent on others, and that person's only consideration should be, does he want to be a part of the venture?

HOW TO GAIN THE ATTENTION OF PEOPLE WHO ARE MORE SENIOR AND FAMOUS THAN YOU.

In his excellent 2002 book, *Make Your Own Luck: Success Stories You Won't Learn in Business School*, Peter Morgan Kash, one of the top technologies and venture capitalists in the United States, recalls an incident that happened to him while he was promoting the interests of pharmaceutical companies.[2]

Kash arrived at a prestigious fundraising event, along with several dozen businessmen. As part of the event they were scheduled to meet with then California Governor Arnold Schwarzenegger. The dozens of business professionals who were there, along with a few journalists, were waiting to talk to Schwarzenegger.

---

2   Peter Morgan Kash, *Make Your Own Luck: Success Stories You Won't Learn in Business School* (Prentice Hall, 2002)

As soon as the governor entered the room, dozens of people surrounded him in an attempt to get a few seconds of his time.

Kash realized he had no chance of getting the governor's attention, and even if he did, it would only be for a few seconds. That would be just like everyone else—not too effective. He saw that Schwarzenegger had walked into the room with his wife, Maria Shriver. Since everyone was focused on trying to speak with Schwarzenegger, no one paid any attention to Shriver and no one spoke with her; she was standing by quietly.

Kash went up to her, started speaking to her at a personal level, listened to her, and she seemed pleasantly surprised by the attention. She smiled and spoke to him openly and at ease. Kash saw that Schwarzenegger, even though he was surrounded by dozens of people, was looking at them out of the corner of his eye, perhaps wondering, "Who is this guy talking to my wife for such a long time?"

A few minutes later Schwarzenegger went up to them, smiled at Kash and asked his wife, "So Maria, who is this guy you've been talking to for so long?" And she replied, "This is Peter Kash. You have to get to know him!" The conversation developed, and Peter Kash got what he wanted, that is, the maximum possible time with the governor, and an opportunity to raise the issue he wanted to talk about.

This story illustrates some key principles of networking, persuasion, self-presentation and call to action: Out-of-the-box thinking and creativity, initiative, and, most importantly, social proof. As soon as Schwarzenegger came up to them, his wife introduced Kash, and he didn't have to introduce himself. That is far more effective and powerful than the alternative.

In the listener's subconscious, the message resonates much more powerfully, and the chances of successful persuasion are much higher, when the issue is presented by someone who is not an interested party, and not the stakeholder.

WHY IT'S IMPORTANT TO TELL YOUR CUSTOMERS ABOUT YOUR SPORTING ACTIVITIES.

Another powerful social proof for the purpose of self-marketing and your own personal branding, is sporting activities. If you take part in a sport on a regular basis, then it's important that you tell your customers about it. Whether it's an intensive or "extreme" activity such as Ironman, running in marathons or half marathons, competing in professional competitions, or whether it's "just" going out regularly for a run, yoga, swimming laps, why is it important to tell your customers about it?

First of all, if the clients themselves train in a sport or like sports, it's a great icebreaker to start a conversation, or to connect with the customers through common hobbies or common interests. People like to do business with people who have something in common with them.

But beyond creating chemistry, there is of course also social proof because when you tell people during conversations, meetings and lectures (and sometimes in your marketing material) that you do sports regularly, what do you broadcast to the other side?

That you are someone who perseveres. You do things consistently. You don't lose patience, and you don't lose interest quickly. You are dynamic and have high energy. You are a winner. You aren't a quitter. You do things that challenge you. You are healthy. You will be around for a long time. You will serve your customer for many more years.

Obviously not all of that applies to everyone. Not everyone who does sports is dynamic, energetic, and consistently a winner. Sports aren't a guarantee of a long life, but that is what your customer is feeling about you at that moment. The customer is saying to themselves subconsciously, "If you are a winner, you persevere and are energetic in sports, then those are probably characteristics you will bring to the service you give me! So I should pick this guy and not someone else."

Sporting activities, like certain other extracurricular activities that suggest you take pride in yourself and your community, are in fact very much related to your business and career if you take advantage of them properly. The problem is that most people don't use these assets and don't translate them into successes. They may not understand that it's important, don't feel comfortable doing it, or don't want to share their private lives with their customers because they don't want to be seen as arrogant. And for many more reasons. But you don't want to be "most people." You want to use all your marketing ammunition and to provide the greatest possible information about yourself (all true of course), in order to increase your chances of success in life, career and business.

HOW VOLUNTEERING INCREASES YOUR REVENUES.

Let's say you donate your time through participation in a non-profit, helping to hand out food to the homeless, sporting activities with a population in need, or shifts at a hot line for at-risk youth. Or it could also be for things like active reserve service late in life, being part of leadership of the parent's association at your kids' school, and more.

It is important from a marketing perspective to tell your customers about this. They need to read about this on your website and in your marketing materials, and/or hear about it during calls or meetings with you. Social activities such as volunteering can greatly increase the likelihood that customers will buy from you, that people will appreciate you and will see you as being reliable, and that your branding will strengthen. In fact, social activities and volunteering are some of the strongest social proofs that exist and the most effective from a marketing perspective.

When you communicate that you are volunteering

and contributing to the community, the message you are broadcasting to the other party of the conversation is that you have values. You are "good people." You are reliable. You are dedicated. You think about others. The other party thinks to themself, "If they volunteer, the chances of them cheating me or giving me incorrect data are lower." The likelihood the customer will trust you with their money and dreams.

Next, when you tell your customers about your social activities/volunteering, what are you transmitting to them from an economic-financial perspective? That you have time and money. That you make a good living. Again, it may not be true. But that's the vibe the other party to the conversation will pick up from you. A business that is fighting for survival won't have the money to donate to others. A large company that is having a hard time paying its employees and making payments to suppliers can't afford to let employees go out for a day to volunteer to paint homes with Habitats for Humanity.

In the Hierarchy of Needs that came psychologist Abraham Maslow's work, there are five levels or stages of universal human needs. The lowest level is basic physical needs. Someone who is starving, and all that is important to them is to bring home food for their kids at the end of the day, is preoccupied with survival. The highest level of the Hierarchy of Needs on the other hand is self-actualization. Social and volunteer activities attract people at this level. When you say you are volunteering and contributing your time and money to others, you are conveying to customers that you have enough of your own. "If that's the case," the customer thinks to themself, "then he is probably good at what he does." The chance of the customer closing a deal with you of all people increases significantly.

WHAT SHOULD YOU PLACE IN THE BACKGROUND WHEN FILMING VIDEO, TAKING PHOTOS FOR FACEBOOK, OR SHOOTING PR PHOTOS?

One of the topics I researched in my PhD in law was how judges establish professional authority and convince the parties in a trial, along with public opinion, that they are right and that their ruling is correct. At the time it was considered a revolutionary topic to write about, and while still a student, I was sent on behalf of the university to lecture about it at international academic conferences. The "product" that the court system actually markets to us is called "public trust in the justice system." Without public trust, the system collapses.

A courtroom is built just like a theater, with a stage and reserved seats, and the rules of the game are clearly set out. When you enter the courtroom, you are actually entering a different set of rules from the ones you were used to just a moment ago in the "outside world." When the judge enters, everyone stands. The judge then sits center stage. What is particularly interesting is that in every courtroom, the state emblem and the state flag hang behind where the judge is seated. On the face of it, an unimportant detail that almost no one in the audience noticed. In fact, it is very important. That is what awards professional authority to that judge. Now, sitting in the courtroom and as the person conducting the proceedings, the is no longer my neighbor or someone I once played golf with. The judge is a representative of the state, who is representing it right now against me, and I am far more likely to comply with their decisions.

In the marketing arena, what's in the background is equally important. A picture, as we know, is worth a thousand words, and a video is worth a thousand pictures. What many people and businesses aren't careful about when they take publicity shots, upload photos to social networks, or take videos is what is behind their subject. You have to pay attention not only to the messages you broadcast in the video, not just to the location you pick to shoot the photos or video, but also what is behind or next to the subject while you are filming. That has a big impact on the subconscious of the viewers, builds your brand and authority and is itself part of the process of persuasion.

In 2014, I was at the World Cup in Brazil, the World Cup being the biggest sporting event in the world. What I noticed as soon as I landed in Rio de Janeiro, were the sponsors. The biggest sponsor was Coca-Cola. That might sound logical to you because they are a massive and profitable company, but just to remind you, we're talking about a sporting event—a symbol of health. By the way, the second largest sponsor at that world cup was McDonald's. Two products that are about as far away from health as you could imagine. That's precisely why these companies chose to provide sponsorship: They wanted to draw a connection between their products and health.

One image that I particularly remember from back then is of Cristiano Ronaldo, one of the greatest soccer players of all time, giving an interview at a press conference, a day before his team, Portugal, was due to play at the World Cup. Behind him, and in front of him—yes, you guessed right—was a row of bottles of Coca-Cola and Coke Zero. Anyone familiar with the biography of this legendary player knows that he doesn't touch those things and treats his body like a temple. In his personal life, he would never drink a Coke, but the image is stronger than everything, and when Ronaldo has his photo taken with bottles of Coca-Cola line up behind him and in front of him, what is branded in your consciousness is that Coca-Cola equals health, and if you want to look like that, or to be as successful, drink Coke.

Consciously, you know this is not accurate, or at least you doubt it, but what has a stronger pull in the brain, the conscious or the subconscious? What has more of an impact on our habits and actions? Obviously, the subconscious is powerful.

Pay attention to the small details and accessories that participate in these games called video shoots, publicity shots, live broadcasts, putting up a post or uploading a story.

Do you want to look **intelligent**?
Have your photo taken with a library of
"serious" books (biographies, business books,
etc.) lined up behind you.

Do you want to look **important, popular, a celebrity**?
Have your picture taken with people who
admire you—a large audience, your staff,
political activists, supporters out on the street.

Do you want to look **cool**?
Have your photo taken next to cool things
like surfboards or a painting.

Do you want to look **patriotic**?
Have your photo taken next to the national
flag or state symbols, or a top state official, or
with a historical site in the background.

Do you want to look **sociable and a family person**?
Have your picture taken in the living room
or in a homely atmosphere with your kids or
with friends.

I could go on and on, but the point is clear. Along
with the verbal messages you convey—out loud and in
writing—your photos and videos convey potentially
powerful non-verbal messages. What can be seen in
a photo is important, perhaps even more so because
it's seared into the subconscious part of the brain and

constitutes the social proof that you need for persuasion and sales.

WHAT ARE THE FOUR MOST PERSUASIVE WORDS YOU CAN SAY TO PEOPLE TO MOTIVATE THEM TO TAKE ACTION?

Imagine I want to persuade someone to come to a certain event like a business conference, a wedding, a political rally, or a concert. I can, and should, talk about the value they'll receive, what they'll get out of it, how great the experience is going to be, and so on. But there's one thing I can do that's even more effective.

I can utter a four-word sentence that will seal the deal for her and for me, and make it completely clear they should definitely come to this event.

Those four words are: "I'll be there, too!" (Or, if I've already been to a similar event, "I was there, too!")

What is the power of these words? They are authentic and believable. Meaning, I'm not just "pushing" someone into something, I myself also plan to be there or use the product or service. In other words, the other side can see that I practice what I preach and that I believe what I'm saying.

The most difficult form of persuasion is self-persuasion. If I myself am not persuaded of something, it will be very difficult to sell it to others. And, anyway, if they ask me, "Are you also going to be there?" and I say, "No," the chances of persuading the other side decrease dramatically. Because if you're not persuaded enough to go to the event yourself, why should the other side be persuaded and take the risk?

The same goes for selling products and services. I can talk with a lot of enthusiasm about a certain product until I'm blue in the face, but here, too, there are five words that will close the deal: "I also use this product!" That's why, for example, clothing chains "force" their employees to wear only the chain's clothes.

Imagine this: You go to buy clothes at a certain retail outlet and the sales clerk is dressed entirely in the competing chain's clothes. Would you be persuaded to buy the clothes they were selling you? Not so much, according to market research.

So, if you want to make the other side see that you actually believe what you are saying, and if you want to make them aware of the value and benefit: Project, show and demonstrate to them that you yourself apply what you're selling to them in your own life.

HOW DID WE CHOOSE A NANNY FOR OUR ELDEST SON?

In 2009, when our eldest son was only a few months old, my wife and I decided to hire a nanny. We started interviewing candidates for the position. We found them on the Internet, through other parents in the neighborhood, and also through a placement agency we had hired for the task.

Because it was our first child, we were pretty nervous, and we also did not completely know what was important to check for in a nanny. We seriously considered every nanny that came in for an interview; we also looked at what we did not like about her (they all happened to be female), not only at what we liked about her. We met and talked with several nannies. Some of them impressed us, and some of them did not impress us that much. Still, we were debating whom we should pick. And then along came Avital.

The truth is that what grabbed us about her in the meeting was not only the fact that she told us about herself and her experience and the fact that she seemed authentic, professional and completely honest. What really persuaded us was that she proved it to us.

Avital did not come empty-handed, as all the other nannies had. She brought along a well-organized binder packed with documents. There were warm and detailed letters of recommendation from every family she had worked with over the past fifteen years, and there were formal certificates from all the courses and professional training programs she had completed in the field of childcare, including, for example, a CPR for infants' course. All that really impressed us.

There were other nannies who had taken similar courses and who told us similar stories. But Avital provided us with social evidence. It is nice if you tell us about yourself, about how the families you have worked with were always very happy with you. (Though your evaluation then comes across as a subjective assessment, because you are the one who is talking about your qualifications.) It is far more professional and persuasive if you also show us a letter of recommendation and if you let us see for ourselves how qualified you are. (The assessment becomes objective.) You can tell us that you completed such and such a course, but if you show us a formal certificate with the logo of the institute that certified you, then that really seals the deal.

Do you want to persuade your customers and impress them? Provide them with social evidence about yourself: Letters of recommendation, testimonials, your client list, pictures of you with an audience and your products, certificates, degrees, and awards you have received, pictures of you with famous people and experts in your field.

The social evidence she brought with her made us choose Avital as a nanny for our most prized "possession," our son, and this kind of approach will also make your customers choose you.

IS IT GOOD WHEN CELEBRITIES RECOMMEND YOU?

If I tell someone else like a customer, investor, or voter that I am amazing, professional, and intelligent, that doesn't go down very well. Besides the fact that my sales pitch sounds arrogant and aggressive, it also sounds less credible because I testified about myself. The message is perceived as subjective. But if someone else says the same thing about me, it will sound completely different. It will be an "objective" message, and therefore it will sound credible and true.

Why did I put the word "objective" in quotes? Because I can be the one who creates a situation in which someone else talks about me. It could be through publishing photographed customer testimonies, sharing thank you letters and recommendations I have received over the years, screenshots of my books on bestseller lists, certifications hanging on the wall documenting my educational qualifications, and through high-profile people I work with who testify how much I helped them.

Celebrities, opinion shapers, influencers, famous people from all sorts of fields, usually constitute very strong social proof because of the halo effect around them. Why did I write "usually" and not "always"? Because once in a while people make inappropriate use of celebrities, and the resulting damage far outweighs the benefit.

A notable example is the final straits of Hillary Clinton's campaign for the presidency of the United States in 2016. In the last weeks before the election, when Clinton led Donald Trump in the polls by a small but steady margin, she publicly harnessed American celebrities such as LeBron James, Lena Dunham, Lady Gaga, and Beyoncé to support her. She appeared with them at public events, where they hailed and praised her as she stood next to them. At the same time, she did not attend many of the events in person, but sent three "star players" in her place, namely, her husband and former president Bill Clinton, President Barack Obama, and First Lady Michelle Obama.

At first glance that seems like a smart move from a media and marketing perspective. A move that most campaign advisors would encourage. But in fact, the results were not favorable for Hilary Clinton and none of the events featuring celebrities increased her poll rankings.

Why? First, Hillary Clinton was perceived as someone who was not strong enough in her own right, and who needed the halo effect of celebrities projected onto her. And physically, when she (as an older and relatively short woman) stood next to a huge sportsman like LeBron James or a figure like Beyonce, it did not look good.

Second, because the events were structured so that the star talked for a long time alongside Clinton while she was standing beside them excitedly. Then Clinton would speak after the celebrities, sometimes for less time than they did. A situation was created whereby some of the audience came to the election event to see the star, and not to see the candidate.

Third, politically, she was perceived as unable to win the election alone, without her husband or the current president to help her.

And what was Donald Trump doing meantime? All the political events he attended were based on him and on him only. Here and there he also brought along celebrity supporters, but they were part of his show and they certainly didn't introduce him at events. He based all his political and public events on himself, his personality and his bravado. At most, members of his family stood behind him as a backdrop.

The message Trump projected by doing that is that he was strong on his own. He was in control. He had all it wrapped up. He didn't need anyone's halo effect; he had enough of it on his own. And that corresponded perfectly with his catchy message of "Let's Make America Great Again."

Social proof is a good and powerful tool, provided that it is a complementary marketing tool, and not the principal point.

You are the main deal. Yes, you. (Recall Commandment 4 and the importance of taking center stage.) Your presence—physical, online, and in the media—is important, no matter whether you are promoting a product, service, idea, or yourself. The fastest and most effective way for you to succeed in life is to put yourself center stage in front of an audience and in front of clients. All the other marketing tools, they are just a bonus.

I WANT YOU AS A CUSTOMER, I DON'T NEED YOU AS A CUSTOMER.

What does it mean to achieve economic freedom? It means you make decisions in life according to what you want, and not according to how much money there is in it. Perhaps you work in the job that you want, and do not compromise on a job you don't like because you make good money there and have expenses to pay. Or you have decided you want to travel to the Caribbean for two weeks; you can do it whenever you want, without saving for two years. Or you live where you want to live, and not in some distant town or suburb, because that's where you can afford to buy or rent a place.

Financial freedom is not about how much money you have. It's about your preferences. Any sum of money, no matter how big it is, will be sufficient for some people to live as they want, while for others it won't be enough for almost anything.

You want to be in a situation in life where you can allow yourself to quit your job, or fire a customer, or turn down offers if something doesn't seem right to you, because you do not depend on them for a living. The marketing term I use to describe this kind of situation is called, "I want you as a customer. I don't need you as a customer." If you are in survival mode in your business or under financial pressure, and you are interviewed for a job or are marketing to a client, you transmit pressure and the other side picks that up, and then it costs you money.

Because of the pressure, you lose money. But if you turn up calm and relaxed, and transmit to the customer that you want to work with them, but you don't have to work with them, and that you have other alternatives, then precisely by doing so, you increase your chances that the customer will be persuaded by you and will close a deal with you, or that the employer will hire you and you will receive the salary you want. Because you are putting out a vibe of confidence and success at the meeting or interview.

It is a question of state of mind, of transmitting a feeling—contrary to what most people do, which is to act automatically and to show that they are under financial pressure and are willing to compromise on almost anything in life, while you play a completely different game. You set the rules.

The way it usually goes is, for example, that when someone has written a book and wants to get it published, they will send the book to a publishing house and ask them to invest money in it and publish it. Then they will usually receive lots of rejections, refusals and excuses and phrases like, "There are a lot of books in the field like yours," "Now isn't the time," "Perhaps toward the end of the year," "Previous books in your style didn't sell," and so on. A best-case scenario is that they manage to find one book publisher who believes in them and is willing to publish the book. But if, for example, the writer first carried out a successful crowdfunding campaign for the book, raised all the money needed to produce and market it even before the book was published, and then offered traditional book publishers the opportunity to publish the book (showing them the results of the campaign they did), the situation would be reversed and the likelihood of the publisher wanting to publish the book will increase significantly.

Why? Because that shows success. Because that shows that there have been significant sales before the book has even come out. Because that proves that there is demand for this kind of book and that there is interest. Instead of chasing after publishers, the publishers will chase after the author who will then be able to pick and choose.

A colleague who is the owner of a start-up company did a successful crowdfunding campaign for software his start-up was developing. Before launching the campaign, he knocked on the doors of some of the biggest venture capital funds in the world. None of them would agree to provide the finance he needed and invest in his start-up.

But then he offered his venture to the public, and raised hundreds of thousands of dollars from a few thousand supporters. An amazing thing happened: suddenly all the venture capital funds were interested in him and willing to meet him. He displayed success, and a significant number of users, and proved that there was demand for his software. What's more, he could then choose who he wanted to work with and who he didn't. And it is obvious that he would then get much better terms, no matter which venture capital fund he chose to work with.

A crowdfunding campaign is just one example of how to reach a situation of "I want you, I don't need you." Have you had achievements in life, in any field? Document them, use them, show them to others,

leverage them in order to create even greater achievements. And then document and leverage future greater
achievements, and do that over and again.

WHAT THE BEST UNIVERSITIES IN THE WORLD DO NOT WANT YOU TO KNOW.

In 2004, a good friend of mine was accepted to
a Master of Business Administration (MBA) program
at an American university that is ranked as one of the
leading institutions of higher learning in the world. The
studies are very expensive and the program is of two
years' duration, during which time the students are not
allowed to work, which would be impossible anyway,
because of the heavy academic workload.

The students who register for this master's program all hope that, at the end of those two years, they
will land a desirable position where they'll earn a very
good salary that will be well above the average. That will
compensate them for the two years in which they did
not work and for the high tuition fees. In addition, their
high salary will enable them to pay back the huge loan
they had to take out in order to pay for the expensive
tuition fees and for their living expenses during the two
years of their studies.

When my friend was accepted, he was delighted.
However, as part of the investigation he carried out, he
tried to find someone who had been admitted to this
prestigious program of studies, had taken out a big loan
to pay for the studies and was then unable to find a good

job immediately after graduating. Which would mean that this person would be stuck with a very big loan that had to be paid back, without the means to do so.

My friend, who was planning to take out a very big loan at the age of 27, wanted to find someone like this who could tell him about the difficulties and about the worst-case scenario. He wanted to find someone who would not simply sing the praises of the academic institution and the MBA degree that it granted.

He searched and searched but could not find anyone. Not because those people do not exist. But because these prestigious universities have no intention of revealing such graduates. In other words, at all of the meetings that were set up for my friend before his studies began, he met only outstanding students, successful alumni and CEOs of major international corporations—all of whom had graduated from that same institution and who came to talk to the students to give them guidance and inspiration.

Why do these academic institutions conduct themselves in such a manner? Because they are employing a marketing strategy called *winner's bias*. This is a broad concept; I will simplify it for our purposes. In order to persuade you to enroll in a program for an MBA degree in the United States, to pay high tuition fees and to take out a huge loan to cover those fees, to move to and live in the U.S. for a few years and perhaps relocate your family, what must the university do?

The university sells you a winning image and

promises you excellent chances for success, with almost no risk. It shows you only those alumni who have succeeded and it "hides" those who have not. (Often these people are "in hiding" themselves because of the shame and the unpleasantness.)

The university hides people who have failed, because failure doesn't sell. People are attracted to success and constantly compare themselves to others. People today are less satisfied with their lives—even with an abundance of opportunities in the world—and technology is only intensifying that trend. Thus, for example, there is a phenomenon known as the *Facebook illusion*, which involves looking at profiles and business pages of other people that we know on Facebook and seeing lots of positive things. Smiling faces, abundance all around, beautiful scenery, children who are always happy, the dinner table laid out and the fireplace burning. It's like an illusion. In reality, alongside those happy moments that we all experience, there are also a lot of times when we experience disappointments, when we are depressed or sad, or just bored or boring. But people don't tend to document those moments. Let's say a couple goes on a romantic vacation to Paris. During their holiday, they argue, are tired and get annoyed with each other. What will they show on Facebook when they want to put up a post about the vacation? Of course, the part of the vacation when everything was going well. Their friends will see a photo of the couple in a romantic pose, with the Eiffel Tower in the background, smiling from ear to ear, and say, "Looks like they are having a great time! They are on vacation again! They look so in love! Why isn't my life like that? Why do I argue with my partner when we go on vacation?"

Then the need arises for "more" and for them to reveal their "secrets." (Remember Commandment 7.) The truth is that reality is much more complex, but people prefer not to see it. They prefer to see success rather than the lab hours and work at nights and weekends. They prefer to read about other people's lives and not to meet the challenges of their own lives. And so they worship celebrities and famous people and they prefer to think about some magical solution right around the corner that will save them from hard work (and so they aren't satisfied with their lives, even if, objectively, they are living very good lives).

The Facebook illusion is a reality that is not going to disappear from the world. The phenomenon will only grow stronger.

So the questions you should be asking yourselves are:

» How do I leverage this phenomenon to my advantage?
» How do I put out an image of success and show the advantages of working with me?
» How do I present testimonials of satisfied customers and create social proofs about my activities?

Your customers want to see your successes: Make them stand out. It's obvious—to them and to you—that there are failures, but failures don't sell.

Credibility is above everything, but from a marketing point of view, it is important to present (true!) information that is convenient for you. For example, it is obvious that you have customers who are less satisfied, but your testimonies will show only those who are the happiest.

Winner bias is being used on you as customers in practically every field, and it is time for you to employ it as well. You should highlight your winning customers, those who have used your services or products and have derived considerable value and benefit from them.

KEY ELEMENTS OF COMMANDMENT NO. 10

Create confidence and trust in you.

✓ Customers are attracted to proven success. People by nature will prefer what is familiar and safe to them—or what they perceive as familiar and safe—over taking risks and buying a new product or service before anyone else.

✓ Take objective data about yourself and present it when you market yourself as part of a presentation, job interview, lecture or sales meeting.

✓ People believe that if others do something, they should and can do it too. Present them with actions and examples of other clients.

✓ If many people around us think something, we will tend to think the same thing.

✓ In order to convince a group of people, you should give each one of them a sense that all the others have already signed on and you are waiting just for them, or that there is something here that will definitely work out.

✓ The likelihood of successful persuasion is much higher when someone without an interest presents the issue, and not the interested party.

✓ People like to do business with people who are like them.

✓ Sporting activity, even though it happens in your free time, is very much related to your career and business, if you take advantage of it properly.

✓ Social activities and volunteering can greatly increase the likelihood that customers will buy from you, that people will appreciate you and will see you as being reliable, and that your branding will be strengthened.

✓ You must pay attention to what is behind or next to you when you are filming promotional videos or advertisements.

✓ Practice what you preach and believe what you're saying.

✓ Have you attained achievements in life? Document them. Use them. Show them to others. Leverage them to achieve greater accomplishments. Failures don't sell. Credibility above everything, but from a marketing point of view it is important to present only (true!) information that is convenient for you.

AUTHOR BIO

Known to the world as Doctor Persuasion, economist and attorney DR. YANIV ZAID acts as a business consultant to government departments, private firms, and public organizations. He holds a PhD in law and utilizes his rich knowledge and experience to help others achieve success.

Dr. Zaid is recognized worldwide as an expert in the fields of public speaking, marketing, sales, negotiation and persuasion, and placed 3rd in the 2003 world ranking of public speakers.

Following twenty years of international success, Dr. Zaid is the author of eleven bestsellers including

Public Speaking and *Creative Marketing* and is often invited to lecture and consult around the world.

Email Dr. Zaid at yaniv@yanivzaid.com, visit his website (drpersuasion.com) for more information, and discover other books by him at his Amazon page.